Why I have written this book.

This is a true story documenting my pe[rsonal experience of] abuse. To the outside world, this was a pe[rfect marriage and he] was an amusing, charismatic man. But behind closed doors life couldn't have been more different.

Living with a **Jekyll and Hyde personality**, who turns from the caring, tender person you fell in love with, to someone with dark morose moods, intent on inflicting hurt, is disconcerting. Then bam, there are flowers or theatre tickets, so you think you must have over reacted, then you are reeled back in and the cycle starts again. From one hour to the next, you are never sure how it's going to be, so you try harder to make every aspect of their life perfect, but enough is never enough.

Intimidation through **psychological control** is a pernicious form of abuse. They say when you are in the woods you cannot see the trees. I certainly didn't recognise what was happening to me for years, because it's a slow insidious creep, an attack on the personality, rather than the body. Intimidation and an ongoing sense of fear is the name of the game, and somehow you are made to believe all the issues you are berated for, are your fault.

Coercive control, is a complex tapestry, it is a classless, silent abuse without witnesses. The degrees of control seem trivial at first and to make life more confusing, they are often disguised as loving behaviour. Then, there might be the **silent treatment**, a passive-aggressive method of control, where for no apparent reason, you have become persona non-grata and can be ignored for days. We do everything to appease this person, to make life right again, so we are reeled back in, and the cycle continues. **Mind games** have a serious effect on every aspect of our lives, mental and physical, as well our social interaction with the outside world. Manipulating situations, causing us to question our version of events, constitutes a severe form of psychological abuse, known as **Gas Lighting**. Persistently sowing seeds of doubt, almost brain washing, wore me down to a compliant, withdrawn woman.

My experiences have motivated me to write this book, in the hope that if anyone recognises any of the behaviour, I have described, the scales will fall from their eyes. I am incredulous it took me so long to understand what was happening, but I gather this is not unusual. Locations and the names of the guilty have been changed, to protect the innocent, whose names have also been changed.

Only *cry* on Fridays

Escaping Coercive Control
A true story

ALICE WAITE

Copyright © 2018 Alice Waite.

All rights reserved. No part of this book may be reproduced, stored, or transmitted by any means—whether auditory, graphic, mechanical, or electronic—without written permission of both publisher and author, except in the case of brief excerpts used in critical articles and reviews. Unauthorized reproduction of any part of this work is illegal and is punishable by law.

For my girls, because you had to know

Every time we impose our will on another, it is an act of violence.

> Gandhi

Contents

Chapter 1   Christmas 2001 1
Chapter 2   Sicily 5
Chapter 3   New Office 11
Chapter 4   Guardian Angel 16
Chapter 5   She's Leaving Home 22
Chapter 6   Silver Service 26
Chapter 7   Aftermath 30
Chapter 8   Settle into Working Life 38
Chapter 9   Ballister & Burns 43
Chapter 10 House on the Market 46
Chapter 11 Time for a change 55
Chapter 12 Rolo Hargreaves 63
Chapter 13 The fax 73
Chapter 14 Mary Collins 80
Chapter 15 Annie 84
Chapter 16 WDFA 91
Chapter 17 Delays 95
Chapter 18 Nadia 101
Chapter 19 FSA Ombudsman 113
Chapter 20 Run up to The First Hearing. 120
Chapter 21 The First Hearing 128
Chapter 22 Hettie visits 135
Chapter 23 The letter 145
Chapter 24 The Package 153

Chapter 25	Move to Edgar Place	158
Chapter 26	Hugo Steele	165
Chapter 27	New Year	173
Chapter 28	Second Hearing	181
Chapter 29	Life continues	187
Chapter 30	The Determination	193
Chapter 31	War Cabinet	200
Chapter 32	Final Hearing	208
Chapter 33	Final Hearing 2	218
Chapter 34	With Wings	225
Chapter 35	The Move	234
Chapter 36	The Move 2	240
Chapter 37	Is anything familiar?	246
Chapter 38	Sources of Help	257

Chapter 1

Christmas 2001

No one has any idea of the fortitude, the strength and the mental process involved, in my decision to purchase this Christmas tree. Its 5pm and dark, the fine drizzle makes the road glisten. My marriage of 30 years is over. I am dealing with Christmas on my own in a rented flat, ten miles away from my lovely home. My husband is still there. Our three daughters will have to divide their time between their home and my little flat. Optimistic the flak will be over in no time, I'm certain I will be waving a Decree Absolute, in a lovely home, with a real fire and a real Christmas tree by next year. It's a watch this space situation and for all the baubles on the Christmas tree, I don't want to be in this space.
Making the effort is *so* hard but I cannot leave it any longer. I have walked past the local Spar Shop so many times this week, watching the line of scrubby, bed sit Christmas trees diminish. Today, there are only three specimens left. These trees aren't for grand entrance halls or gracious drawing rooms. These trees are for those who use the local Spar shop, with the same regularity as others use Waitrose. They will not know the joyous family gatherings or the countdown to Christmas Eve. These trees are for those souls who know a different Christmas, in below par rented flats, shared houses and bed sits or studio flats as they are more optimistically called these days.
Wilfully veering myself into the shop, the smell of bananas turning black, cigarettes and newsprint greet me. The young gay guy behind the counter looks up, takes my £12.50 leaving me to choose any one of the three green prickly stumps for myself. All have seen better days. I could have taken all three, he is unconcerned, returning to reading Hello the moment the transaction is over.
Hoisting my handbag straps onto my shoulder to lift this evergreen number, I discover the black plastic pot is filled with clay to give weight

to the base, causing my hysterectomised (yes, I know that's not a word, but it should be) tummy muscles to take the strain they shouldn't.

Making my way along the dark pavements, filled with the last struggle of Christmas shoppers, I envisage the baubles and expensive silver stars, waiting in readiness, to decorate this darling. Fifty paces forward, after navigating the rubbish sacks outside Clarke's Wine Bar, I approach my front door. Placing the pot on the top step while I find my keys, my arms throb with relief. Now, with the tree under my left bosom, I put the key in the main front door lock and push with the other available shoulder, press the light timer switch and stagger towards the stairs.

In this Grade II listed townhouse, these stairs are known to the residents as *the back stairs at John Lewis*. This exemplary 18c stone staircase, sadly has been embellished with black and white lino tiles, in perfect harmony with the mushroom coloured woodchip wallpaper, simply light years away from the original 1772 genteel ambience. Now, Building Regulations insist on a rubber and metal nosing on each stone step, along with reproduction Georgian fire doors. This is now an HMO. A House of Multiple Occupancy. Sadly, no one from Building Regulations has been around lately, to tick all the other boxes, including emergency lighting.

My knees are quaking with the weight of this seemingly little tree. There are four steep flights of stairs to negotiate. This is the pay off to achieve elegant ceiling heights. As I start the second flight, the prickly green beast has sent friends and family into my bra. My arms are yearning to release, for what is, my small frame, an extreme weight. The shoulder straps of my handbag, have slid down to my elbow, so the bag is now dragging on the floor in front of me. Every step forward is like an obstacle race, but with weights. What the hell is in that handbag anyway? I have only managed a few steps of the third flight, when the light timer switch gives out. Save the world! Hey, let's not waste electricity.... It's pitch black. When I say pitch black, I mean deep inside a cave, prehistoric pitch black. Farrow and Ball do not even have a name for it. This is an internal staircase. There is not a chink of light from any source. I am in no man's land. Its one and a half flights to the next light switch and with Christmas prickles stuffed into my face, I try to negotiate the next step.

One minute I knew where I was going, the next, I am in a black place, unable to see the way forward. I falter at every turn and cannot organise one step in front of another. Had there been less pressing things on my mind, I might have seen the irony of my situation. The next step, isn't quite where I thought and as my handbag hits my knee, I reel trying to restore my balance, then the tree makes a lunge at my face. Fast forward to Christmas day when my girls will arrive, and they will think I have been in a fight with a cat.

Now well and truly stuck between landings and more importantly, light switches, I am in intimate contact with prickly pine needles. My breathlessness takes in the fir essence, and a wave of unbearable sadness overtakes me. The tears start to roll. My whole body gives way to sobbing, then my legs sink to the step I'm so precariously, pivoted upon. Sitting in the dark, hugging the tree, I weep, overwhelmed by a complete sense of hopelessness, as I try to convince myself that this is just a culmination of physical exhaustion. But, I know it's about so much more. I feel utterly alone, I must move forward without a backward glance, all *so* much harder than it sounds. Since September, I've been fighting my corner and if, at this stage, I had any comprehension of what was to come, I'd have probably just stayed on those stairs, hugging that tree. I have a firm word with myself. 'Stop feeling sorry for yourself Alice! *It's unbearable.*'

After what seems like hours, the front door opens and a second later, the light is back on. Mustering myself upright as quickly as I can, because it might be the young man from the floor above me, who runs up these stairs two at a time and I don't want to be seen like this. Catching sight of myself in the half landing mirror, I am confronted by a red eyed, dishevelled woman, but mercifully manage to make it to my front door, before someone wishes me a Happy Christmas.

After an Earl Grey recovery, I fish out the Paperchase bag and the decorations I have bought. Silver stars, silver birds, clear lights. In monetary terms I thought I had bought enough to decorate a tree in Trafalgar Square. When I hang the precious pieces on my mini Spar tree, they look frugal and silly. I really can't spend any more money. Then the tears come again. *Do get a grip girl!*

In another life, there were boxes containing beautiful gilded angels facing right and left, holding ribbons, to support garlands, which draped elegantly over the fireplace. In that other life, there were more boxes, saved from when my girls were little. They were filled with hand drawn glittering Santas and a Baby Jesus, crayoned with such love. Multi coloured beads threaded on string and jolly snowmen made from cotton wool covered yogurt pots. The tree, always huge, was in the latter years decorated elegantly in one colour, but we simply had to open the childhood boxes to reminisce. These tokens of childhood were everything. They transported me back to happier days, busy days, dealing with the demands of three little girls under five. They were so loving and brought real joy into my life. Now here I am, years after the crayons and the glitter have been put away, having to acknowledge what I would not contemplate then. In the blink of an eye, my girls are fully grown responsible young women and angry with me. I have upset their beautiful applecart, ruined their perfect family life. They knew behind the scenes, it wasn't anywhere near perfect, but best behaviour always prevailed when they came home from school and university.

It's 10pm and my building is silent. Looking across St Phillip's Square there is barely a light on, in the myriad of flats occupying five floors of these Georgian houses. Echoing from the basement kitchen of Clarke's, I can hear plates clattering, as the washer uppers beaver on. The University's empty Bendy Bus glides around the fountain. Don't the bus companies know the students broke up ages ago? It's nearly Christmas Eve for heaven's sake.

Chapter 2

Sicily

I'm on a plane, on the way to Sicily, alone, despite having booked two seats. A week before we were due to leave he decided he would not be coming. Looking back this was clearly a ploy, to force me to beg him to come on this holiday. He knew I was nervous of driving on the continent, not only because having driven an automatic for some 15 years, (the only automatics available were at the top of the range, so were too expensive) but also because I found driving in Italy nothing short of terrifying.

Months before, I had found a lovely villa not far from Syracuse on Sicily's Ionian coast.
Facing the sea, it seemed idyllic. Sleeping up to eight, I had hoped my girls would join us with some of their friends, but somehow, not only was the timing not right, but neither was the quiet location and to cut to the chase, they simply didn't want to come. So, it was just us, and for three weeks… this was either going to be kill or cure.
I hoped for the latter. Moving on after 30 years seemed out of the question. At fifty-three, the upheaval of a divorce filled me with dread. Hopefully, we could just rub along together, if he would just stop being so unkind. He was nice in the early days, maybe he would revert to his old self after a holiday? I knew I was kidding myself but had to cling onto something when I booked the villa.

So, the joint holiday was not to be, and my mind went into overdrive, calling girl friends who jumped at the chance of free accommodation in Sicily. I spoke to Diana, just back in the UK after a five-year stint working in Geneva, with the World Bank. In a nanosecond, she volunteered to be our driver.
'Darling I've been driving on the right forever, no problem!'
Flights were booked, dates confirmed, so no more worries about the

driving. My first guest was to be Diana, her flight arrived thirty minutes before mine. Sitting on the plane, my heart in the pit of my stomach, I could not begin to think how my future was going to pan out, now there was not going to be a Sicilian reconciliation. Opening my suitcase, that night, right on top of the clothes was a small bunch of roses, now looking rather sad, together with a card he had written saying *Have a lovely holiday. I will miss you.* This man throws me hand grenades, then roses.

The next three weeks were a maelstrom of girl friends coming and going. The local taxi driver ferried them back and forth to the airport. Long leisurely lunches were followed by siestas in the shade. Diana's white-knuckle drives took us to the delights of Noto and Ragusa, leaving us happy to recover at the villa for days, listening to the therapeutic sound of the sea, from the safety of the terrace. Eventually cabin fever would take over and with the indomitable Diana at the wheel, we would don hard hats for the drive to Syracuse.

Old Syracuse town is a honey coloured medieval gem, with narrow winding streets leading to the sea. There are dazzling Baroque piazzas at every turn, the limestone seemingly reflecting centuries of sunlight. Map in hand, we find the shady calm of the Basilica di Santa Lucia al Sepolcro before crossing the bridge to Ortiga. Can this place get any better? A Greek theatre built within the curve of the land, then palaces, more fountains and the sea at every turn.

We have lunch courtesy of Fratelli Burgio in Ortiga market. Part deli, part Enoteca, perching on plastic chairs around tiny tables, we are grateful for the shade of the awning. The food is sublime. Char grilled artichokes, roasted long red peppers, chicory filled with soft cheese. Greedily, we sample so many dishes and decide to take more home, as we now call the villa.

Evenings on the terrace are long. With the sound of the sea behind us we talk, look at the stars and I start to regain a sense of who I was. For so long my husband's behaviour has had a serious effect on my well being. My confidence has taken such a battering. I have become isolated from friends and lost all sense of what behaviour towards me is acceptable.

My girlfriends give me overwhelming support and are so reassuring. These are people who have known me for years and have my well being at heart. 'Alice what are you thinking?' 'Do you want to spend the next twenty years walking on eggshells?' 'We've all noticed how you've lost your sparkle, you've turned into a mouse… sorry to say that, but it's about time somebody did.'

They patiently listen, night after night, as I pour it all out, trying to come to a decision and then a plan how to implement it…

I tell them about the watch. Several years ago, I had fallen in love with a very beautiful watch. Completely out of my league, I tore pages out of Vogue and scrutinised the detail. Designed by architect, Gae Aulenti for Louis Vuitton, the face showed the time, worldwide. I was certainly not a world traveller, but loved the clever design, which also showed the phases of the moon. Several times, I was taken into Louis Vuitton shops to look at it. Once I even tried it on. Now, knowing what I know, about abusive behaviour and coercive control, I understand what was happening. But then, I was oblivious. Every time we walked into Louis Vuitton my hopes were built up and then when we left the shop, I felt crushed. It was the humiliation of his control. I *could* buy you this… but do you know what, I am not going to. These are mind games and were second nature to him. Of course, the first time we sauntered into Louis Vuitton in London, I didn't understand this. I thought of it more as an exploratory visit, with a maybe… well, Christmas isn't too far away… But Christmas came and went, and I pushed the thought right out of my mind. We were in Paris one autumn on business and lo and behold as we walked along Boulevard Saint Germain, Louis Vuitton's flag ship store came into view. We'd had a good year and when he suggested we should see if they still made the watch, my heart took a leap. Attentive assistants unlocked the glass case and placed the watch on a velvet pad. We listened to the sales patter until they had delivered every syllable memorised by heart. Then, silence…. A very awkward silence.

'Thank you, *I'll* think about it' he said.

And following him like a lamb, we left the shop.

I'll think about it said everything. Power and control. *I* hold the purse strings here. This purchase won't be a joint decision. *I* will decide, *if and when, I* am ready.

That Christmas his twisted behaviour escalated. On Christmas morning there was such excitement when we started unwrapping presents. The girls ripped off the paper with squeals of delight. Treasures they had hoped for and surprises too. I had bought all their presents as usual and of course his presents. The girls had bought me lovely hand crème and smelly things for the bath, but the ones I treasured the most, were the things they had made themselves. A needle case, embroidered Mummy. A pen case made from felt with huge blanket stitches around the edge and an egg cosy. In the confusion of wrapping and ribbons, no one noticed, their father had neglected to buy their mother a present. He *knew* exactly. His eyes would not meet mine as he unwrapped smart shirts, after shave and his favourite chocolates. Eventually, that evening, when the girls were in bed, he said something about he didn't know what to get….

This was perverse to say the least. In the run up to Christmas we had gone into Selfridges and as usual, parted at the front door with the arrangement to meet for coffee, in an hour. Hence some privacy to buy each other presents. I had done quite well and then made for the ground floor to look at a new wallet for him. Then, I spotted him at a jewellery counter handing over his card. Golly I thought, moving quickly out of sight as he tucked the parcel inside his overcoat. I never saw any jewellery that Christmas or any in the future and could never put my hands on the December Credit card statement.

Back to the watch: Fast forward, several Christmases, it appeared completely out of the blue. You could have knocked me down with a feather, I was so excited. I had put it out of my mind completely and couldn't quite believe it. Little did I know how significant this watch would be in my future life. It's a Boxing Day drinks party and he has gained mega brownie points, all round, by regaling our friends with the story of how he had put out a search for this watch, because it was a limited edition.
'And Louis Vuitton, well… they eventually tracked one down for me in Durban.' he said, putting his arm round my shoulder.
'Steve you're a star' they said.
'You lucky girl!' they murmured.
His kindness was universally endorsed. Everyone else thought he was amazing. Kind, considerate and *so* caring! What a gem! I knew something was terribly wrong, but I didn't understand what. I just couldn't articulate the problem. Maybe it was me. Am I too sensitive? Maybe he was right about that? It's all in my head. Why, when you have so many good things in life are you so unhappy? I'm numb inside and drowning, meekly standing there, while the conversation buzzes all around me. Someone comments that I'm quiet, but before I can utter a word he says
'Yes, she's worked so hard to make Christmas amazing for everyone, she deserves some cosseting and I'm going to make sure she doesn't lift another

finger this week.' 'When we get home, I'm going to run you a lovely deep bath darling with some of that bath oil you like so much… then an early night I think?'

'Ah' they mutter, 'how lovely Alice.'

I smile, knowing that the chances are, he will actually do this… run the bath that is, and even light candles. And this is why I find myself confused, I question my own instincts. He can spend hours, trivialising my existence, followed by acts of kindness. When he realises he has gone too far, my eyes are dull, I do not speak, I'm inwardly crying, with my protective wall all around me, he will appear with a cup of tea.

'I've booked theatre tickets for Wednesday and I thought we could get an early bite at that Italian.'

Now, previous experience tells me, that no matter how I am feeling, I need to show gratitude or there will be a price to pay. If I don't muster up enthusiasm pronto, there will be punishment. There will be more ranting.

'Just look at yourself, you're so miserable.'

Then, I'm simply ignored. Here comes the silent treatment. He won't speak to me for days on end or won't answer my questions

'Shall we eat about 7.00?'

He will just glare at me in an intimidating way. The atmosphere is menacing and it's best to make myself scarce. Over the weekend, he disappears to his work shop for hours. He has parked his car directly behind mine, so he knows I'm trapped. If I go to the workshop to get him to move it, he apparently doesn't hear me banging on the locked door.

I therefore quickly lighten up.

'Yes, I really wanted to see that play.' 'Thank you, that's lovely.'

Gratitude is important. It makes him feel good. It endorses his self belief that he is really such a nice person.

A couple of years on, when the clocks change for autumn, changing the hour on my watch, I find the winder has dropped into my hand. The watch is returned to Louis Vuitton. They in turn, return it to their maker, in Switzerland for repair, in all it takes nearly three months. The winder problem happens a second and then third time.

In the intervening years, his behaviour has become more destructive and is taking its toll. When the winder dropped into my hand a fourth time, I wrote to Louis Vuitton documenting all the repairs and request a replacement. As luck would have it, I meet the postman on the drive with an envelope embellished Louis Vuitton, in his hand; I tuck it into my pocket. In the privacy of my office, I open the envelope. There are no replacements available, but they offer to repair my watch one last time, then if this problem happens again, they will refund the purchase price in full. Wow! This takes my breath away. This is like having a substantial cheque around my wrist. Every time I glance at the time, my heart flutters, because now, I just might have choices.

When the Captain declared we are preparing to descend to Syracuse airport, he announced local time; I naturally attempt to adjust my watch. As I do so, the winder drops into my right hand. I flinch, this is it…. I will have funds, can I, do it? Can I be brave enough? How will I survive? I carefully put the winder into my purse. Fasten my seat belt and prepare to meet Diana.

Chapter 3

New Office

He had decided to pick me up at the airport and this allowed me to think positively. Maybe you have missed me, and want to make amends? I really want to believe this, because the alternative is unpalatable, even if now, I will have the means.
On the journey home, I chatter away, but try not to point out how much he would have loved Sicily. I don't want to rub salt into any festering wounds, so talk about the friends who joined me, but quickly realise this is dangerous territory, when through gritted teeth he says
'I can't stand that woman ....'
Thank heavens, he hadn't been there. There would have been no laughter, we would have been at the mercy of this man's behaviour and I would have been deeply embarrassed, because he would have lashed out at my friends. So, for the rest of the journey home, to travel without any more agitation, it was easier to relapse into silence and feign sleep. The sticking plaster that I hoped Sicily might provide, could not heal this deep festering wound.

When we arrived home as soon as we pulled into the drive of The Rectory, I knew something was different. Everything was much lighter. The sky was in full view at the top of the garden. It suddenly dawned on me, the trees had gone.
'What on earth.' I said. 'You've chopped the trees down, how crazy!' 'You know the land behind has been sold for building.' 'Now we will be overlooked… not to mention the noise and mess when all this work starts, what were you thinking for God's sake?'
'Well you should know this house is going to be sold.' 'I've had Threadwells around to value it and it goes on the market next week.' 'I feel sorry for *you*, because *you* won't have anywhere to work, will you?'
He delivers the news in a spirit of self- interest. I was aghast, this bombshell was doled out full of venom.

'Hold on here.' I said. 'This house doesn't just belong to you.' 'It belongs to both of us.' 'You just can't go instructing estate agents on your own.' 'That's what is going to happen, you can sort yourself out.' He said, pushing the front door open and closing it behind him. Mr Nice guy leaves me unloading my suitcases and looking for my front door key. I will not ring the bell to enter my own house.

The next day, I drive into town, post my watch back to Louis Vuitton, but with a change of address (to my friend Barbara). I cannot risk their monogrammed envelope with it's cheque for my future, dropping through this letter box. Then I go to the council offices for the commercial property register. This is a monthly list collating all the commercial properties on the market. Dear reader, yes, we are pre-internet, and this is how things were done. Sitting in Waterstone's café, I trawl through the list, page by page. It's about as thick as your thumb, there are so many huge offices and shops listed. Then I see something that looks remotely possible. From my mobile I call and ask if I can view it. We fix a date and time and I start to do the sums. There's rent, plus business rates, plus electricity, plus, plus… Can I make it work? I have a small stash of cash, I have been secreting away for years. (I'll come to that later) I never really knew why, now I know why. The money from Louis Vuitton might take a while. At this point I have not envisaged moving out of my home. Even if we are parting and it is to be sold, it will take time and that will save me money, but it will be a living hell.

To leave him mentally *in control*, I don't mention anything about looking for premises. His menacing agenda and personal demons, make the atmosphere tense. We are on a collision course. After visiting the premises, I immediately know the space could work for my School of Media Studies. There are four rooms, which will give me an office and three studios. There is even a courtyard garden. Without giving myself time to change my mind, I sign a two-year lease and pay the deposit. I can move in, in a week's time. Now to drop the bombshell, he will be furious I have taken the reins. There is already an unbreachable chasm between us and I am extremely anxious about his reaction to this news.

Feeling furtive and deceitful, my tummy is in knots with so much inner turmoil. There are arrangements to make to move the existing studio furniture into my new premises, but first I must do a bit of a paint job, to freshen it up. When he is in his workshop, I secrete steps/ brushes and old painting clothes into the boot of my car. Picking up Cornforth White en route, with a sandwich, coffee and milk, it means I can spend a whole day there with Radio 4 and just paint and think, but I'm so scared.

Soon everywhere is looking smart but my arms ache and so does my back. I'm just not used to this kind of exercise. My landlords are graphic designers and use the rest of the building. They are pleased to have another creative soul in the basement and have kindly left plain white blinds at all the windows, saving another expense. I must watch the pennies like a hawk, but I know all the tricks of the trade, so applying them to my own project, is rewarding. Later, I splash out on a pair of Box trees for either side of the front door and hang a silver framed sign to one side.

Dreading that I must tell him I'm moving my business into the town centre, I comfort myself with the thought that this is something I've talked about before, to attract more students. Running the Media Courses from our Coach house in a village is charming and cost effective, as it is rent free. However, it does mean I have to organise lunch everyday for ten to twelve and when some courses last up to eight weeks, the burden is huge and the cooking falls upon me. I would take a week to cook 90% of the food and then freeze it. A local girl would then come in to put it in the oven, make the salads, serve and clear up. It seemed I spent more time worrying about the catering, than running the courses. By moving into town, everyone can pop out for a sandwich or whatever and I can charge the same price, which will cover my new overheads. Now I must drum up business… I need more bums on seats. Some students who booked for the autumn term, earlier in the year must be told about the change of address, my head is buzzing with a long *to do* list. Suddenly it feels like I'm on the starting blocks with a *new* business and although it's scary, it's also exhilarating.

We're having another silent supper. I decide I must tell him…. to get this over with, because I've booked a man with a van ……. So, I blurt out,
'You'll be pleased to hear, I've found somewhere for my business, so no worries on that front.'
He stares at me. His eyes become even more cold and angry.
'Where, what do you mean?'… 'How are you going to pay for it?'
I think he is going to choke on his food. His mouth is hard and the nasty furrow between his eyes deepens.

'I decided *it would* be a good thing.' 'You told me, remember, I wouldn't have anywhere to run my business from.'
I wanted him to feel reassured he was in charge.
'And anyway' I said, trying to smooth the waters
'Anyway, I've talked about moving into town for ages…. So, this seems the right time… I think, don't you?'
I said this, almost trying to elicit approval, but my heart was thudding in my chest.

He is furious I have dealt with this on my own. I haven't referred to him, discussed it with him, and sought his approval.
'Are you nuts?' He said, 'Taking on overheads you can't afford.' 'What ever you've done, you need to cancel it.'
'Can't be done.' I say feeling stronger. 'I've signed the lease.'
He explodes. His power has been undermined. I have taken control, his face turns red. In the interest of self preservation, I attempt to reassure him that I've done this as a direct result of his decision, to put the house on the market, but he's not having any of it.
'You *stupid* woman' (anyone who disagrees with him, is always stupid) 'Just cancel it, just cancel it.' 'Anyway, where did you get the money?'
'Diana loaned it to me.' I fibbed
We are not going to have that Louis Vuitton moment, that's for sure.
'This office… Where is it?' He blusters
I tell him, but he doesn't know the street and that makes him feel even less in control.
'What about all the studio furniture, how do you know it will fit?'
He can't be serious! Does he think he is the only one who can draw a floor plan to scale?
'Well I won't be doing any of the teaching.' He rants.
'Don't worry.' 'I've got that sorted.' I reply.
This isn't true, but I'm sure I can find someone to teach the odd slots he would cover, if not, I can. After all I won't be worrying about all the catering now.
'Who?' He is ranting now
In a quiet voice I say,
'No one you know.'
His control has been eroded further, and he's been given his P45. It's getting ugly. Deciding its time to make a move, I start to clear the table. This isn't going to be a meal to linger over.

'Don't expect any help from me, in any shape or form.' He continues nastily.
'Of course, I won't.' 'I have organised the move.... I have a van coming on Thursday.'
'You've what!' He screams
Then he smashes a plate on the floor close to my feet.
'Stop this!' I shout.
'Look.' I say, 'What do you expect me to do?' 'I come home from holiday and you want to put The Rectory on the market, telling me, I will have nowhere to work...'
'You obviously want to split up.... ....Although we haven't discussed it.'
'These are things we should have talked about.' 'It's not for you to ...'
'You double dealing little shit.' He screams and storms out, slamming the front door behind him. He will be in his workshop, throwing tools around, smoking furiously. In his hasty stage exit, he hasn't taken the obligatory cup of coffee, so I know he will be back. Clearing up the shards of china, I load the dishwasher and head upstairs for a bath and an early night.

Thursday arrives and so does the van. He is unpleasant with the men and runs around after them, checking everything going into the van. He looks deranged, his hair badly needs cutting and he's wearing an old sweater that has stretched nearly as far as his knees.
'No, not that, not that.' He yells.
I remonstrate 'Of course we must have the swivel chair for the desk.' 'Don't be silly.'

I'm trying, not very successfully, to soften the whole episode but he *so angry,* his face is turning purple. It's as if a hurricane is sweeping through the village and he can't stop it.... it's happening all around him, he's caught up in the vortex. I just want to get the last things into the van and to be off as soon as possible, leaving this hideous farce being played out on the drive to every dog walker in the village. I do not want to explain anything to those loitering with intent, poo bag in hand.

Chapter 4

Guardian Angel

I have known Andrew for more than twenty years and we've always got on well. For years he lived with Roger, but now they were no longer an item, he had moved to a double fronted Georgian town house with five floors including a light and airy basement. Andrew had all of the first floor, with four large windows to the drawing room alone. The rest of the house was let to professionals to give Andrew an income. There were so many embellishments from his time with Roger. Chandeliers, candelabras, a Blackamoor or two, tasselled tie backs, and antiques at every turn. You get the picture, Sybil Colefax and John Fowler would have been in seventh heaven here.

I had popped in for a cup of coffee. Andrew knew instantly, something was up because I didn't generally call in, unannounced. But I was in town and my mind was a melee of fragmented thoughts. Not knowing which way to turn, although my office was signed and sealed, I would sit in Waitrose's car park, until my parking ticket ran out, not wanting to go home. I had a thought, Andrew always knew somebody, who knew somebody… I remembered he had a connection with the Rasborough Estate so wondered if he knew the Estate manager.

'Now darling, what's up?' 'If you don't mind me saying, you look all in.'
'Andrew, I have to leave.' I said
'What do you mean…leave?' He quizzed
I explained my situation. We were sitting at his kitchen table, which had a Persian rug thrown over it. He pulled a small linen cloth out of a drawer, smoothed it out, then brought, a flowery melamine tray to the table. Pouring instant coffee from a silver coffee pot, he looked puzzled.
'What's going on?' He said, 'I didn't realise there were problems.'
I started to cry. 'Nobody does.'
'It's all behind closed doors.' 'I have to have a brave face, for the outside world… I'm so sorry.'

The tears came, with real sobbing, I was shaking.
'My dear.'
Andrew came around to my side of the table, putting his arms round my shoulders. Now I was really blubbing and so embarrassed, but just couldn't stop. He found a paper napkin for me to dry my eyes.
'Look.' He said, 'Go to the little girl's room, put some cold water on those eyes and I'll make some more coffee.' 'Don't worry we can sort this out.'
When I returned from the loo he gave me a big hug, I thought I the tears would start all over again. *Stop it right now.* I said to myself. *Get some control Alice.* Andrew, ever the pragmatist, started discussing the sale of The Rectory, how long it might take and where I might live.
'I was wondering if there might be cottage to let on the Rasborough Estate?' 'Didn't I meet the Estate manager at one of your drinks parties?' 'Could you put in a word for me...?' 'I just don't know if I can live there any longer, he's so angry, I've signed the lease on these studios.'
'What studios?' Andrew looked confused.
It seems in my weepy state, I had forgotten to mention them.
'Garrton Street?' He said, 'that's just down the road.'
'Yes, that's right... I've got the whole basement with a little courtyard garden.' 'It's so light and airy.... I've been decorating it... I'm very excited, but scared at the same time.'
He picked up the phone to ring his friend Mark, the Estate manager.
'Hey Mark, it's Andrew, how are you doing?' 'Good good...' 'Look, I've got a friend who's looking for a nice little cottage to rent... have you got anything?' There was a pause as Andrew listened 'I see... a waiting list, goodness, I didn't realise.' 'Well if there's any chance of you ... you know, reorganising the waiting list... if you get my meaning. ....' 'Of course, of course, but you would give me a ring if anything changes...? 'Yes, it would be good to catch up, let's get a few people together for Bridge, shall we?' 'OK... I will call you.' 'Thanks anyway.'
'Sorry darling, as you probably gathered, there's a waiting list. Mark says it's as long as his arm and he's not sure if he can wrangle something.' 'So, it's not looking very positive.' 'You're sure you can't stick it out sweetheart?' 'I really don't have any choice then do I?' I said shaking my head. I couldn't trust myself to say anymore for fear of breaking into sobs again. Andrew knew, so didn't press me further. Never was my silence so articulate.

On the drive home, I start to develop a strategy to protect myself. Gauging his moods, raises my anxiety levels, so I am always on the edge, feeling physically sick with apprehension, when I hear his foot on the stairs or his car return. I am being driven out of my own home. It isn't a safe place and in truth, I am terrified this abusive behaviour will boil over into something else.

Once, when he wanted a document signing, (a second charge on our home to fund another brilliant idea) and I wasn't willing, he drew a knife from the knife block. The sort of knife I call a sandwich knife, with a long thin blade. He remonstrated with me as I said I thought this loan wasn't a good idea. He flexed the point of the knife in his fingers. Tapping the point of the knife on the worktop as we talked. He used the very tip of the knife to point to the line marked with a pencil X indicating where I should sign. Had I no faith in him? Why was I making him feel worthless? Why wouldn't I back him?

'Do you know, how low, *you*'re making me feel?' 'You are knocking my self-confidence.' He said in a saddened voice.' 'Don't you realise how hurtful this is?' 'I'm trying my best…you, you are so cruel… I'm just trying to do the best for *us*.'

He cleverly twisted and manipulated the whole situation, by proclaiming, that by not signing this document, I was undermining him, driving his self-esteem into the ground. This was a great opportunity to develop his new product and I was standing in his way. His artful and divisive ability to engineer a situation to his advantage was a strategy I eventually learnt to recognise, but at the time I wasn't analysing anything. My full attention was on the blade of that knife. As low self-esteem was likely to turn into uncontrollable anger, without warning, I really had no choice but to sign the paperwork.

Pulling into the drive, my heart is in my mouth again. Opening the front door, I am greeted by a ghastly smell that is all too familiar. He's had another fry up for lunch, so I know exactly what I am going to find. All the pans on the hob, lumps of poached egg in the sink, a plate heavily smeared with HP Sauce on the work top and grease everywhere. It's like a punishment for going out, for leaving the building. On the plus side, he's out, so I don the rubber gloves to make a start clearing up his mess. You may be thinking, why don't you just leave it? ….. But I am the only one who will be inconvenienced. It's just easier to capitulate.

Next, heading for the basement to unload the washing machine…. Eeeh

Gods, there is a familiar sight. I remember at some point, when the IRA were in prison, they protested by hunger strikes and something called 'the dirty protest' where prisoners refused to slop out and smeared excrement over the walls. This is a similar protest, an expression of dissent and of confrontation, but from my husband. He has at least mastered the skill of taking his washing to the basement... well most days. However, he has found a way of using this accomplishment to his advantage. If, I must insist he delivers his washing to the laundry basket, I can jolly well pay for it. Right on top of the basket, 'face up' so to speak are his soiled underpants. For some time now, he has started to deliberately, leave serious amounts of excrement in his underpants and what's more he wants me to know about it. There they are.... again. It is not *an accident*. If he had had *an accident* surely, he would be keen to deal with it... it happens to us all and yes, it's embarrassing but we get on and clean up. Anyway, this is happening on an almost daily basis and always the pants are on top of the basket to greet me. The front door slams. Finding courage, through anger, I run up the stairs. How dare he do this to me? How vile an action? Why am I putting up with this?

'Look here.' I say

He looks bewildered, as I hold the offending pants on the end of an old walking stick, I have found downstairs.

'I am not dealing with these *disgusting* pants anymore!'

And I fling them towards him. They drop on the floor by his feet. He steps back looking aghast. Has this woman flipped?

'Deal with them yourself!' 'Anymore of this nonsense and they will go in the bin, just don't ask me to deal with them.'

He tries the *Poor Me* card.

'I've not been well... ... My tummy... it's all this upset *you* cause.'

Here we go again, turn the tables. It's all *my* fault; of course, well don't I just know it?

'Well get to a doctor or wear disposable pants.... I mean it, I *will* bin them.'

After this shout out, I feel stronger. I've taken charge. I am pleased with myself. He's embarrassed, but if I think I have solved the problem I am wrong. The following week it starts again. So, I say nothing. Each day the pants are bagged and hit the wheelie bin. After about ten days, he complains there are no pants in his drawer.

'Am I supposed to bring them up now, as well as take them down to

Alice Waite

the basement?' He queries, as if he has been asked to descend and climb Everest, with his washing on a regular basis.
'Nope.' I reply, '*You* just need to get to M&S to buy some more.'
He looks perplexed. Then the penny drops. He is *so* cross.
'How dare you throw my pants away!' He rages.
Walking into the kitchen leaving him to contemplate his underwear crisis, I don't recognise myself. There are no winners in this game of control, however I validate my behaviour. No one comes through this hell unscathed.

A few weeks later, Andrew phoned my mobile.
'Can you pop in sweetheart?' 'I've had a thought.'
It's mid-afternoon, the same day and I'm back at his kitchen table. China tinkles as he proffers a pot of tea and hands me a plate of Garibaldi biscuits. Andrew is always immaculate. I am contemplating his Navy-blue Cashmere V neck and crisp blue striped shirt, as he says,
'I'll be mother, then shall I?'
'Sorry Andrew I was miles away.'
'I take it things aren't any better at home?' He said
'No.' I shake my head, 'no, no and no again.'
The tea is so strong it could be alcohol, but a Garibaldi rises to the challenge as I gulp it down.
'Now listen darling, a tenant upstairs has given notice.' 'They will be leaving before the end of the month.' 'What do you think?'
At first the idea does not register. Why is he telling me this? Then the penny drops.
'You mean I could move in… rent it I mean?'
'Exactly that.' He said.
'I've got a spare key and permission to show prospective tenants around.'
'Finish your tea and then we'll take a look.'

Andrew took me up to the next floor and opened the door, to what could have been a Laura Ashley showroom. Lots of flowery fabric tied back at the window and all in peach and cream. Clearly, he is proud of the furnishings he has chosen, so I bite my lip and compliment him on the scheme. As a thwarted interior designer, he beams. There is a Sitting room with a teak dining table in the window. On the opposite wall, a darker peach sofa with a single green Parker Knoll wing chair and a couple of side tables. The walls sport a random collection of watercolours, hung in a haphazard way.

There are two bedrooms, a galley kitchen and bathroom. Two bedrooms, meant I could at least have two of the girls to stay, but then, one could always be on the peachy sofa. My mind is overdrive. Andrew watches my face as we wander round. Then we take in the view, over the square. Such a beautiful square and five minutes' walk from the new office. This must be the right thing to do. I turn to Andrew and say we must talk about the rent. He closes the front door, as we make our way down the stairs back to his flat or apartment as he likes to call it, he says,
'Look darling, you will be safe here.' 'There is an entry phone at the front door, so he can't just walk in and I don't put names on the bells anyway, just the apartment numbers.'
He makes a fresh pot of tea and we discuss money. He kindly offers to let me have the flat at less than the going rate.
'Because I like to have people in the building I can trust.' 'That's important to me.' He said, pointing out that this flat is directly above his.
'You can rely on me not to have wild parties.' I laugh. Some hope of that, I thought.
We chink our tea cups in celebration and I know it was meant to be, as we girls are so fond of saying.

Chapter 5

She's Leaving Home

It is D Day. I'm busying around as usual, on a Saturday morning, changing beds, loading the washing machine, clearing up the cat sick, along with the removal of a dead vole, a present from Betty our cat, so nothing unusual here. He was in a fickle mood. Not wanting to go. I impressed upon him, nothing ventured, nothing gained and if it was really a dead duck he could just come back on Monday. His friend Nat, (otherwise known to my girls, as Scratch and Sniff, for reasons too vile to go into here) had offered him space on his stand at the NEC to try out another of his…
'This is going to be a winner!' products.
For example, let's think of a recent one… Ah yes. Coffins for Hamsters. These were marbled, flat pack, cardboard boxes, to keep on hand for when the dear little rodent pegs it. Of course, no parent wanted to contemplate buying a coffin at the same time as their child chooses their hamster at the pet shop. The sales pitch *He's done his best, now lay him to rest… in a Celestial Box,* didn't really cut the mustard with the pet shop owners either. They certainly didn't want this sales promo board, next to the golden furries.
The trouble is, when you strive for month after month on *another winner that the public will go nuts for,* sooner or later, you must get out there to test the waters. But, when you test the waters and they were not as expected, depression sets in. Morose meanness sets in, and then metaphorically speaking, you can justify kicking the nearest dog. I was that dog. The person who took upon her shoulders everything you were not prepared to own up to. I opened the brown envelopes, juggling teaching three evening classes a week, as well as my day job, to put food on the table, while you came up with *another* brilliant idea, shutting yourself in your disgusting shed for months on end, to create it. To be fair, some of your brilliant ideas had been successful, to a degree. But your enthusiasm lasted a nano

Only cry on Fridays

second or six before the next *brilliant idea* was on the drawing board and you pushed the last one off a cliff.
The beauty of *this* current idea and my new enthusiasm for it, was that when you return from the NEC, I will not be here to smell the all-pervading stench, of your failure. The brown envelopes will be yours. So, will the blocked dishwasher. (It is NOT a waste disposal unit, combo). The piles of socks left by your side of the bed, could form a pyramid or art installation. The contents of the milk jug you left in your shed, could be made into cheese. Hey! Another, *brilliant idea*?
I am happy to leave you with these thoughts as I potter about, moving A to B, folding towels, scouring the hob… Gosh that's something else to think about. The air is still blue from your huge fry up this morning, and every plate and pan has been left for the Skivvy to clear up. Tell you what! Today, I might just be too busy today, to deal with this.

I am a woman of lists. Heaven knows when/if I get to the Pearly Gates I will have a list of questions for St Peter about my accommodation, the rules, dress code et al. The lists I now held in my sweaty hand, had been weeks in the making, hidden away from prying eyes, in places no man would consider going. The cleaning cupboard, the linen cupboard, the basket of ironing. The lists were organised into groups. Household: with sub headings: Baking/ chopping/saucepans /utensils/ china/ cutlery/vases. Linen: with sub heading: Sheets/ pillow slips/ duvet covers/towels/ bath mats. General: Photographs/ Art/ Books. You get the idea. Detail, detail and tick boxes to boot.
Finally, he was in the car and had driven off. From previous experience I knew an hour was the minimum time between him leaving and turning back, because he had forgotten something. I bided my time making phone calls. White van man, only had my mobile, so could never blow my cover. I phoned to confirm 2.00pm.
'We could come over now love if you like?'
Tempting though it was, I declined.

Having already moved the clothes I was taking with me, into one section of my wardrobe and linen to a couple of shelves of the airing cupboard, I was as prepped as I could be. Some things had already been sequestered into the boot of my car, week by week, to my new abode… small things we weren't using on a day to day basis. Silver serving spoons, photograph albums, that kind of thing. The hour passed by remarkably quickly and

soon Barbara was at the front door. What could she do? I set her to work with a list. I had been hoarding newspaper for weeks, but in no time, as it was layered between plates and glasses, it ran out. So, my collection of scarves was called into play.
White van man arrived at 2pm. Two burly lads, wearing shorts and tees. Walking them round the house pointing out pieces of furniture, just small items they were to pack into the van before the boxes, the clothes and so many things I did not have boxes for, I could almost see their brains ticking over, as they eyed up antiques, paintings, five bedrooms, plus attics and the ambience of a good life. I was not prepared to explain, this was a business transaction, two men, their van, with five hours labour. The van was quickly filled and so my car was utilised to take suitcases and some boxes. Barbara's took still more. Her battered VW was filled to the gunnels, I worried about her seeing out of the back window.

My handwritten letter of some two A4 pages was on the dining table. Next to it, I piled numerous small plastic boxes, that had contained wax ear plugs. Wax ear plugs? I can hear you muttering. Emotional abuse is a complex tapestry. It is an incredibly skilled form of torture. No black eyes or broken noses, just hidden psychological, brutal behaviour, meted out with such aplomb, that the person on the receiving end, starts to doubt their sanity. So, when in my deepest sleep, vile words and phrases started to slip into my consciousness, as the person who promised to love and cherish me, moved closer and closer, I thought I was having a nightmare. But when his damp, warm breath and the extreme vocabulary became ever louder, as it permeated my ear, I knew I was not dreaming. This was in fact a waking nightmare and it became a recurring one.

You may ask, why I didn't remonstrate and writing this now, I could ask myself the same question. But rewind to the depths of a systematic and persistent pattern of abuse, when I regularly questioned my own judgement, instincts and sanity. Yes, I could have moved to the guest room, but part of me was trying not to let him see, how upsetting I found his behaviour, because it meant, I would be acknowledging my predicament and his control over me. So, night after night, with the aid of over the counter sleeping pills and wax ear plugs I managed to block out the verbal abuse and withdraw into a deep silent chasm of peace. Hence, the pile of empty ear plugs boxes, which I referred to in my letter.

Just then, I heard an unexpected and familiar voice.
'Mum, what's going on?' 'Mum, where are you?'
It was my middle daughter Hettie. I was not expecting her home from University this weekend. She was with her friend Sam and both looked alarmed at the sight of the van and the cars spilling with general household effects. I led her into the dining room, Sam made herself scarce. Crying, as I started to explain, I couldn't go on any longer, she started to cry. I begged her not to phone her father for at least a couple of hours after I had left. She was genuinely shell shocked, that it had come to this, but reluctantly agreed.

No one can ever get inside anyone else's relationship or behind those closed doors. Their loving Daddy, what could be wrong? They have never known anything but his kindness. As she picked up my letter and started to read, there was a look of incredulity on her face. I sensed she thought, I was making it all up. Then she took in the pile of small plastic boxes, labelled ear plugs, but chose not to acknowledge them. Giving her a big hug, I walked away to load the last few things into my car.

All the trips to van and car were watched by our twelve-year-old cat, Betty. She had a bouffant of ginger, unruly candy floss for a coat. Her vivid green eyes, followed every arm load that walked past her, as she sat on the kitchen steps. My greatest sadness, was that I couldn't take Betty with me to a city centre flat. At least now Hettie was home, I didn't have to set the automatic cat feeders and I hoped in my heart of hearts, I would be able to reclaim her when I moved back to the country, in no time at all. As I pulled away, with the van following, I glanced up at a window where she had finally taken up residence. It was the thought of leaving her, not my home that brought the tears to my eyes.

Chapter 6

Silver Service

Driving straight into a parking bay in St Phillip's Square, I fed the meter. Barbara's VW and the van are double parked; it's the only way on this busy Saturday. Taking a suitcase, plus holdall up to the second floor, I unlock my front door. Seconds later I am followed by the men with a side table. They now know the extent of the staircase climbing, they are in for over the next couple of hours. Barbara appears with an armful of clothes and lays them on the bed. Nervous of traffic wardens and tickets, she returns to her car, getting the men to empty it while she keeps watch. Meanwhile the contents of the escape convoy, are stacking up around the flat in disorganised piles. It's going to take forever to find homes for everything. Barbara calls my mobile. 'I just can't park Alice, I think I'll head home.'
'But, it's gone half past five.' I say. 'Spaces will become free as the shops start to close.'
'I know, but Linda is coming over and I need to get back.' She explained. This is the first I've heard of this. Struck by a feeling of abandonment, there is a lump in my throat, then a tear trickled down my cheek. Somehow, I had quite wrongly thought, Barbara would be helping me unpack into the evening, perhaps we'd get a take away. I do not have chance to discuss this further, as the men require more instructions. Then, looking out of the window, I see her car exit the square, I can't quite believe it…
Just when my heart is in the pit of my stomach and tears are welling up, I hear the rattle of china. I turn around to see Andrew standing with a tray, laid with a silver teapot, pretty china cups and saucers, milk, sugar and a plate of shortbread. He puts it on the kitchen worktop and gives me a bear hug. I can't hold back the tears any more. He quietly tells me,
'It will all be alright darling, it will all be alright.'
White van men appear, and gratefully gulp down Andrew's tea.

So, everything is unloaded, the men have been paid and gone. Standing, surrounded by a small part of my life in bags and boxes, strewn around the floor, I feel unbearably sad, as I reflect on the enormity of what I have done. With shoulders like a bent coat hanger, I mentally shut down, to set about the task of moving things from A to B in the hope of getting some semblance of order; after all its work as usual on Monday.

My phone starts ringing as I knew it would. I can see it's *him* and do not answer.

It rings again and again… I bury it under the sofa cushion. Occasionally I check the missed calls to see there are new numbers, but I know, with certainty, he is using other people's phones to get me to pick up.

Then one of my girls called. 'Mum where are you, what's going on?'

'I presume you have spoken to Hettie?' I say

'Yes, Mum…. why have you done it like this?' 'You should have talked it through with Dad properly'. 'This isn't the way to go about it'. 'What are you thinking of?'

'Do *you* think, if I had thought, reasonable discussion with your father was possible, I would have left like this?' 'Can you begin to think, just how bad it has to be, to leave my own lovely home?' 'You just don't know the half of it my darling.' 'You just don't know.'

There were lots of tears on both sides, but I held firm. I was not going to apologise for leaving or not sitting down to have a reasonable discussion, as she put it.

It was only when I said, 'I had to leave this way.' 'I was too frightened of Dad to do it any other way.' She drew breath and there was a slight pause. This was not what she wanted to hear or indeed believe. There was no comfort blanket I could give to her.

I can only begin to guess what was going through her mind. Will The Rectory have to be sold? Where will all my stuff go? What happens at Christmas/ graduation? She can't have been unaware of the difficulties between us… but then I thought perhaps she could. The quips around the dining table that seemed *so funny,* but they were at Mum's expense. Somehow, his charisma managed to draw them in, to play his games. On the surface, it all seems so innocent, just banter. Except the underlying tone of this banter had history and long reaching consequences. It had changed the way I lived and behaved over a sustained period of time.

'So, girls, let's get the table cleared please.' I would mutter after preparing and serving a meal.

Alice Waite

'Just leave it' he would assert…. 'We can do it later.' Code for, *she* can do it later.

'No let's just get it done now.' I would chip in.' 'I need the table... anyway, I want to sort out some paperwork.'

'Some people' he would say in a derisory tone. 'Some people just can't let other people have a relaxing time.' 'They just want to put everyone else under pressure, to suit themselves.'

'It's nothing to do with that.' I said fighting my corner 'I need the table to sort out some paper work for tomorrow *and* it's perfectly reasonable to expect *some* help.' 'After all, I've produced the supper while you all sat by the fire …. *please,* let's not make a song and dance about a little job like loading the dishwasher.'

'Well if it's *so* little… we'll do it later, hey girls!' he quips.

He's making it easy for them to be complicit with his behaviour. They have an ally in their laziness.

Everyone, but me thinks it's *so* funny.

'Mum, take a chill pill.'

'Yes do!' He says, 'At Mum's time of life, *some* women do need chill pills.' He laughs in a derisory tone and continues 'don't worry girls, it's also the time when *they* can go a bit ……' He taps his head and makes a contorted face. 'Go a bit loopy if *they* can't get their own way.'

Everyone finds this hilarious. I find it utterly humiliating. Tears are pricking my eyes. He sees and seizes the moment. He gives me one of his looks, turning my body cold. I am fearful and swallowing hard, I turn away. He's ready to deliver the next line of my humiliation and in a withering voice says

'Then, women like *this,* use emotion to get their own way.' 'But we won't be drawn in to this la la fantasy world…. will we?'

He wipes the floor with my dignity. More gesticulating… with fingers tapping the side of his head again. He's playing to the gallery, he's centre stage. Our daddy is *so* funny! They see him as the outside world does. A most congenial man…. 'He's so affable.' 'You are so lucky!' 'He's such a laugh.' Accolades from our friends are never ending. They do not see behind closed doors and your suffocating behaviour, trivialising every nuance of my existence. Sniggering, my family leave the room, to go back to the comfort of the fireside.

I cannot blame you, my girls, although I wish there had been more sensitivity to my plight. You were easily sucked into these seemingly playful exchanges, because they suited your Sunday indolence, justifying your release from domestic trivia as you saw it. You were not mature enough to read the distress signals.

After hours unpacking and breaking down boxes, I have run out of space. They are stacked on their sides in the hallway, until I can't get past. Eventually with relief, bed linen comes to light, so I can make up the bed. I am utterly drained, not only physically, but emotionally. I can hear my phone ringing and ringing but can't face having to justify myself and go over and over the same conversation, when no one will consider this situation from my point of view. Ask yourself girls, just how bad does it have to be, to uproot yourself from a lovely home? Just how scared would you have to be, to feel you couldn't discuss this with your husband? Really…. Just ask yourself those questions, before you remonstrate with me about 'Having a proper and rational discussion with Daddy.'

These conversations are whirring around in my head, but then I wake with a start, in the small hours as a door bangs on another floor. The noise bounces off the internal stone staircase, through five floors. So many unfamiliar sounds punctuate the rest of that fitful night. HMO. House of Multiple Occupancy. I have to get to grips with this new way of living.

Chapter 7

Aftermath

The enormity of what I must deal with, races into my consciousness, the second I open my eyes. Retrieving my phone from under a cushion, there are twenty-six missed calls. I can't deal with this now, there are more pressing matters, such as finding a towel and discovering how to work the shower. There is a shower curtain on a rail over the bath, which the moment the shower starts, is sucked towards me, swaddling my naked body in a cold nylon craziness. The shower is a plastic box, with a very short hose, the antithesis of the power shower I had known, in a former life. It seems like a lifetime ago, but it was only yesterday morning.

Ryvita and jam, plus coffee make a quick breakfast. As I survey the carnage around me, it is clear there isn't going to be enough storage. There is a hall cupboard with an ancient Hoover dumped on the floor. I muse about getting a hanging rail in there for coats, but I must take care, money is tight, especially now, because I now have the rent for this flat to find, as well as everything else. This has been a leap of faith into unchartered territory and I feel sick with the enormity of it all. Then I am sick. Not a good start to the day with so much to do. Eventually some semblance of order is achieved, but realising I feel faint with hunger, hotfoot to Waitrose around the corner to get some supplies in. The courses haven't started yet. There's another hopeful six weeks to fill the places, which I absolutely need to …cash flow is everything. Money or lack of it, is constantly on my mind. At least I haven't had to pay Andrew three months' rent in advance and an inventory deposit.
'On the first of the month darling, just push a cheque under my door.'
I'm unpacking my carrier bags, calculating my bank balance, minus the groceries I've just bought when an unfamiliar buzzing punctuates my thoughts. Jolting back into the here and now, I realise it's the intercom phone. Hettie has arrived. She had phoned earlier, asking to come to see

me. I gave her the flat number with firm instructions, not to tell her father. Already, I have put her in a difficult situation. Buzzing her into the main door, I hear her making her way up the staircase. Standing in my doorway, she bounces in.
'Mummy'! She exclaims, and we hug very tightly. Her elder sister, Antonia is in London and Cesca is still away visiting the boyfriend. Clearly Hettie has been sent as the envoy. She looks around the flat.
'It's *so* not you Mum!'
'I know' I say, 'But it won't be for long I'm sure' 'We just need to get everything sorted out in the next couple of months and well… I'll be able to buy a cottage maybe….'
She interrupts 'Mum… Dad's in bits.'

I can imagine, I think. As of yesterday, he has no one to blame for his failures. No one to bully, victimise and hurt. The unpalatable reality is that emotional abuse knows no socio-economic boundaries, nor do the abusers look dysfunctional. They are to all intent and purposes, perfectly ordinary looking. The abusers do not show their bullying and undermining tactics in public, to the outside world, they are extremely loving and caring, truly entertaining characters. Pure Jekyll and Hyde. Except once, he did mistakenly show his true colours to friends, but managed to recover the situation quickly. Our guests were leaving and on the drive the conversation turned to cars. At the time we only had one car between us, known as *his car*. This was rather strange because my business had paid for it, but he quickly made it his own, with the smell of cigars, an over flowing ashtray, sweet wrappers and general detritus. I longed for my own car, which I knew I would keep immaculate.
I had to negotiate to use the car and this was persistently monitored with 'How long will you be? 'Do you need to go there now?' 'Well, I need the car.'
And all too often,
'I need to go into town, so we can go together.'
I found this constant surveillance of my comings and goings extremely difficult and sometimes didn't go out for days.
'Someone asked 'so what car do you drive Alice?'
Oh, I don't have a car, at the moment.' I said
Embarrassed that this had been noticed, quick as a shot, he quipped
'Ha! Where would she want to go without me?'
There was an awkward silence, which was quickly broken when he realised

his joke had not seen as funny, but a rather strange comment. He retrieved his position with 'Ha! Only joking!!'

Embarrassed, everyone including me, laughed rather too heartily. I did not want the outside world to see my humiliation. There was also a sense of shame, I was being treated this way. I felt guilty, I must not be a good enough wife/ mother, and this is why he is behaving like this. It's my fault. He then told everyone he was about to order me a Mercedes estate.

'How super is that Alice?' Someone said

This was the first I had heard of it, but I beamed, as if I had known all along.

They cleverly lure us, yes us… even professional women, into damsel mode, under the guise of kindness. We accept these gestures, because we feel looked after and loved. For example, he insisted on doing all motorway driving

'So, you can relax.' But the upshot is, at this point I was so inexperienced, driving on the motorway, I avoided it. He always dealt with the big financial stuff, like the mortgage, tax and the accountant. And, because you trust your partner in life who pretends he knows what he's doing, like a lamb to the slaughter, you…. '*Just sign here.*' Now I ask myself, 'where did all this erudite financial knowledge spring from?' Well, I can tell you now, and I know to my cost, for the most part, its unqualified guff.

So, Dad's in bits? Well, I was pretty scared and fearful of his reaction. He might just wait outside the front door until I came out. Or turn up at the office, to cause an embarrassing scene. My fear of his angry backlash was very real, and I was genuinely terrified of repercussions. The anxiety was making me physically sick. Hettie didn't want to hear anything against her father. Therefore, trying to explain why I had been driven to leave, wasn't making any sense. I was painting a picture she didn't recognise or certainly didn't want to recognise. Despondent with the enormity of dealing with two warring parents, she looked at me with pained incredulity, just as she had the day before, when confronted with the boxes of ear plugs. She seemed to pity my plight, but I suspected she was also questioning my mental health. In fact, after that visit, I didn't see or hear from her, again for weeks.

Work hummed on like a well-oiled machine, I put in the hours, but was always looking six months ahead, proffering my services for talks to

Ladies' Luncheon clubs, or organising Readers' day events for the glossies. I didn't have a computer (which, by the way were only just superseding typewriters). I didn't even have a typewriter and was so tight on funds, I couldn't buy one for ages. Hazel, my ever-faithful book keeper would turn letters around overnight for me. It seems farcical now, but I would handwrite a letter, then fax it to Hazel. She kept a stock of my letterhead and would type it up, then put it back in the post for me to sign. This way we could get by on a two to three-day return basis, better than many professional companies including my solicitor. Hazel, had also typed a series of *Master letters* with details of all the courses I offered. Dear…. Blank, I would then personalise the letter with a hand-written flourish. I had a stock of photocopied versions ready to sign and send out. To all intent and purposes, I had a secretary who was managing the admin.

When I was leaving school (and sixteen was considered sufficient education in my family) my mother had wanted me to take a typing course. The thought that her daughter might become a secretary filled her with pride. Nothing as grand as a Secretarial course you understand, because we were not grand, we were ordinary, and my mother made sure I knew that. I did not want to be a typist or even a secretary, so I refused the offer of the very rudimentary typing course.
'This will be such a useful skill' she said, 'It will stand you in good stead, until you get married'.
She meant, find a meal ticket. What I really wanted to do, was to go to Art College, but that involved staying on in the Sixth form to take A levels and then heaven forbid a Foundation course, followed by a three-year degree course. In your dreams Alice! I must have been an early feminist, although the word was not in use in my immediate working-class circle. Books such as, The Female Eunuch were for the intelligentsia, not for shop assistants, which was my alternative destiny.
'Well if you won't type you will HAVE to go into a shop' declared my mother.
After a spell working backstage at the Hippodrome operating the lighting board… which I loved, I finally found a job in a design shop. Now remember, Habitat had only just opened its first store in London, so a shop filled with Scandinavian furniture and bold orange and brown prints, in the provinces was very cool.
So, in declining to learn to type, I learnt lots of other skills and through evening classes at the local Art College a new world opened to me. Over

a year or two, I gained confidence in my abilities, sufficient enough to build a portfolio to apply for a full-time degree course. Still living at home, bringing in a wage, which was all my mother really cared about, I applied for my courses using my work address for all the correspondence, I could not risk the melt down that my unreasonable desire for further education would bring. In those days there were grants available. Yes, the local authority actually gave students funds to further their education…. And there was no mention of paying fees. It seems unbelievable in today's climate. Now, in order to get a grant, your parents were required to fill in forms giving their financial details, so I knew I would hit a brick wall. Then I discovered there was such a thing as an independent grant, based on a mature student's income. At twenty, I was now considered mature, but had to demonstrate I earned not less than £425 per year. Hard to believe now, I know, but you could buy a small house for about £1500 so it's all relative. I always had a strong work ethic, so taking on two extra jobs to make up the shortfall, was the answer to my dilemma.

On a Sunday, I took three buses to work in a friend's Coffee Bar called Downtown. Then for five evenings a week, I was an Usherette at the local flea pit of a cinema. I finished my day job at 5.30pm and then raced out of the door to start my shift at the Gaumont cinema at 6.00pm. The word, Usherette has all but disappeared from our vocabulary, but in those days, uniformed ladies would show customers to their seats in the cinema with a torch. Arriving at 5.55pm there was the uniform to do battle with. Made of dull brown serge material, the jacket and skirt were so stiff with the B.O. of previous workers, both could have stood up on their own. There were gold buttons up to the neck and gold braided epaulettes on each shoulder of the jacket. The stiffness of the serge and the design in general, meant movement was limited. Our duties included, checking the tickets of the customers at the door, then tearing the said ticket in half, so that there was no possibility of reuse. Another usherette would then show the customers to their seats. Sometimes, when we were showing a block buster, there would be queues outside, and we had to physically count the number of free seats available. That's right, no computerised tills…

Of course, we saw the films numerous times from our positions at the very back of the cinema and naturally became bored. We knew every line verbatim, so when block busters were retained for several weeks, our tedium knew no bounds. Once, when the film was well under way, I was given the task of showing a couple to available seats. In the dark they meekly followed, as my torch light guided them through the auditorium. I spotted *seats* in the middle of row M and left them to interrupt probably twenty people watching the film, to make their way to the centre. With much under the breath grumbling, everyone had to stand up for the couple to pass. Unfortunately, as I well knew, there was only a single seat in the middle of row M where they were left stranded, and then had to make an exit with even more kerfuffle. You can imagine, the fuming and complaining from those involved … but by now the giggling usherettes had made themselves scarce…… to head for the freezer room, where the Draconian red headed Pat would be giving orders to stack the freezer trays, for the interval.

Pat handed out handwritten chits with our requirements from the freezer. She kept a carbon copy, so under her beady eye, we could count the unsold stock, back to the freezer and reconcile the money we had taken, along with our float. We diligently followed the list, stacking our trays ready for the interval. Each night, Pat would make the monumental decision as to who would be *the chosen one*…. Who would be The Fruit Parfait Girl? I scanned my list and saw to my utter dismay, that tonight, *I* was the chosen one. *I* was The Fruit Parfait Girl. Reader, let me tell you, in those days, I was a slight soul and found it hard enough to carry the normal insulated freezer tray, loaded with choc ices, ice cream et al. But the Fruit Parfait Girl had an extra-large tray filled to the gunnels, with the dreaded concoctions of raspberry ripple ice cream cones, topped with jam, then whipped cream, with a glace cherry on the top. Not only was I required to walk backwards down the slope of the auditorium, navigating the occasional steps, but I had to wear a yellow nylon overall and tricorn hat, which informed everyone *I was* The Fruit Parfait Girl. The indignity didn't stop there. I wore a torch around my neck which shone down onto the tray, so my face was in darkness. However, my anonymity was to be short lived. At the appointed time, towards the end of the B film and before the main event, we would struggle out of the freezer room, along a labyrinth of maroon gloss painted corridors, to our appointed positions of entrance to the auditorium. The Fruit Parfait Girl would be given the hallowed position of the centre aisle. When we were given the signal, the doors were opened and turning around 180 degrees to face the audience, started to make our way very slowly and backwards towards the screen. The weight of these trays filled with frozen goodies, was enough to induce serious back and

shoulder strain. But as the Fruit Parfait girl, I had to wait until all the other girls were in position at the front, before making my entrance, down the central aisle. Any hope of not being recognised faded, as I was lit by a huge spotlight, when the manager boomed through his mic
'Look for the Fruit Parfait Girl NOW'
The spotlight followed my wobbly steps down through the auditorium. I shuffled backwards, constantly looking over my shoulder, terrified of missing one of the steps and ending up legs in the air, covered in the wretched Parfaits. Dying a thousand deaths, I hoped no one I knew, was in the audience. Within seconds, long queues snaked up the aisles, as the audience chose its favourite interval refreshments. The Fruit Parfaits were sold out in no time. At last when the music for the main film started, we made our way back through the cinema and to Pat in the freezer room.
'Not good enough!' she bellowed at me. 'You took forever to get to the front!' 'You looked like a rabbit, caught in the headlights.'
Then, 'There has been a complaint' 'Some of the Fruit Parfaits sold were missing the glace cherry from the top!' 'How can this be?'
Her face was red and her hair on fire.
'I really don't know' I stammered.
My face and neck were now also on fire.
Pat started slamming freezer trays around and for a moment, as she pushed a box of choc ices into the massive freezer, I thought I might be spending my last days beside them. Of course, I knew how the cherries had vanished. While we were waiting for the doors to the auditorium to be opened, some of the clear plastic lids to the Parfaits had been eased off and several glace cherries eaten by hungry young women, rushing from one job to the next.
'If this ever happens again' she continued starring at me '*You* will be given your cards' 'Now form an orderly line, count the ices you haven't sold and cash up… look sharp now!'
Months later, I did get the sack for reading 'War and Peace' with my torch at the back of the cinema. Fast forward to the next financial year and my PAYE slips would show I had earned £450 in the previous year, so at last, I could apply for an independent grant.
Following a huge row with my parents, leaving home and taking my degree course, here I am, thirty years of marriage and three children later, still unable to type… other than with one finger, which incidentally, is how I am writing this. In sombacke ways my temerity has backfired on me, but in many other ways, I have been able to develop skills and nurture innate talents, that would have been latent, had I been dispatched to

typist's school. But hey! I can drive a car, but don't know what goes on under the bonnet. I can turn on a light, but I can't rewire a house. We all have individual skills which we must make the most of and should not feel guilty if we need to pay others, to fulfil areas we neither have the inclination, or the skill to deal with.

Chapter 8

Settle into Working Life

As I had moved into my offices a month or so before I left my home, everything is ship shape, ready for the autumn term's courses. I already have some bookings but anxiously court more for the first course which starts mid-October. Over the phone, I talk prospective students through the curriculum and then, by first class post they receive the prospectus the next day. Money, or indeed the lack of it, causes so much stress, so many turbulent nights. Every debit card transaction, is subtracted from the bank balance carried in my head before the card ever reaches the terminal.

I haven't dared ask for an overdraft but know I'm going to need some working capital sooner, rather than later. Picking up the phone to my bank manager, a date for a meeting is arranged. This is the first time I have had a meeting with a bank manager on my own. On previous occasions, usually pleading for an extension to his business overdraft, I would sit mutely, beside my husband while he, with the gift of the gab, would regale the man behind the mahogany desk with a sales pitch about his latest brilliant idea. Occasionally I might chip in with some enthusiastic remark, but otherwise my presence was merely decorative. Indeed, I was always instructed what to wear.

'Not trousers…!' He would advise.' What about that suit with the little pleated skirt?'

This time, and with a new manager, I wanted to present myself in a much more serious vein. This is *my* business. *I* am in charge, so I arrive in a smart trouser suit (as matching trousers and jacket were known) and stride purposely into Nat West's Business unit, sited next door to the bank itself. Our separation is something I draw a veil over, simply talking about the new premises and the great opportunity I have, now the courses are based in the city centre. He seems happy enough with last year's figures and signs off a small overdraft, with immediate effect. This feels incredibly empowering and I skip back to the office.

Carolyn and I are meeting for lunch at the wine bar along the road. Over the years we have shared many a lunch and like agony aunts, have listened to each other's marriage problems. She is still *working on her marriage* although we both know, this means, she will never leave. When I phoned to tell her I had left, I could hear the disbelief in her silence on the line. Eventually she mustered 'When? ....' How did it go?' 'What did he say? OMG!'
I couldn't risk telling her beforehand, because our daughters are good friends and one careless remark would have been a disaster. So, its lunch at Clarke's with Carolyn. I know she is intrigued by my situation, if not a little jealous, I did, finally get up and go. We sit in Clarke's with a Brie salad until pretty much the last of the lunch time stragglers have gone. I know Gary the owner, he clears the table and then brings our coffee over. Ten seconds later he's back with the most catastrophic news. There's just been a news flash on the little TV he keeps behind the bar.
'The World trade centres.... have been bombed.' 'A plane has just gone into one tower!'
I assume there has been a dreadful accident. At this moment, I have no idea there has been an act of terrorism and how the world is about to stand still, not venture out unless absolutely necessary. Everywhere was in deep shock and incredulous this could really happen. Where would be next?
The extra students I had hoped to enrol for the October courses, simply never materialised. From that day onwards, my telephone did not ring, the streets were all but empty. Economic inertia set in, it was like a plug had been pulled and a haunting malaise paralysed the world. All my financial forecasts to keep afloat until spring might as well be put through the shredder. Thank heavens for the new overdraft, but I knew that was not going to be sufficient to carry me through. What if I couldn't find the rent for the studios, the rent for my flat? Then there were business rates, electricity. ... ...It was imperative I found another income stream.
I had previously held courses for several Further Education Colleges, so resolved to approach them again, with a view to starting a run of Spring Courses. Everything is quiet, terribly quiet, the world is in such shock. No one misses a news bulletin, just in case. There are no enquires about any upcoming courses, in fact the phone barely rings, I wish someone other than One Biz would phone.

Alice Waite

I worked through the October course, keeping chirpy for the students, but all along knowing, I haven't passed my breakeven point. Distraught with worry about my overheads, the overdraft has almost reached its limit, but the bills keep coming in. To make matters worse, I receive bills for our home, forwarded by my husband, for gas, electricity and rates. He really must be joking! He will be sending me his grocery bills next. They all went straight back in the post, return to sender. What do I do? I have a couple of credit cards with decent limits, but I need money in the bank to pay the bills and I can't use a credit card for these. One card sends a flyer with my statement offering 0% on purchases for twelve months. I stare at the flyer and then suddenly think, what if use my own terminal to process *a sale* with my own card? The money will go into my own bank account … This moment of clarity helped keep me afloat until at last, the enrolments for the Spring Courses started coming in.

Meanwhile America is in crisis and there is footage daily of what remains of the twin towers in New York. Such ugly scenes and then the raw emotion of voicemail messages to loved ones, is heart rending. My memories of New York are mixed, I have been several times, every trip filling me with elation. I particularly loved the buzzy (and then) edgy atmosphere of areas like Soho and Tribeca.

The last time we went, only a couple of years earlier, proved to be a different experience. From the start, he was not in the greatest mood, but after a seven-hour flight without smoking, I assumed once he had had a cigar, his spirits would be lifted. This was a business trip, but the business just didn't materialise. We had stand at a trade show and so were indoors at the Javitt centre from 9.00am to 5.00pm. At the end of the day, I always wanted to return to the hotel, to freshen up before dinner, which was almost the highlight of the day. He wasn't having any of this. He wanted to go for food on the way back to the hotel, sit in front of the TV and pass out having emptied a good part of the mini bar. Thus, there was no possibility of making dinner, a little occasion, when perhaps we might enjoy conversation in relaxed surroundings. I was still living in hope we might get through a bad patch and rekindle what we had, many years ago. Always trying to win his approval, my increasing efforts to please him were less and less successful. So, I would go along with his choice and we would stop off somewhere uninspiring to eat, on the way back to the hotel. One evening we were walking back after a meal, when he started picking on me. He was berating me over something or other and became increasingly hostile. To get out of earshot, I walked faster, so I was a few paces ahead. He continued hurling abuse and had to raise his voice to ensure I could hear him. I was pacing ahead, every bullying, scathing word felt like a blow, a physical attack on my person. I covered my ears with my hands and walked faster. Then a woman who was walking towards me, stopped at my side to ask if I was OK. This act of kindness pulled me up short. I was so used to his outbursts (admittedly not in public) I was embarrassed someone else had witnessed them. How could I be embarrassed? I was not the perpetrator, but I felt so ashamed of my predicament. Some inner voice was telling me I must deserve to be treated in this humiliating way, because it had become the norm in my life.

'Are you sure you're alright Mam.' The woman persisted.

'Yes, yes, thank you.' I said in a small voice. I wanted the earth to swallow me up with embarrassment. There was no way I could tell the truth, admit what was happening. I had no dollars on me, nowhere to go. I had to smooth the way and carry on. Withholding currency on a foreign trip was a continued form of control. He was the man who prior to a trip, would organise the necessary currency. It was what we did in our house… he would fill the car with petrol, check the oil tank, oversee the heating thermostat and then… the foreign exchange. I hated the fact that at passport control, he would hold all the passports and in 'head of the family' mode, stand in front of us all, at the passport booth. Like chattels we just stood there, until waved through. Even to buy a postcard, I had to extract cash from him. He would always hand over just enough or ask for the change if he had given a larger amount. By holding onto the money, he could vet every possible purchase, and ensure he was in charge. Yes, I had a credit card, but I knew, if I went out on a limb to buy something and had not involved him in the decision there would be repercussions.

Finally, one evening we did go out after returning to the hotel first. I had searched the Zagat guide and found an Italian several blocks away, but an easy cab ride. Trattoria Dell'Arte was booked for eight o'clock and we were shown to a table in the second room from the front. The whole restaurant is a series of interconnecting rooms painted striking colours, displaying oversize, white plaster body parts. Our meal was delicious and quite relaxed, considering the trade show had not been a great success. Towards the end of the meal, he did seem a little crestfallen, and I tried to cheer him up, speculating the trade show was good publicity and … Suddenly without a word, he got up and walked into the next room, I assumed to find the loo. I poured myself some more wine and watched the waiters rushing around with platters, piled with delicious food from the adjacent antipasti bar. Suddenly, I saw him approaching our table wearing his coat. Without any acknowledgement, he walked straight past me and in a second was in the first dining room and then had vanished out of the front door into the night. I was completely thrown, what was he thinking? Had he paid the bill? My coat had to be found from the cloakroom, but he had the cloakroom tickets. So, I found myself telling the cloakroom lady he had had to leave in a hurry, while inside I'm dying a thousand deaths. Oh God, why am I in this awful situation…? I didn't even have a dollar to leave her. I half hoped, he would just be outside, smoking a cigar, but as I opened the front door to flurries of snow, the reality was, he had vanished into the night.

Quickly buttoning up my coat, and putting on my gloves, I frantically, look right and left, trying to assess the situation. Here I am on 7th Avenue, abandoned and without any money for a cab. (There were no card terminals in cabs in those days.) It's after 10pm and although everywhere is brightly lit and busy, I felt discarded and vulnerable. I know I need to keep walking to the right and do so for three blocks or so until I pick up familiar landmarks. It's snowing on and off, the flakes swirl into a vortex between buildings. Over an hour later, the street to our hotel comes into view.

I decide not to go straight to our room but head to the cloakrooms for a tidy up.

Standing in front of the mirrors, I wonder what has happened to me. Once I was a feisty woman in control of my life, now my life is controlled, my freedom curtailed and my self esteem in tatters. How did this happen? A slick of lipstick picks me up, I head for the piano bar. I find a quiet table and after a couple of glasses of wine, which I sign to our bill, make my way up to our room on the eleventh floor. At least I have a key, so do not have to ask for entry. He's lying on the bed watching television. Looking towards me, but without making eye contact, I think there's just a modicum of unease in his voice.

'What took you so long?'

Without giving him an answer, I go into the bathroom, close the door and start to run a bath. I am not going to mention I have been sitting in the bar for the last hour or so and idly wonder if I have given him *some* cause for concern. Hopefully my bar drinks won't be noticed in the confusion of our final invoice.

Chapter 9

Ballister & Burns

It's two months since I left home. I know, he's been thinking I was just having a moment of madness and would be back, tail between my legs. How do I know? Well, when you've known someone for thirty-four years, you just know. Clearly, he doesn't know me, because wild horses wouldn't drag me back, to the hell of my marriage. So, I need to make a move, fire a shot across the bows, to let him know there is no moment of madness and there will be a divorce. In my head, I think this will be a simple if painful matter of selling the house and moving on. What I hadn't taken into consideration (Spoiler Alert….) was just how low he would sink and just how stupid he thought I was.

I need a divorce solicitor, so ask around

'Does anyone know a name, someone that's pro- active…?'

A name comes up. Lucinda Gibbs at Ballister & Burns. I telephone and make an appointment for the following week. Ballister & Burns are in Princes Square, with offices in a fine Georgian building. Reception is more like walking into a private house. There is a large antique desk with fresh flowers in a Delft china vase. I half expect the receptionist to be scribbling away with a quill pen, but I am reassured when I spot a laptop on a side table. The lighting is soft, with table lamps in abundance. Sitting on a velvet button back chair, waiting for Lucinda Gibbs, my surroundings suck me in, everything seems convincingly proper. After a few minutes she emerges from behind a heavy mahogany door. She is older than I expected and wears a grey woollen skirt, with blouse that has a pie crust collar. Her grey hair is scooped up in a bun, she looks like she was born here. We discuss my apparently straight forward divorce and the assets we must divide. The existing valuation of the house by Threadwells is noted. She tells me about her charges and I gulp as she advises Ballister and Burns will need a substantial cheque, on account 'To open the file'.

I pull out my cheque book and pass the cheque across the desk. This month

Alice Waite

is going to be very tight. Lucinda is going to write to my husband, advising of my intention to divorce. She is very forthright and matter of fact about the whole process, which I like. This is what happens, this is what we do. This reassures me it will be straightforward and over in no time. I think I have been here before…. In the distant past, some part of this is familiar.

Yes, now I remember. Those National Childbirth anti natal classes. All very matter of fact. This is how it happens, this is what you do… every aspect of the birth, in neat boxes. Like the farce of The Birth Plan. The visualisation techniques, to make the pain go away, the deep breathing, ah yes, the deep breathing. When I was expecting my first child, we went to see a lovely obstetrician who would take care of everything throughout my pregnancy and deliver the baby. At our first meeting, my husband started talking to Mr Hillier as if I wasn't there. He was clearly expecting a man to man talk about *his* wife and *the* birth.

He started 'Well, *we* want a completely natural birth.'

'No, no.' I said, 'I want an epidural.' 'Can you arrange this for me Mr Hillier?'

Harry Hillier turned to me. 'Of course, Mrs Waite… I work with Richard Locksley, who is an excellent consultant anaesthetist; I will write to him and make the arrangements.'

'I thought it was so much better to have a natural birth.' My husband butted in.

'Better for whom?' Mr Hillier responded, sounding a little irritated.

'Well it's all in the press… water births and all that deep breathing…'

Mr Hillier turned his attention back to me and we talked medical history and dates.

Unused to being ignored by another man in favour of his wife, my husband was flummoxed and started again.

'Natural births are the way forward these days…. I mean using essential oils, calming music and foot massages you know.' He expertly advised us.

Harry Hillier had had enough. He swivelled his chair to meet my husband's eyes.

'Who's having this baby Mr Waite?' '*You* or *your* wife?'

'Well of course *she* is!' He thought this was a joke

'Well shut up then!' Hillier boomed, so no joke…

I must admit, I was rather thrown by the last comment, but secretly liked the fact Hillier had spoken so plainly, private patient or not. My husband was not used to being spoken to like this and like a dog with a bone, the birth expert continued,

'But I have read epidurals can be dangerous ...and, *I know* visualisation techniques reduce labour pain.'

'Really.' said Mr Hillier '*You know* this do you?' 'So, when you last went to the dentist for a filling Mr Waite, I expect you had an injection for pain relief?'

'Well yes I did.' He said, like a lamb rushing towards his imminent slaughter.'

'So, you didn't try any visualisation techniques instead?'

'No, well no... but that's different, isn't it?'

'Yes, it is very different' Hillier sighed 'Childbirth can take twelve – twenty-four hours ...even more.' 'And, it's a very different kettle of fish to a quick filling, for which we all have that pain numbing anaesthetic.'

My husband knew he was on the back foot and sat silently, with terror in his eyes, as Hillier went on, 'Imagine Mr Waite....Imagine, having your top lip stretched slowly.... Ever so slowly, over twelve, maybe, twenty-four hours or more.... Your top lip is stretched over the back of YOUR HEAD!' He made his point firmly, staring at my husband and continued

'Because, Mr Waite, that's how much the uterus has to stretch to get this baby *out*!' 'And if your wife, quite reasonably, in my opinion, wants pain relief, and I for one wouldn't blame her... I will make sure she gets it!'

'Now, Mrs Waite' he said swivelling his chair towards me once again, 'We were discussing due dates I think.'

Inside I was beaming. Harry Hillier was listening to me. He wasn't going to be railroaded by this accomplished natural childbirth guru. He was his own man and I admired him from that day onwards. He subsequently delivered all three of my girls, *with* epidurals and *without* visualisation.

I leave Lucinda Gibbs at her desk and wander out into the bright light of Princes Square. I am ambivalent about just how straight forward this can be, but nevertheless use my positive visualisation techniques to imagine myself living in a cottage by next summer.

Chapter 10

House on the Market

The Rectory had been viewed by Threadwells while I was away in Sicily. The valuation was pretty much what we thought and therefore, now a month after leaving my lovely home, it seemed appropriate to get the ball rolling, by putting the house on the market. Lucinda Gibbs had the valuation on file, so I was waiting to hear from her with his response to the neat tick box divorce, I was about to embark upon. A couple of weeks later, I opened a letter from Claytons Estate Agents with an invoice for a valuation. My mouth went dry. Reading on, I can see the instructions have come from Ballister & Burns.
'Why?' I shout out loud. 'We have a valuation; I don't need any more bills....'
On picking up the phone to Lucinda Gibbs, I discover she is not in the office today, so leave a message, asking for her to call me, the next day. This is my first experience of dealing with an absent legal profession. Should I be practising my deep breathing to alleviate the frustration that has yet to come? Of course, I know I am not Lucinda's only client, my simple straight forward divorce will be small beer to Ballister & Burns, but the word divorce should ring just a couple of emotional bells, shouldn't it? If we telephone, we have a problem, we need advice. In my parlous state, an unexpected invoice, is enough to throw me into complete panic. Granted you aren't offering a service called Relate as it is now called. (Marriage Guidance if you are over the age of fifty) But like it or not, you are in business dealing with a highly emotional situation and believe me, a little empathy, and a return phone call would go a long way.

In the depths of my despair and long before I had heard of the term, emotional abuse, under the illusion our marriage problems were entirely my fault, I contacted Relate. There was a waiting list of a couple of months, which seemed like an eternity, when I was in such pain. Eventually, I received a call offering a date and time, and this gave me three weeks to prepare myself. I had long conversations in my head, this situation, that scenario. His mood changes were unpredictable, disarming me with kind gestures one moment, then refusing to acknowledge me, with the silent treatment the next. The turmoil I was living in daily, should not be under estimated. This was nothing less than artful, two faced, manipulative behaviour, administered with guileful aplomb.

Simple things, such as, my car keys would go missing. I am a methodical person, well organised, always prepped the day before client meetings. All my files are double checked, waiting with my handbag in the hall. My car and house keys, always on the hook in the kitchen, except when I am ready to leave for my appointment, my keys aren't there.
'Have you seen my keys?' I ask
'No' is the monosyllabic response.
'But they were here last night… I know they were.'
'Well they can't have been or they would be here now' he remonstrates, unconcerned. He starts to head off to his workshop.
'But I'll be late for my meeting.' I am now panicking.
He shrugs again, apparently indifferent to my anxiety.
Rooting through my handbag, all the time, knowing they can't possibly be there, mindful of my meeting and with time ticking by, I am becoming distraught.
'Look they can't have been on the hook!' He repeats with a sigh.' 'Or they would be there now, wouldn't they?' He booms 'You must be careful with these things.'
He opens the front door to leave.
Astonished at his uncaring attitude I ask,
'Aren't you going to help me look for them?'
'You really must get a grip you know…. this isn't the first time …. This key business… you clearly aren't coping with all this work, as well as you think.'
At first, I am sceptical of his opinion. I am fine and think, what *is* he talking about? But when there are repeat incidents, such as a file has gone AWOL or an important drawing is missing, I start to doubt my sanity.
'You must have left the drawing at the photocopiers.'… 'You fool!' He would boom.
Over time, with the slowest burn, uncertainty starts to kick in. At the time, I couldn't see how his resentment of my success, was fuelling such

bitterness towards me. Day after day, he was creating situations, to reinforce self-doubt. They were subtle issues that seemed meaningless at the time. Gradually, the resulting insecurity creeps into my psyche, insidiously reinforcing my anxiety.

What is happening to me? Am I going crazy? No wonder he's exasperated with me, I must try harder. He's getting so upset with me. I'm making life difficult for him.

My self esteem battered, I pondered, are these incidents proof of my inadequacies or madness? I started to double and treble check everything, which had the effect of making me look crazy. Like a headless chicken, the night before a client meeting, I would go back and back again to the kitchen to see if my keys were on the hook. When one morning they weren't there, and I knew, yes, I really, really knew, they should be, because I had triple checked, just before I went to bed, I began to see the light. And what I saw, was so disconcerting, I couldn't begin to contemplate such an intolerable truth. To overcome some of these situations, I learned to be ever vigilant and proactive with day to day, self preservation strategies. But these fuelled my anxiety and made me feel underhand. Underhand? … Yes, underhand and devious. Hiding my own car keys? What *are* you doing? I would question my own actions, but as I started to understand the reality of my situation, I played him at his own game. My files, all triple checked would be put in the locked boot, the night beforehand, then the car keys were hidden with my underwear, ready for the morning. This worked well for a time, but what is the point of having the car keys, if someone has blocked in your car, with his car parked immediately behind, on the drive? 'Well' I hear you say, 'Just tell him to move it'.

If only life was that simple! Just like Macavity, he would disappear. He would make himself scarce at his workshop, a rattling old building with two floors and three entrances. I would rush into the front door, calling out,

'Steve, Steve.'

To hear his footsteps on the boards upstairs. Rushing up the stairs, I would find the interconnecting rooms empty and race down the back staircase that has facilitated his escape… And so, this hideous farce of hide and seek continued, until I would find him nonchalantly making coffee back in the kitchen. But this wasn't farcical, it was a heart breaking, an insidious attempt to control my life and undermine my business.

My Relate appointment was in some rather sad offices above a clothes

shop. The nice lady at reception ushered me into a side room, to take some details. As I started to launch into my problems, she stopped me and said 'Ah … no.' 'I am not your Councillor…. I just assess your situation, so we can allocate you the right person.' 'Didn't someone explain this?'
'No' I said.
Overwhelmed by the whole build up to this appointment, I started to cry. 'Now' she said firmly, turning from the nice lady at reception, into a brusque Sergeant Major talking to a hapless Squaddie.
'You have waited this long, a few more weeks won't make any difference.' She clearly hadn't the slightest idea about the agony of a marriage in tatters. Totally disheartened, I asked,
'How many weeks?' Turning on a chirpy voice she replied, 'Let's go back to the desk and look at the diary, shall we?'
Drying my eyes, I followed her back to reception. Wearily, leafing through my diary to seven weeks ahead, dates were fixed for a further six Tuesdays, as my Tuesday morning yoga class, would provide my cover. Feeling despondent and pushed to the edge of endurance, I made my way out onto the street.
Seven weeks ahead, Janice who is my allocated Councillor introduces herself. First of all, she wants to hear about my childhood.
'Were there any problems with your parents?'
Well only the fact they didn't want me to better myself and further education was out of the question.' I replied
'So, they didn't want to see you succeed…. How odd?'

In that moment, the penny dropped. How could I have not seen this before? I had married someone just like my parents. I had seen the term Family Behaviour Patterns, in some of the Self Help books I had been reading. In that moment, to my horror, I realised, on an unconscious level, I had sought in my marriage, someone with the same expectations of me, as my parents. We are all subconsciously, comfortable with what we know and are reassured by it. My mother, was a difficult character. I never knew what kind of mood she would be in when I arrived home from school. It was a life walking on eggshells, so it was important to keep her on an even keel. To win something that passed for affection, I would take on little household jobs, before being asked. Eventually, no matter how many little jobs I did for her, how many errands I ran, I was never going to be able to please her. There was an innate jealousy of the educational opportunities, I might have, and she did everything in her power to stall my future. She even remonstrated with the local authority, to stop my independently won grant for Art College. Ten minutes into my forty-minute appointment I realised my marriage was following a predetermined destiny. I would produce his favourite meals, drop my work in favour of his, have sex when I didn't feel like it, get up at night to sooth small children, all just to enjoy his reasonable or normal behaviour. Now I could see, I was following the same behavioural pattern, I had followed in my childhood, when enough is never enough. This is when jealousy reared its head and he would try every which way, to stop my career from flourishing. *His* work was the important work and yes some of his projects were financially successful, until he grew bored with them, lavishing all his time and attention on the latest *brilliant idea* to the detriment of the last.

I explained my situation while Janice listened patiently, offering tissues as emotion overwhelmed me. She advised, several times over, I can't change other people, *only* myself. Janice stands up to draw our session to a close, suggesting before next week, I write a list of ways *I* can change. I am so confused. Should I be changing my behaviour in some way to make him behave differently? Does this mean I haven't tried hard enough? I emerge onto the High St, holding back the tears and head straight for the car park. Three weeks into my six-week allocation, I'm floundering. We seem to go round and round in desperate circles. I am not sure what these sessions are giving to me, apart from a weekly outpouring of sadness. One week, Janice asked me to swap chairs with her and then tell *me* (in the opposite chair) what to do, how to cope. I was all in and looked at her with incredulity. Not in the mood for musical chairs of any description, I just wanted to walk out, but lacked the courage and the confidence to do so. I wanted to tell her her my life wasn't about Councillor's party games, but instead, I dutifully swapped chairs to endure this rather silly conversation, where I was the Councillor and she was me. I told her (me) to get a grip and regain control of her (my) life. But I didn't have a strategy, Janice that's what I needed from you.
The following Tuesday, my daughter was away from school with flu. She had a temperature but then is freezing cold, plus ear ache and is miserable. Although she is old enough to be left for a couple of hours, it seems pretty mean to announce,
'I'm off to yoga' when she could do with some TLC. I decide to call and cancel my session. The following week Janice hauled me over the coals for cancelling. I am quite taken aback. It feels like being at school again,

making excuses for being late. She told me my daughter was old enough to be left on her own and I should have given more notice, so she can fill the slot. I soon gather, this is really all about money, as she won't be paid if someone doesn't turn up. None of my explanations are going to satisfy her, so the session gets off to prickly start. As we approach the end of my allocated time, she declares, she needs to see us both together next week. I explain my husband knows nothing of my sessions with her. As she shows me to the door she is still insistent. I am starting to feel bullied. Do I have the kind of personality that gives people permission, to treat me like this?

It's time to talk to Steve. The reason I'm going to Relate, is to make things work again, so where can be the harm? After all he's surely going to want to keep things together? The alternative is too awful to contemplate. As ever, we have an almost silent supper. Staying silent is a coping strategy I've developed. If I stay silent, there can be no reason to criticise me. I therefore do not comment on conversations I've had with friends, current affairs, or simply anything, then I can't get into trouble.
So, to break the silence to announce, I have been going to Relate and his presence is requested next week, fills me with dread. At the weekend he seems in a better mood, so I pluck up the courage and begin
'I should tell you...errh ... I've been going to see Relate.'
'What' he screams.
I've clearly misread his mood.
'Look' I say, 'We've obviously got problems we need help with.' 'You can't pretend this is how things used to be?'
'What have you been saying?' 'How dare you discuss private things with other people?' 'How dare you....?' He boomed.
'OK, OK.' I say... leave it.' 'I'll tell her you won't come.'
'What do you mean... come where?' 'Tell who?' 'What have you been saying about me?'
Ahh... there is concern about his reputation.

The following week, neat as a pin, he accompanies me to my Tuesday meeting.
'Hello Janice, so pleased to meet you.' 'I've heard so many good things about you.' He gushes.
She smiles like a 15-year-old being chatted up by a prefect and organises our chairs on either side of her. Leaning forward towards him she says

Alice Waite

'Now, as I've been seeing Alice for a few weeks on her own, perhaps you would like to start today, by telling me how you see your relationship.'
'Well, I'm not sure where Alice is coming from with all these problems?' He sounds concerned. 'I just don't understand what's wrong with her.' 'You know Janice, as far as I'm concerned we've got a good marriage.'
He engages her with his kind smiley eyes. I don't know when I last saw his eyes looking like this. She's holding her head just slightly to one side and regards him sympathetically, absorbing every syllable, like molten honey. You just couldn't make this man up. He's a professional, a star player. Within ten minutes of this session starting, she's eating out of his hand.
'I mean' …. He continues 'Our children are at private school… I bought Alice a *lovely* Mercedes…. We've got a house in France and of course our lovely Georgian house here.' 'I just can't see what the problem is…? 'You know…. Janice, *I'm* as confused as *you* must be… and you're a professional?' Janice's eyes are now the size of grey moons because our finances sound very healthy. I've been paying a slightly reduced amount each week, as I quite honestly declared, my personal funds were limited. She turns towards me, presumably to hear my thoughts, but as he continues her eyes swivel back towards him, as more pearls drop from his mouth.
'I don't know about *you* Janice' he gushes '…but I think all these things *I've* worked so hard to provide for *my* family count for a lot… don't you?'
I butt in
'Now look, we need to get some clarity here' 'You should know, that I pay the School fees and…our life…. Well….'
But no one is listening. He continues
'Now, now' 'Let's not start splitting hairs darling…. I *really* appreciate you do your bit…'
He leans across and holds my hand.
Janice beams. Her eyes are the eyes of a woman in love… I don't know why I bothered coming. I am the invisible woman in this room. It's a conversation a deux and I swear if he asked her out to dinner she would be out of the door in a flash.

Then, la piece de la resistance. Janice draws the jolly session to a close, indicating its payment time and queries that I've been paying a special rate. 'Oh darling, that's not right.' 'Now Janice, I'm sorry if you've been misled here…'
'There really is no problem.' 'We can't have a wonderful service like this,

short changed, can we now?' 'Don't think of arresting her will you Janice?' 'There's clearly some misunderstanding.'
He nudges Janice who has flushed slightly. She makes an embarrassed giggling sound, then laughs. Then they have a good laugh together….
Then, I get out *my* cheque book and pay up.

We drive home in silence. Nothing has changed.
He clicks his fingers abruptly, right in front of my eyes.
'What are you thinking…. what's going on in your head then?'
At least this part of my life I can keep completely private. Thank God, he has no access to my thoughts. I sigh and do not answer. If I do not speak… yes, I know you know, but there it is, the perfect game plan for survival. My silence cannot be twisted or argued with. My silence cannot be wrong. My silence gives me refuge. I broke my silence the following morning to cancel my last appointment with Janice.

A few days pass before, after telephoning Ballister & Burns again, I manage to speak to Lucinda Gibbs about the second valuation invoice.
'I'm not sure why we have this second valuation?' I say
Lucinda's voice is firm and has a *don't question my opinion,* tone to it.
'A second valuation is always a good thing.' She says, 'It gives us clarity across the market.'
'But look.' I reply, 'I have an invoice for £500 + vat here….'
She interrupts 'In the big picture of things Mrs Waite, this is inconsequential.' 'Your husband will have to pay half of it.' 'I'll mention it in my next letter to his solicitors.'
'Do we know who they are?' I question
'Yes, it seems he's got Legal Aid and has retained Mark Kenny of Douglas Kenny & Maggs.'
'Legal Aid?' I say, 'How can he get Legal Aid?' 'I don't understand'
'Well that's something between him and Douglas Kenny & Maggs.' 'I don't know the details.' 'Now, if you'll excuse me Mrs Waite….'
'Yes… ….'
The phone is already purring before I can say
'…Of course.'

Within a couple of days, I receive a letter from Lucinda, outlining our telephone conversation and enclosing an end of the month invoice. It seems the phone call cost £86 + vat and the letter confirming said phone call a further £148 + vat.

Plus £… Plus ££…. Plus £££…. + Vat. In fact, why not write two letters…? When all the questions could have been asked in just one. These are my first dealings with Solicitors. The Legal profession seem to exist in a parallel universe and know when they are retained it's because we are in a desperate situation. I might as well leave my credit card and bank details behind reception, so they can help themselves.

Chapter 11

Time for a change

Sometimes, positive thinking and visualisation are not enough, we crave more, more, from other sources. Sometimes a heavenly facial or back massage will lift the spirits. Sometimes it won't. When the enormity of what I have done, sits like a leaden weight on my shoulders, in fact, it encases every fibre of my body, no amount of aromatherapy oil, will change the way I feel. At fifty-three, I am in the middle of a nightmare. I have jumped into the abyss, leaving my lovely home, filled with antiques, beautiful works of art and yet also, intolerable misery. Has anyone asked themselves, just how bad does it have to be, to remove yourself from this seemingly perfect life? This is the bravest thing I have ever done. Looking for any sign of optimism, I have started reading my weekly horoscope in the Sunday papers, with more than a cursory glance. Then one week, at the bottom of the page, I see I can receive a fax from Jasper de Souza, giving a more detailed insight into the next month for Aquarius. In my current frame of mind, it's too tempting a suggestion and it will only add a couple of pounds to my phone bill. I fax my details to Jasper and wait anxiously by my fax machine. A few minutes later, it whirrs into life and I am enthralled as the pages flop onto my desk.

Jasper tells me, that January is going to be a very important month. I will be entering a new, dramatic and exciting cycle. And, as someone who is intuitive, I've already sensed these changes coming. Jasper continues to advise, I won't be able to see in what direction, the developments will be coming from, because, Uranus is involved, and the circumstances can be unexpected. Jasper has me mesmerized as I read on. 'The wiser Aquarian will take things slowly, enjoying what it feels like to be in this new period of your life.'
I am hooked... how can he know all this, just gazing at charts with stars dotted around?

I read on… 'Examine every area of your life, from purely personal relationships with friends and family, to your financial well-being, as well as your self esteem. And do reflect on your plans for the future. Decide which areas of your life make you happy and where you feel something is lacking or that changes would be appropriate. You may decide there are some things you would be better off without and therefore need to begin all over again.'… I'm on that one already, Jasper.
'With Uranus in your sign, such profound advancements, are not only viable they are attainable. The more flexible you are about this situation, the better chance you will have to take up the opportunities this cycle will bring. Half way through this month, Venus will meet Uranus and while this may suggest, unexpected encounters or surprise developments on the financial front, it may be to your advantage or less straightforward and to your loss.'…...
Spoiler Alert, spoiler alert!

At this point (Another spoiler alert…) I cannot envisage, how the mental pain and anguish can get any worse than I am feeling right now. It's coming up to Christmas and all that family time, how will we deal with it, in the flat yet again? City centre life isn't for everyone. While I was grateful for the refuge Andrew's flat provided, it couldn't be more convenient for my office, it was safe, and Andrew had been brilliant about keeping my rent below the going rate, but I did struggle with the constant noise of traffic and also the parking nightmare. I had bought a resident's parking permit, but this didn't guarantee a parking space, so once I had found one, I didn't want to move the car, or go anywhere in fact, because I wouldn't be able to find a space on my return. The alternative was to find a meter but then I was limited to two hours. Meters were free from 7pm and overnight but had to fed at 7am in the morning. At 6.50am traffic wardens were circling like Vultures waiting for any hapless fool who had pressed the snooze button on their alarm clock…. you get the picture… On Saturday mornings, I would look out of my window to see residents in their dressing gowns feeding meters on the dot of 7am, just to give them another two hours, before circling around in the hope a resident's space would become available. One day after Andrew had seen me racing down the stairs in my dressing gown, he phoned with a suggestion.
'Look, my friend Leslie… he lives just down the road in Grafton Row, well he has a lovely garden apartment there… and it has a garage.' 'The thing is, Leslie can't drive anymore because his eye sight is deteriorating.' 'Why

don't I ask him if he wants to rent his garage out to you...?' 'I'm sure he wouldn't want much for it.'

The thought of another overhead filled me with horror, but the parking fiasco was driving me crazy, never being able to leave my space. Not wanting to commit myself, I said,

'Well, would you ask about it Andrew and then I can see?'

In no time at all Andrew had introduced me to Leslie and the garage was a done deal. Leslie must have been eighty if he was a day. Every time I popped the rent around he was so pleased to have company, the kettle was on or he was opening a bottle of wine, insisting I stayed....

'Just a few minutes darling, do tell me your news.'

In truth it was always an hour. It was sad to see this fragile, gay man, with his failing eye sight, bereft because his partner, Leonard had died a few years ago, so pleased to have company. Over our wine he told me all about his former life. He and Leonard had owned a fashion shop, which in its day, sold the trendiest men's clothes. This is why he always looks so stylish I thought. A lady came in to clean and do his ironing and a nephew brought his shopping, but he spent many hours alone with his radio blasting out. (He was slightly deaf too.) Sometimes, I would drop in and be asked to help him chose an outfit because he couldn't make out the colours.

'Darling does this sweater look right with this shirt?'

He had several options laid out on the bed, so I was charged as his style assistant.

'Paul is taking me to my club this evening you see... oh and I will need a cravat too.'

Looking at the clothes on the bed, I could see some had food stains on them. He would die if he knew he had been wearing grubby clothes. I quickly moved these into the laundry basket and made my choice from the rest.

The garage was a godsend. It literally changed my life, because I could zip off to see a friend or go to yoga, knowing I could park my car when I returned. As I popped in to see Leslie more often we became good friends, he so loved a proper gossip.

'Now dear, what's Andrew been up to?' 'Any parties ...? You would hear them from your flat.' 'Come on *do tell*!'

I admit when I was pressed for time or just feeling so low and couldn't be jolly, even for Leslie, I would put my envelope with the rent cheque in Leslie's letter box. I felt so guilty about this, because I knew he would be looking forward to a proper catch up, as he called it.

Alice Waite

When it was Leslie's birthday, Andrew organised a little gathering at his flat.
Of course, there was champagne, a birthday cake and then presents. When Leslie opened a CD from Andrew he looked dismal.
'What's this?' He said waving a Rachmaninov concerto in the air.
'I thought you would like it.' said Andrew, now a bit perplexed. 'It's Rachmaninov…'
'This is more like funeral music… what are you thinking Andrew!'
Leslie got to his feet
'For my funeral, I want YMCA…'!
Then standing in front of his chair, swaying his rickety hips, hands waving above his head, he launched into his favourite song.
'*Young man*, there's no need to feel down
I said *young man,* pick yourself off the ground
I said, *young man* 'cause you're new into town
There's no need to be unhappy
Stay at the Y…M…C… A! I said Y….M….. C….A…!.Y…M…C…A…!
(Come on, I know you can hear the tune in your head)
By now the whole party had joined in 'Y…M…C… A …!'
'I said Y…M…C… A …' '*Young man…*'
His hips were positively pulsating now, hands waving, Leslie was in his element. He was twenty-one again, having the time of his life.

Andrew passed me on the landing, he asked about my Christmas.
'What's the plan darling?'
'Well, the girls are having a brunch with their father and then coming to me, late afternoon and we will have our Christmas then.' I replied
'You are not staying up there on your own until then… you will jolly well come down for drinks about 11'o clock and then sit down with us, for lunch… no excuses.'
'We've got loads for lunch, one little one like you darling, won't make any difference!'
He's such a sweetheart. The reality is, I don't want to be the stray at his party, but I know he will come up to get me if I'm not there for the popping of the first champagne cork. There will be of plenty of time on Christmas Eve to make the flat lovely and prepare our meal. What I haven't had the heart to bother him about, is the thermostat on the oven and come to that the one on the fridge. Cooking is very hit and miss, especially when the fridge decides it's a freezer, wrecking everything overnight. We'll manage

somehow, I think. I'd better get a cheap electric heater, because by 5pm all the heat has gone out of the storage radiators. I must make it as cosy and homely as possible for my girls.

Lucinda Gibbs has sent another missive with copy correspondence from my husband's solicitor. Every time I see an envelope marked Ballister & Burns, my heart starts pounding. I must put it on one side until my lectures are completed for the day. The last few students finally leave, so with a heavy heart, I return to my office and stare at the envelope. Tearing it open, I panic as my eyes glide across the text, not really understanding what Lucinda Gibbs is telling me. I glance at the enclosed letter from Douglas Kenny & Maggs. Now I get it, this can't be right…? *He has decided,* he will stay in the marital home until Hettie has finished her degree, the following year. Hold on a minute, she doesn't even live at home in term time. What's more, he wants me to pay half the mortgage and household bills. Further, he is going to make claims against my business, as he is (on paper) still a partner. I don't know whether to have a heart attack or make a cup of tea. I make tea, but my heart is still thumping. Think, think… I look at the clock, it's 4.40pm.
I can still speak to Lucinda Gibbs. I quickly dial her number, the phone rings and rings, then clicks onto the answering machine. How can this be? Why isn't someone picking up?
I try again, telling myself the receptionist has just left her desk for a moment. But no, here we go again….
'Ballister & Burns Solicitors. Please leave a short message after the tone.'
I slam the phone down.
'For pity's sake' I yell with frustration 'Its Friday… Don't send me stuff like this on a Friday.'
I am about to learn, that on Thursdays, solicitors like to clear their desk of the week's outstanding detritus and so make a concerted effort, to dictate as many distressing letters as possible. This means their clients either receive the post when they arrive home from work on Friday evening, or even on a Saturday. Either way, the timing dictates, nothing further can be discussed, and we are denied those questions, that might have allowed a night's sleep. In no time at all, we have unwittingly, memorised by heart, the contentious contents of these letters and no matter how hard we try to disconnect ourselves from them, they permeate our brains like canker. There can be no release from the ugly monologue going around and

around in our heads, for at least forty-eight hours. These anxieties fill my head just before dawn.

Monday at 9am before my students arrive, I try to make an appointment, so I can discuss the letter with Lucinda. I explain to her diary secretary, I am teaching until 4pm so the earliest I can get to the office, is 4.30. I can tell she is not enthusiastic about the timing, but given no alternative, she reluctantly pencils in Thursday.
At last, it's Thursday, I usher the last stragglers out of the studios, grab my coat and files to make the dash across town. I walk through the doors of Ballister & Burns at exactly 4.28pm. Promptly, Lucinda guides me into her office. She leafs through the files in front of her.
'I am concerned how my husband thinks, he can dictate when the house can be put up for sale.' I jump in.
'Well given it's in joint names, if he wants to be awkward about it, the only way to deal with this is by a court order, as part of your divorce proceedings' She advises.
'But how long is that going to take?' I say
She clasps her hands on the desk and tells me,
'We can write to his solicitors and let them know we disagree with his proposal… and see how they respond.'
I can see this bat and ball scenario going on indefinitely, with invoices to match. We briefly discuss the mortgage payments he has requested.
'Look, I am paying for a flat along with all the expenses that entails… I don't see why, he expects me to pay for him to live in luxury, in our home.'
She responded, a little wearily
'The mortgage still has to be paid, doesn't it?'
'Yes, I appreciate that, but we will have to deal with who has paid what and settle everything when the house has sold… I can't afford to pay rent and a mortgage.' 'And anyway, where is the incentive for him to get on with the sale of the house if he's being financially helped to stay there….'
Why is it *me* thinking everything through, I'm not the solicitor. She's supposed to be on my side…. that is, working for *me*. She looks at her watch and standing up, starts to put paperwork back into files.
'Then, there's this issue of him claiming half the income from my business.' I continue.
She closes the large lever arch file.
'I am sorry, Mrs Waite; we will have to discuss that matter another time.' I look at my watch its ten to five. She sees my disconcerted face.

'If you can ring my secretary to make *another* appointment, maybe next week we can talk this matter through more fully then.'
'I will have the same timing problem next week.' I say, 'I am teaching every day until 4pm.' 'There's just nothing I can do about it.'
'Well' she replies reaching for her silk scarf from the coat stand behind her. 'I'm sure we'll work something out.'
I can't believe she has just ignored everything I have just said! I am ushered into reception and notice many of the table lamps have already been switched off. I have been railroaded out of the office, mid conversation. This is nonsense, how can I manage a divorce with snatched exchanges? This is not boding well. I navigate my way across Princes Square and head home.... No... I mean back to my flat.

Christmas comes and goes with everyone on best behaviour. No one discusses anything contentious and this is probably the best way forward, but there's no doubt the elephant was in the room with us, the whole time, sucking up the joie de vivre of the season. I don't doubt, this is immensely difficult for them, watching a marriage of thirty years, being dismembered before their eyes. They do not want to take sides and the minute I say something inappropriate about their father, they insist I stop. They must have had a sisterly conference about this, as they inform me straight away, the same policy is applied to their father. They are wise beyond their years.

In the dog days between Christmas and New Year, I start some serious thinking about my legal representation. This divorce is emotionally hard enough without having to beg for an appointment with Lucinda Gibbs. Further, *I* seem to be the one, really thinking about our strategy, not my solicitor. Gibbs is formidable, and she could be a real presence in court, but then I'm hoping we can just get this resolved between us, without court. After all, she did seem to think it should be a pretty straight forward division of assets. But my instincts are telling me, something about her laissez-faire attitude isn't right. In my experience, women are incredibly intuitive and if, knowing what I know now, I could give advice to my younger self, I would say
Listen to your instincts... trust your gut reaction. Don't dismiss these thoughts as rubbish, because no one else agrees with you.... In your heart of hearts... you know when something is amiss.
In evaluating Lucinda Gibbs' performance to date, I even start worrying if I change solicitors, I will offend the friend of a friend who suggested her.

Alice Waite

'Really!' I hear you say… 'REALLY!'
I have a firm word with myself.
'Get a grip girl!' 'You can't have this apology for the Legal profession acting for you.'
I resolve it's time to change solicitor before I get in any deeper.

Chapter 12

Rolo Hargreaves

So, with the decision made, I must exit gracefully from Ballister & Burns to make an entrance somewhere else… but where? I gather some girlfriends round to the flat for a pasta supper to get some feedback.

Dee was introduced to me by Andrew. She is a blond whirlwind of irreverence, who manages an up- market bridal shop. Every week the area manager sets her a sales target, to beat and every week she manages it. She could talk bridal corsetry, peplum waists, boned bodices, Rouleau loops and tiaras until the bridesmaids have all left school and grown up. She calls everyone 'Darling' even if she has only known you for five minutes. Presumably, her brides and their mothers, get the same treatment and judging by her sales figures, they love it.

Annie, I met at a local Business Women's association and I have just started to employ her as a tutor on my courses. She is confident, sassy and great with the students. She runs her own media practice but like any self-employed designer, is pleased to have the certainty of funds coming into her bank account, even if it means working late into the night on her own projects.

Lucy, was an ex-student of mine. I had trained her, several years before and we became firm friends. Lucy didn't have to work, Max saw to that. He was on the 6.10am train into Paddington every morning and didn't return until nearly eight o'clock in the evening. If Lucy's latest passion was a horse, then in no time at all, there would be a thorough bred, with new stables and all the horsey accoutrements Hermes could provide. Ditto, the pottery passion, which produced an outbuilding, converted into a studio, complete with potter's wheel, kiln, work tables et al. Even if she is spoilt, she is a bright, intelligent and fiercely loyal friend.

We sit down to eat and discuss my next move as if we are writing a new episode for a Soap Opera. Lucy, the trimmest of all of us all, is demolishing her pasta Arrabiata, as if she hadn't seen food in a fortnight. She chipped in

'A woman in my Dressage class, has just come through a divorce, why don't I ask about her solicitor?'
Annie waving her fork around, broke in
'Well it's all very well, but frankly we need a solicitor with balls, not one who takes two weeks to return a phone call and is just playing the tick box game.'
'Yes, it's Balls and Proactive we want' said Dee
'Do you think we could find one listed in The Yellow Pages?' I said half joking.
'What about Balls Proactive & Cheap Ltd!' Spluttered Lucy
'What about Legal Rats & Rottweilers.' threw in Dee?
'Yes, yes!' I said' I'll take them all, I'll take them!'
'Or what about… Smug, Slack and Sluggish?'

We all collapse into Chianti fuelled laughter. They say laughter is the best medicine and my goodness what a release it is from all this stress. I so badly needed a Solicitor working for me, taking the situation seriously. In the meantime, the support of my girlfriends made life so much more bearable.

Literally, clutching at straws, I ask everyone on my radar, if they have heard any good reports of anyone's divorce solicitor. Eventually, another friend of a friend came back with Williams Rossiter & Phipps. I simply didn't know what to do, where to turn, so decided to give them a call. The name at this firm I had been given, was Victoria Buchannan. On the phone she seemed pleasant enough, so I arranged a meeting. Their offices, couldn't have been more different to Ballister & Burns. Reception, was a cubby hole with a couple of stackable chairs squeezed along the wall in front of a high counter with lots of typing going on behind it. Victoria appeared and took me along a Fluorescent lit corridor to another characterless cubby hole. I started thinking, without the plush trappings of Ballister & Burns their hourly rate might be cheaper. No, it didn't seem to matter; they were in fact, a few pounds an hour more expensive. Victoria seemed to think she could help me and hopefully speed things along. The trouble is when you are desperate, you hear what you *need* to hear. I agreed to ask Ballister & Burns for a closing invoice, which when paid, they will forward the files onto Williams Rossiter & Phipps. When everything was dealt with, my files were sent across and I waited. And waited…. I thought
'Well, she's got to get up to speed on the files…'

Over three weeks later, I received a phone call from a Sally Grafton.
'Hello Mrs Waite, Victoria has passed your files to me. I will be looking after your case.'
'I don't understand.' I said, 'Victoria said she would be handling everything.'
'Well, one of her cases has escalated, so I will be dealing with your file until such time her case load reduces.' She continued
'I see.'
She must have heard the disappointment in my voice, because she chirpily replied
'Don't worry about it. "I'm starting on your file today and will be in touch soon.'
'Starting on my file *today*...Victoria has had everything, for over three weeks.' I said
'Well, I'm afraid she was on leave for a week, but she is going to bring me up to speed later today.'
'I see.' I said again 'When will I hear from you?'
I will be writing to your husband's solicitors this week and will copy you in.'
Not exactly bouncing around the office with sheer enthusiasm, I put the phone down. My husband will be smirking all the way to his Legal Aid solicitors, with the thought, I have employed useless solicitors and must start all over again. I seem to have taken several steps backwards, because Sally Grafton, now must familiarise herself with the files. Eventually, I receive a letter simply establishing what we already know.
'Give me strength!' I explode.
Where is this leading? What is our strategy? Then, another couple of weeks with no communication, until a letter arrived informing me, that 50% of funds from the sale of a property in our pension have been allocated to my personal pension fund.
'What!' I yell out loud.
For years we had a property nearby, my husband used as a workshop. The property was bought through our pension fund with Pension and Mutual as an investment. We paid rent for the property, which was then invested in our pension fund. Between bright ideas, when times were difficult, rent ran into arrears and months before I left, we had decided to sell the unit. With planning permission, it would convert into two dwellings, so in a village location it was very saleable. The information advising me the property had been sold, was a complete surprise, as the property was in joint names. How can this be? I haven't signed any document releasing this property.

Before I made my leap to freedom, I wrote numerous letters with my change of address details Then, I arranged for all my post to be redirected. The Pension property was on the market for a significant sum, so along with Pension and Mutual, I also wrote to the estate agent, David Ellis, asking to be notified of any offers made on the property. How could this property have been sold without my signature? I was about to learn about Trustee Law and so much more.

Firstly, I called Pension & Mutual to get some answers. A rather flummoxed person on the other end of the line seemed slightly alarmed that a property jointly owned, had been sold without my knowledge, but advised,
'Pension & Mutual are The Trustees of this property and therefore they sign off any sale.' 'But you *will* have been advised prior to the sale.'
'I can assure *I have not* been advised.' I said' 'My husband and I are separated, I wrote to Pension & Mutual with my change of address details in September 2001 and I have received no communication from you whatsoever.'
There was silence on the line, then,
'Madam, I suggest you write to us with your complaint, so the correct department can deal with it.'
'I'm sorry.' I said, 'I want to speak to whoever deals with the sale of Pension fund properties now.'
'Who in your organisation dealt with this sale?'
'The person heading up the team was John Rawlings.' I was informed.
'But please *do* write to us at the Reading address and your correspondence will be forwarded to the correct department.'
'Well just hold on a minute.' I said, 'The amount credited to my fund, does not reflect half the figure the property was on the market for.'
There was a short intake of breath, then he replied,
'I can assure you Madam this is exactly half of the final sales figure.'
'This figure is significantly less than the property was worth… I don't understand!' 'Who decided to *give it away* at that price?' I said
'These decisions are all in the hands of The Trustees Madam.' 'Please write to us.'
He was almost pleading now. I took his name and made a note of our conversation. Little did I know, this was the first page of many lever arch files, I was about to compile. I was concerned about the figure the property had been sold for, why was it sold so cheaply? I raised my concerns with Sally Grafton, who couldn't have appeared less interested.

Only cry on Fridays

'Look, property prices aren't great now and at least this money has gone into *your* pension fund.' She said

'Yes, but I should have been informed …. I should have been given the opportunity to agree to this reduced price.' I remonstrated.

'Well take this up with Pension & Mutual… see what they have to say.' She replied

I was being left to deal with this on my own. This problem was clearly not one Sally was going to tackle. It didn't fit into a neat box called divorce. A few days later, I called John Rawlings at Pension & Mutual to try to get some answers.

'Trustees office, Susan speaking, how may I help?'

'John Rawlings, please.'

'Who may I say is calling?' Said Susan

'Alice Waite.' I replied

'And can I ask what it is in connection with?' She continued

The Sale of 42-44 Holden Street.' I said

The line went on hold to the usual Vivaldi Muzak. When the line opened again, it was the same voice

'I *am* sorry, Mr Rawlings is in a meeting now.' Susan lied.

'When is he likely to be free?'

'I don't know I'm afraid.' She continued

'Well please ask him to call me.'

I made sure Susan had my details and got on with my work. Over the next few weeks with the sale price whirring around in my head, I decided to make some enquiries through the Land Registry in Weymouth. I spoke to a helpful young man, who said I could buy a copy of the Land Registry certificate of ownership for a few pounds. I wrote a covering letter, enclosing a cheque and SAE. Within a week, I was holding the certificate. My mouth went dry as I read it.

Sale of 42 -44 Holden Street.
Purchasers name: Roland Hargreaves
Purchase price: £115,000

'Rolo Hargreaves! ROLO HARGREAVES' I repeated 'My God, Rolo Hargreaves!'

Rolo Hargreaves was an Insurance Broker and a friend of my husband. We had been introduced to him by Anna a secretary, who had worked for us some years ago. In fact, he was her on, off, boyfriend, but he was *not* a boy.

Divorced, with three grown up children, he was a bit of a man about town. I never liked him, not least because of the way he treated Anna, but also, he seemed a bit of a slippery character. His dulcet tones could charm the birds off the trees, sell snow to Eskimos… you know the type? This lothario wined and dined Anna, sent flowers to the office, brought her bottles of super expensive perfume back from his business trips and then there were those luxurious weekends away. Rolo always looked after his women and I do mean women in plural, because when Anna found out she was one of many, there were fireworks and tears at the office, as well as flowers that were thrown back at the poor delivery boy. Other rumours about his womanising were always in circulation and what's more, he wore them as a badge of honour. He was always known to have a younger model on his arm, mainly I thought, because they were too ditsy to see him for what he really was, or what he really wanted. That is the older man, looking for some firm young flesh. He even regaled us one evening with a story, that I thought at the time I should report to the NSPCC, but no crime had been committed, it was just the flavour of what was in his mind.

He was apparently mowing the lawns at the front of his ex-wife's property when,

'I saw this beautiful girl walking down the road towards me.' 'Well, I can tell you, she was quite something…. you know, lovely figure, hair down to her shoulders and wearing shorts… so I could see she had fabulous legs…'

'So, I started to take the mower closer to the foot path, I wanted to get a better peak at her.' 'And low and behold, she turned into the drive and said, 'Hey Dad!'

He thought this was *so* funny.

'Imagine.' He said, 'It was my Emma!'

Someone said, 'Time to get new glasses Rolo.'

'Well it might have been helpful if I was wearing them….!' He laughed

Emma was all of sixteen and this episode, just for a second or two, had brought him up sharp. Men with libidinous motives, just like him, were eyeing up his precious daughter. But when the event had conveniently drifted from his mind, in no time at all, he was charming those young fledglings off the trees again.

When their relationship was on, Rolo and Anna would come around for supper, his charm offensive would be on full throttle.

'How pretty the table looks Alice.'

'You've cooked this roast to perfection…. You *clever* girl.'

'This chocolate soufflé is the best I've ever tasted.'

'Your husband is *such* a lucky man.'…..
Rolo, always with a slight tan, looked immaculate. I would normally call a man like this a Silver Fox, but his receding hair was still dark brown, thanks to Grecian 2000 and his smart striped shirts ran amok over his paunch, like the graphics on a Bridget Riley painting. He ran his insurance business from a small office in town. Everyone in his social circle, gave their business to Rolo, because if ever there was need to make a claim, Rolo would smooth the waters, fix the problem. That was his professional life. But the more I learned about Rolo Hargreaves' other life, the less I liked this smooth-talking reprobate. I knew from Anna, he rubbed shoulders with some low life characters. He was not a man you would want to cross. He had people who could fix things, and I don't mean the likes of a plumber or a handy man.

As soon as I read his name on the Land Registry form, my heart skipped a beat or two. Now I had huge misgivings about the sale of our property. Why was Rolo involved? Not for any altruistic reasons I could be sure. I called Pension & Mutual again. John Rawlings had never returned my call.
'John Rawlings, please.' I said
'Who's calling?' I recognised Susan's voice
'Alice Waite….in connection with the sale of Holden Street.' I pre-empted her next question
'Oh, yes.' she said rather meekly.
I'm sure she knew exactly why I was calling
'Mr Rawlings didn't return my call.'
I wasn't telling her anything she didn't know.
'I see.' She said
'So, is he available now?'
'I will find out.' She pressed the Muzak button.
After a couple of concertos, Susan came back to me.
'*Unfortunately*, Mr Rawlings is out of the office today.' she lied again.
'So, how do I ever get to speak to Mr Rawlings, Susan?'
'I will pass your message on.'
She said not answering my question.
'So, who is his deputy'?
I wasn't letting her off the hook.
'Err, that would-be Mark O'Neil.' She said
'Can I speak to Mr O'Neil then?'
'I'll try his extension.' She said

More Muzak, more waiting, more frustration. I will have gone grey, before I get to speak to some one.
'Mrs Waite?' Susan was back on the line 'Sorry to keep you.' 'Unfortunately, Mr O'Neil isn't available at the moment.'
'Do you know Susan, I had a feeling you were going to say that.'
I heard an intake of breath on the other end of the line.
'Susan, can you give a message to both Mr Rawlings and Mr O'Neil.'
'Of course.' She said
'Can you tell them, that I will not be fobbed off any longer'… 'I will be going to the Press with this issue….'
I heard a sharp intake of breath again, as soon as I mentioned the word Press.
'And the issue is, Pension & Mutual have sold a property in my Pension fund without consulting me' 'Serious stuff Susan!' 'And, I will be like that annoying wasp, buzzing around a jam pot, you will never get rid of me, until I get some answers.'
'Oh' Susan said taking the flack for Rawlings and O'Neil
'So, if I don't get a return call in the next twenty-four hours, be on notice, I will take matters into my own hands.' 'Thank you, Susan.'
I put the receiver down, feeling mean that Susan had taken the brunt of my complaint. She was being used as a human shield by Rawlings and O'Neil. Trying to get answers from Pension & Mutual, was like climbing Everest without oxygen and Sherpas.

Not only was I furious with Pension & Mutual, for not advising me of the sale, but also why hadn't David Ellis our Estate Agent been in touch? I picked up the phone and called him.
'David Ellis please.'
'He's not in the office at the moment.' A young voice said. 'Darren speaking, can I help?'
I realised I had called at lunch time, but continued
'Well Darren, maybe you can' 'You have a lovely property for sale 42 -44 Holden Street'
'Oh no!' He said 'You've just missed it… It was sold last week!'
Last week, I thought? I looked down to the Land Registry details and could see the sale date was three weeks ago. Then without thinking I said 'No… that can't be right…'
But he interjected, 'I'm sure… let me get the file.'
I soon realised that Darren was probably about sixteen and must have been

left alone in the office to cover lunchtime, because Darren was being Mr Super Helpful, office boy and about to give me confidential information. I played the part.
'Are you sure it's sold Darren?' I said… 'It was just what I wanted…'
'Yes... Yes.' He said, 'I'm looking at the file now….it went for £250,000 to Damien Humphries.'
My heart nearly stopped. My mouth went dry.
'Sorry?' I said, 'Could you repeat that? 'This isn't a very good line.'
'No worries.' He chirped 'So £250,000 to a Mr Damien Humphries.' 'Oh, I remember him coming in…. he's that sculptor chap, wanted a big work shop.' 'Doesn't look like he had to get a mortgage either.'
So much information…!
'Well thank you Darren.' I muttered 'Such a shame I've missed it…. you've been most helpful.' 'Thanks again…. goodbye now.'

The enormity of what I had just heard was hurtling around my head. I had to sit down. If there had been wine in the office I would have poured myself a large glass. So, 42 -44 Holden Street had been sold AGAIN, by Rolo Hargreaves, just a couple of weeks after he had bought it. Is this a deal with the Devil? What was going on? An Earl Grey and a ginger biscuit, soon got the faculties working.
The difference between the two prices was a significant £135.000. This clandestine second sale had been engineered by my husband and Rolo. The double dealing, two faced pieces of low life. They had each been complicit in what surely must be fraud, but how to prove it?
I tried to speak to Sally Grafton and when I finally did, she wasn't particularly impressed or excited with my findings.
'Sally, my husband has set this sale up with this morally unprincipled, Rolo Hargreaves.' 'My pension is nearly £70,000 short… it's a lot of money!'
'You don't know that they have set this up… I mean how would you prove it?' 'It's probably just a coincidence.'
I began to realise solicitors, definitely worked in boxes and anything outside their standard remit – well it belonged to another department… think separate bills for specific specialities. I apparently would require a Pension specialist, plus a Litigation specialist. Of course, this would have a huge bearing on my divorce, but it was up to me to instruct more suits, so that the case, within the correct legal framework, could then be presented back to the divorce suits. No chance! The piggy bank was all but empty. As it was, I was sweating at the end of every month, as another invoice hit

the mat. Williams, Rossiter & Phipps were very efficient at communicating at the end of the month, but not so efficient at communicating with their clients at other times.

I decided the best short cut was to hire some Private Detectives. Now, pre-internet, the only way to source someone like this, was to resort to something called, The Yellow Pages, a big fat trader's directory, printed on yellow paper. I pulled my copy from the top shelf.

Chapter 13

The fax

Leafing through the Yellow Pages, I reached the heading Private Investigators. There was a sizeable list of professional sleuths. The one that caught my eye was called Panther Investigations. (No, you couldn't make it up)! I called them, because their ad made much of the fact, they used ex police officers for all their work. What do I know?

A couple of days later Doug from Panther turned up at the office. A rather well built, man, with a patterned pully under his jacket. His tie was greasy at the point the knot met his chins. Has he never checked himself in the mirror? Puffing his chest out, he explained he had worked as a Detective Inspector and was now running his own investigation company. Clearly, he was rather pleased with the name, Panther Investigations. In his mind's eye, I'm sure he saw himself as a sleek Black Panther pounding through the underworld at record breaking speeds, to make an arrest. Whereas, when I looked at his inept store detective frame, I saw Inspector Clouseau of Pink Panther fame, the antithesis of a Kick Ass investigator.I explained the situation and gave him a contact sheet with all the information he would need, then we discussed the way forward for his investigation.

'I will set up a meeting with this Sculptor chappie to see what he knows…' He advised

Slightly alarmed he hadn't retained the appropriate names of those he would be investigating, I reminded him 'Err, Damien Humphries you mean?'

'Yes, yes, but *to avoid suspicion*, I'll *do some research,* so I can commission 'Im… err... as a Sculptor.' 'I have an architect friend, I'll see if he can make the first approach.'

'How long will this take?' I asked

'Well we need to set this meeting up…and to *avoid suspicion*....' His eyes met mine. *Avoiding suspicion* was almost a nudge, nudge moment. Bring in Dixon of Dock Green to save us, pleeese!

Alice Waite

'Yes' I butted in, becoming more than a little irritated. 'I do understand we need to *avoid suspicion.*'
'As soon as I have made arrangements I will be in touch.' He said and clutching his retainer cheque, was on his way to the door.

I was still keen to speak to David Elliot. I wanted all the pieces of the puzzle in some kind of order. How was it, he had resold the property? Why hadn't *he* been in touch about the first sale? I tried several times to get him on the phone, leaving messages. Without a doubt, the messages resulted in a lead draw bridge firmly being pulled up to the battlements. I wrote and faxed and called again and again until one day I lost it.
'Look!' I said to his secretary 'I know he's there and I want to speak to him.'
'He has some serious questions to answer and if I don't get a return phone call today, I shall not only be contacting the National Association of Estate Agents, but also the Evening Post.' Getting into my stride, I continued 'And after notifying the press, I will come to your office, with a large banner explaining just what kind of double dealing estate agents you are!' I slammed the phone down. I thought I might just combust. Taking a sip or two of water, I tried to compose myself as the phone immediately started ringing. My professional phone voice answered, 'Good Morning, The School of Media Studies'
'Mrs Waite?' A voice said.
'Speaking.' I replied. I knew exactly who owned this gravelly voice and I could see his rather lived in face.
'David Elliot here.'
'Well thank you for returning my call' I said in my most charming voice 'I want answers to some questions Mr Elliot, as I'm sure you are aware.'
'Now look here.' He said, 'This is a marital dispute and I am not prepared to get mixed up in it.'
'My goodness Mr Elliot, you clearly have misconstrued why I have been calling.' 'I am not calling on you to be a marriage guidance councillor... I am asking a simple question.' 'Why didn't you advise me there had been an offer made on my property?'
'Well I didn't know you had separated.' He said
'Mr Elliot, my letter advising you of my new address was sent Recorded delivery and I have checked….it *was* received by your office.'
'I see' he said rather quietly.
'So, acting for both my husband and I, *you* have a duty of care to *both*

of us….and *you* have failed *me*.' 'I am therefore looking at negligence on your part.'

'Now now' he said, 'I had nothing to do with the first sale.' He sounded defensive.

'What do you mean?' I said

'Look, I only dealt with the last sale.'

'But you knew about the first one?'

'Look, I've already said, I don't want to get involved with all this…'

'Mr Elliot, like it or not, you are involved up to your estate agent's neck, with some very shady business.' 'I don't know what the NAEA will say about it, when I present them with all the details.'

'Don't threaten me!' He shouted

I realised I was pushing the envelope, but continued,

'I am *not* threatening you Mr Elliot, I am simply stating I have recourse to your professional body and… well any resulting publicity wouldn't be so favourable, would it?'

'Now look here.' He said

'No, *you* look here.' I continued 'I want the facts with dates.'

'I'll send you a copy of a fax I have' he said, 'that should clear up what you want to know.'

The line went dead. I had no idea what he was talking about… what fax? My hands were clammy, my heart palpitating, but somehow, I felt rather powerful.

Minutes later the fax machine whirred into action. A single sheet of paper slid onto my desk. In the middle of this kaleidoscope of double dealing, I was now looking at a heist of diamonds.

Dear David

42 -44 Holden Street

As you know this property has been on the market some time and you have secured interest from Damien Humphries, which looks like it is going ahead.

However, in the meantime, I have sold to Mr Roland Hargreaves who will be contacting you shortly to arrange the sale to Humphries. Rest assured your commission will be paid on this sale.

Kind Regards
Steve Waite

I starred at my husband's signature. OMG! What an idiot! *Unbelievable…!* He can't Typex this one away!

I picked up the phone to my solicitor. Sally Grafton was not available. Over the next ten days I tried several times to speak to her. She was never available, and she didn't return my calls. The continued unavailability of Sally Grafton, caused incalculable stress. The practice was always economical with the reality of her working hours. She was often 'In court' or 'With a client.' So that for a while, I convinced myself, Sally was a high flyer…. So busy, she *must be* good? I later discovered she did not work on Wednesday or Thursday. Therefore, a crisis on a Tuesday couldn't be dealt with until Friday. However, by Friday, Sally Grafton's phone message list was so long, it was the luck of the draw if she managed to return my call. Unbelievably, divorce solicitors do not acknowledge the emotional traumas' their clients are undergoing. And when there is a crisis in the proceedings, when we seek assurance, or maybe clearance on some legal points, *listen sisters*, we need to speak to someone, preferably within twenty-four hours*, not* two weeks. Trying several times, a day to speak to you, we only hear the singy song voice of your secretary, who assures us, you *will* return our call…. Whilst all along, she knows you are at home, with the kids, or doing the gardening, or filling a trolley at Waitrose. This is *so head bangingly frustrating.* Your call list for Friday will take up more than your designated six hours of work time, never mind the files piling up on the floor, around your desk. So, prioritise, we all have to! Some sad souls like me, may not get to the top of your list, or even the middle and another weekend will arrive, without answers and then…more sleepless nights. You just don't get it, *do you*? We are not dealing with dumping the family goldfish, just thirty plus years of marriage and all that this entails. With weeks of this reticence you guys, make it so perfectly clear to gullible fee-paying clients like me, that non-communication is your modus operandi.

After weeks of this nightmare, Williams Rossiter & Phipps reluctantly admit that Sally Grafton is only part time. I ask for my case to be transferred to Victoria Buchannan, who was originally recommended to me. By now, I have a PA called Trish who arranges a telephone appointment for me at lunchtime. I am lecturing all morning and afternoon and it's my only free slot. Victoria sounds sympathetic and I feel a sense of relief as I voice my concerns eloquently. (Little does she know I had a prepared script on my desk?) Victoria agrees to pick up my case. I explain the whole fraud issue;

Only cry on Fridays

she appears concerned, relenting to take my files from Monday onwards… YES! Someone who will bat for me, take charge, answer my queries and even phone calls.

That evening, I draft a letter to her, listing my concerns, issues we must address, not least the fraudulent selling of the property in my pension fund. Trish types it up the next day and sends it to her Recorded delivery. A week goes by and I have no response. OK, OK, I think, let's be positive, she must review the files, make enquiries. Then another week goes by. I make a phone call and speak to another secretary with a singy song voice. Do they train them to sound like this in Secretary's School? It's Gilbert and Sullivan at its worst.

'Victoria is in court today.' She trills 'But I will make sure she gets the message.'

Where have I heard this mantra before…? For all Williams Rossiter & Phipps care, *messages* might as well be the lost earring, dropped between the floor boards or a mouldy piece of cheese lurking unnoticed, at the back of the fridge. In the small hours I have nightmares. There is another fluorescent lit cubby hole in the offices of WRP called *Messages*. It is jammed packed with unloved bits of paper, Post-its, message pads and fluff, copious fluff. Every night, the door is gingerly opened by a laughing singy song secretary and every message of the day is thrown in and the door pushed closed, locked and bolted, lest anything might escape. All the secretaries laugh with glee, as they survey their desks, clean and pristine, ready for another day, trilling on the telephone or typing invoices.

I was familiar with this ostrich style behaviour. My husband would not deal with any post requesting money or information. Cheques were of course rushed off to the bank, but other post, piled up over months, creating a pyramid of brown envelopes on his desk. My requests to 'Please deal with this' fell on deaf ears. Every couple has their own way of dealing with their finances. In the early years when the children were small, and Steve was earning the lion's share of our income, he was most reluctant to have a joint account. Why should I have access to *his* money? Small amounts were doled out to me on a *How much do you need for that?* basis. Alarm bells about power and control should have been ringing then, but the clanging of those bells was well and truly drowned with the demands of three children under five.

Later, this mean-spirited approach was to my advantage, as my business became more successful and *my* account was *my own*. We agreed on who would pay what and it felt like a pretty even distribution of responsibility. It roughly worked out that, I would cover the Gas, Electricity, food, holidays and school fees for two of the girls. He was to pay the mortgage, HMRC, Rates and school fees for one daughter. For years this seemed to be fine, until *another Brilliant Idea* hit the dust. Then the brown envelopes would start to form the all too familiar pyramid on his so-called desk. I say so called, because it was all but invisible with overflowing ashtrays, pen pots filled with dried up biros and broken pencils, old coffee mugs and of course masses of post. You cannot rescue someone who doesn't want to be rescued. But then, he had a way to deal with this irritating disorder, just like my nightmare of Williams Rossiter & Phipps' Message Room, he could make this inconvenient truth of Manila, disappear. One day it would be there in all its troublesome glory and the next, as if by magic, there was a clean desk, empty ashtrays and some semblance of order. Sadly, the magic was not the overnight emergence of super organisational skills, combined with the use of a cheque book. All his problems had been eliminated into large black bin bags. The decks swept clean... Working on the premise, if you can't see the problem, it doesn't exist. He must have felt he had disappeared down a rabbit hole and arrived in Wonderland. But then, the ramifications of this well-ordered desk, soon came by Recorded Delivery to haunt me. Starting with the Inland Revenue and tax arrears, then a repossession order from the Building Society....and on it went. Both our pension funds had to be raided (possible because we were over fifty) and I was left to deal with what the pensions wouldn't cover.

So, back to the Message Room at WRP. The key has been tossed into the back of a drawer and Victoria has not been tempted to go there. She can't be responsible for what she doesn't know. Three and a half weeks later, there has been no contact, either by phone, or letter, not even a pigeon with a Post-it. I am tearing my hair out, going up the wall. I need answers, I need action... This Pension fraud issue has been kicked into the long grass. By now I've been through two and a half months of non-communication with replacement solicitor number three and I'VE HAD ENOUGH!

Here we go again, scattered phone calls to everyone. Do you know any woman who has had a good divorce settlement? Everyone must think I am eating these solicitors for breakfast. Then I remembered Andrew has a friend who is a retired judge. It's a long shot but I call him. He tells me to pop in for a cup of tea when I get home. Ever hopeful, I bound up the stairs and I tap on his door. Andrew puts the kettle on.

'I've called Horace.' He says, as he turns down the sugar-coated voice of Radio Two.

Then he disappears into the dining room and returns with a couple of wine glasses.

'Looks like you need something stronger than tea darling.'

He opens some ice-cold Sauvignon Blanc and we clink glasses. It's only five thirty, but I'm not about to protest.

'Now, Horace has given me the name of a woman he trained…. she's heading up the department he left.' 'Her name is Mary Collins and she's SHIT HOT!'

The Sauvignon Blanc hits the spot.

'Oh God, Andrew, Thank you!' 'She's got to be my Woman.'

Chapter 14

Mary Collins

I made an appointment with Mary Collins at Garston & Welland. Term had ended which gave me more flexibility, so with all my files in (smart) carrier bags, I hopped onto the train. I didn't want the stress of parking and a taxi from the station soon deposited me at reception. Another solicitor's reception I thought, here we go…
A plain, smiley woman came over to introduce herself
'Mrs Waite?' 'Hello, I'm Mary Collins.'
She had a good figure and a pleasant demeanour. Her face was scrubbed and well, we've all had bad hair days. No matter, it's not what this about… It's her brain and commitment I need. In no time at all, sitting opposite each other in the conference room, tea arrives, and we get started. She takes copious notes but was at pains to defend her colleagues at WRH. Professional protocol I presume, she certainly wasn't going to push them under a bus. At the end of an hour's in-depth discussion, I ask her to act for me.
'Are you up to date with your invoices from WRH?' She asks
'There's bound to be another invoice on the way… it's the end of the month after all.' 'But otherwise I've paid everything.' I said, thinking of all the money that had leached from my bank account.
'When you've paid the closing invoice, all the files can be transferred.' She explained 'You know they won't send the files until you've done this.'
'Yes, I've got the picture.' I said, 'I have to pay for months of incompetence, it's the only way I can move, forward isn't it?' ….. 'It's shocking you know.' I sighed 'They can charge what they like and because I need the files, I just have to pay it.' 'It's daylight robbery!'
I realise I am talking to someone in the legal sister hood. They were probably in the same book club and she certainly didn't want to entertain my unprofessional banter at any point. Closed Ranks, I should have known.

Only cry on Fridays

'I'm sure they will only invoice you for work carried out on your behalf.' She said diplomatically.

The tea was cold, but I felt we had had a good meeting. Mary watched as I packed up my files and then escorted me to reception. This was solicitor number four. Crossing my fingers, I hoped she was my woman.

I asked Victoria Buchannan's singy song secretary for a closing invoice and miracle of miracles, in the blink of an eye it appeared. Funny that! How some messages escape the gathering fluff of the Message room at WRH. Alarmingly, Victoria saw fit to invoice me for reading my files after my case was moved to her, because of the sheer inefficiency of her colleague Sally Grafton. It beggars belief, because even if she did read my files, she never did anything with the information, except ignore my messages. I knew by disputing the invoice, it would just delay everything further, so I begrudgingly paid it with a scathing covering letter. The Legal fraternity or sisterhood in this case, are a law unto themselves. The files went across to Garston& Welland the following week. A few less files on the floor for Victoria to negotiate, on the way to her desk.

Mary Collins was all over my files quickly, asking lots of pertinent questions. She suggested, I should get in touch with the Financial Services Ombudsman regarding the negligence of Pension and Mutual and my Pension property. I phoned The Ombudsman and obtained all the paperwork, then set about collating all the evidence I had. I knew I was going to need more detail and wondered what had happened to my sleuth. A month or so had passed and I had heard nothing from Doug, The Pink Panther. I left a message on his mobile and his land line. I recognised his voice on the answering machine, speaking very precisely over a background of barking dogs. Days passed…Nil response…I tried his mobile and again left more messages.

The summer was upon us and while it was good to have a more relaxed feel to the working day, I was worrying about the finances for the next six months. I needed bums on seats for the autumn term. I also had the added commitment of teaching three evening classes a week, so had to be even more organised than ever. Three different classes in three different locations and the nearest, forty minutes' drive away.

After another week or so The Panther finally rung.

'I'm setting up a sting you see…. These things can't be hurried because….'

Let's hear it from the top Doug…

'Because it causes suspicion.'

'Now look.' I said, 'This sting has been going on for nearly three months, I want to know just what you have in place and when you are going in there, to get the evidence I need.'

'Well my architect friend has made some initial enquiries, so we will be calling again to set up a meeting in the next few weeks.'

'WEEKS'! I said… 'No, no… This matter has some urgency to it.' 'I don't think you realise how important this evidence is for me.'

He said he'd get back to me as soon as possible, promising I wouldn't be disappointed. I've been living in a world of broken promises for the last eighteen months, so is it any wonder I don't believe him? Eventually I threatened him with Trading Standards and in no time at all received a cheque for the retainer I had paid him, some six months previously. I was reminded of poignant line in a Bob Dylan song 'You only wasted my precious time…'

Living in the city centre has its benefits and some draw backs. At the drop of a hat I could go out for the evening, the theatre, cinema, restaurants all were within walking distance. The Theatre was rather expensive for my budget, but town centre dwellers knew the score. Half an hour before curtain up, the best tickets in the house were on sale for £10… very doable. So, a group of us would sit in Pizza Express near by and at the appointed time, one would slip out and see if there were sufficient tickets. If not, it would be another bottle of wine and a more prolonged evening at Pizza Express.

Every May, there was an Arts festival when the streets became art venues, with sculpture on traffic islands, alongside jazz bands or chamber orchestras. On the opening night there were Madrigals processing Georgian Crescents with candles and on the last night a firework finale. Given the vagaries of the English weather, it was de rigueur to turn out with umbrellas and Wellies in support.

On the downside, I struggled living in a flat, (or apartment as Andrew liked to call it) without a garden. The late evening town centre noises of those the worse for wear, never mind the rat run, to and from the ambulance station, adjoining my square made my location less than idyllic. Spring brought the Seagulls into the city looking for mates. Their nuptials, immediately followed by screaming matches and fights to lay claim on the best nesting spots in the warm nooks and crannies of the buildings. The Gulls were up arguing from first light. Like braying donkeys on my window sill, the noise was unbelievable. One morning they attacked a poor pigeon leaving it injured outside my window. The RSPCA were called to take the injured chap away.

However, all said and done, I was immensely grateful for my second floor flat. With an intercom at the front door, I felt safe and away from harms way. I enjoyed returning every night to the peace of my own company. No harassment, criticism or cruel words. I won't say I wasn't worried about the future, but I was focused on getting through this. My new life was filled with support from so many friends new and old. To a certain extent, I was in a frozen, numb state. A state of hibernation, waiting for the real spring, when my life would start again, on my terms. By prolonging the divorce with the Pension fraud, my optimistic estimate of getting through this in six months, was now laughable and all the time my husband was sitting comfortably in our lovely house. He was still in my head. I could hear his cruel disparaging words. He was present in my dreams/ nightmares and I wanted him gone.

My frozen state was for Monday to Friday, putting on a brave face for work. *Professional, professional Alice,* you must remain professional. Nobody wants to deal with a tearful woman, on the edge. So, all week I would be the consummate actress, running my business efficiently, with a smiley face from nine till five and also, for the three evening classes on my agenda. But by Friday night, everything was bubbling up to the surface, panic, rage and sadness... so much inner turmoil. It's hard to describe mental pain if you haven't experienced it. It is unimaginably distressing, dealing with a hideous conflict of emotions. The mind resists all attempts of distraction. No matter how I try, I cannot stop toxic thoughts colliding in an alarming vortex. The man I married, who had promised to love and cherish me, had broken my spirit with his twisted behaviour. He infiltrated my soul, manipulated my life, systematically chipping away at my self confidence with pernicious jibes. He's still in my head and there's no way around it. On Friday evenings I didn't have to put on a brave face for anyone. Yes, I was incredibly tired after a gruelling week, but the weekend gave me permission to let everything out. My body overtaken with unrelenting sobbing, I heard myself howl like a wounded animal. Not only was I dealing with a legacy of abuse, I now had the Pension fraud on my plate.

Chapter 15

Annie

Annie had popped into the studio for coffee and an update. I told her I had drawn a blank with the stupid Panther sleuth. He wasn't capable of discovering, a tea bag in a pot of tea. Annie followed me into the kitchen to fill the kettle when I realised she was in a bit of a state, her eyes were red, she looked all in.
'Hey, hey old thing, what's up'?
I gave her a big hug and, as is perfectly normal when you feel low, if someone shows kindness and concern, the sobs turn into meltdown.
'Come on girl, you need a coffee.' I said
I started to make the coffee. Distracted, I must have put the coffee in twice, because the plunger was pretty hard to push down.
'It's Matthew.' She mumbled through the tears. 'He's dumped me!'
I knew things hadn't been great between them for some time but felt it better to express surprise.
'What...why?'
'Oh, you know, I had my suspicions about that woman at work...it seems he's definitely been seeing her and for even longer than I thought '.... 'The sod!'
'So, did you have it all out.... Did you confront him?'
'Sort of... last night' she said 'But we didn't get anywhere, we just went around in circles, you know.... I can't say I behaved impeccably.... I was accusing him without real evidence, just a gut feeling.' 'He was so angry.... then he left, slamming the front door... I thought it was going to come off its hinges!'
'Anger sounds like guilt to me.' 'He didn't like being found out, did he?'
I poured some high voltage coffee. You could have stood a spoon upright in this brew. The contents of the biscuit tin, was not exactly inspiring, but there were a few soft, dark chocolate digestives to help the coffee go down.
'If he is a two, timing bastard then you are better off without him.' I said

'Yes, I know but it makes me feel crap.' ….. 'I mean what's this woman at work got that I haven't?' She started crying again 'I even shaved my pubes into a heart shape for Valentines you know…. He couldn't even buy a card!'
'Come on, Annie drink some coffee.' 'How about we go out for a pizza tonight?'
'And, do you know *how* he dumped me?' She went on, rummaging in her handbag, pulling out a very crumpled piece of paper, which she waved in the air.
'By bloody fax!'
'No!' 'The coward' I yelled. 'Unbelievable!'
She passed the fax over to me and my eyes scanned across the few lines he had typed.
'You know what…?' 'You are SO much better off without him'… He's dumped you in Helvetica.' 'Just *no t*aste, that man!'
She started to smile. 'No, definitely no taste.' She said
Her inner turmoil released through all the sobs, she laughed at last. She knew she was better off without him, but it was his deceit that made her crestfallen. She cleaned up her mascara smudged eyes and we decided to have an early lunch at Clarke's down the road, instead of a pizza in the evening. Annie's eyes were still puffy, so when we arrived, and Gary showed us to a table, she chose to sit with her back to the restaurant, facing the wall and I sat facing the busy wine bar. We ordered our lunch and thought in the circumstances, a glass of wine was an absolute necessity. I had loads of work waiting in the office, but realising there wasn't going to be much afternoon, threw myself into support mode, as Annie had always done for me. As we ate our lunch, she recalled how they had met, good times and not so good times and then launched into a serious character assassination. In her heart, she had always known he wasn't going to change into the person she had convinced herself he was.
Weighing in I said, 'You know he wasn't exactly God's gift Annie.' 'I mean he had become seriously overweight.' 'He looked like the only time he got off the sofa was to get another glass of wine!'
We both had a good giggle, and then she pronounced in a rather loud voice,
'I know, I know, and the sex wasn't that great either.' 'It was like a wardrobe with the key still in it, falling on top of me!'
We cracked up laughing and as I looked towards the lunch time crowd, I could see several people smirking. Something to tell the others, when they get back to work, I thought.

Alice Waite

Annie had left her Art folder at the studios, so we walked back slowly in the mid-afternoon sunlight.
She started singing 'Going to wash that man right out of my hair.'
I joined in 'Going to wash that man right out of my life...'
She was on the mend. We did a little dance along Parson Street, then turned into Garrton St. As I opened my front door she said
'Now look, I've been thinking....'
'Yes... Annie what *are you* thinking?'
'What if I went to see this sculptor.... Damien is it?'
'Yes, Damien Humphries.' I replied, 'But to what end?' 'I know the Panther has failed me spectacularly...'
'So, I will go with my designer hat on and see what I can find out.... why not, we've got nothing to lose old thing?'
'That would be amazing, thank you!'
I gave her a big hug and we started making plans. No internet, no websites remember, so it was back to Directory Enquiries, as Damien had moved in after the latest Yellow pages had been printed. I scribbled the number on a scrap of paper and pressed it into Annie's hand. She said she would phone him the next day.
'I need to be fresh.' She said, admitting the lunch time wine had gone to her head. 'I'll dream up a project and drive out to see him... don't worry I won't blow it!'
And with that, she was gone, back to her studio.

The next day she telephoned me.
'OK, OK.... I'm going to see him on Friday morning!' She bellowed excitedly. 'Poor sod, sounded so enthused when I said I was working on a garden design... I'll report back on Friday!' 'Yeah!'
She sounded so buoyant and happy. Matthew was definitely history.

On Friday, Annie drove out to her appointment with Damien. She had a slick silver sports car, which she leased. We had long discussed the issue of the right car, in client's eyes. Too old and not smart, the client will think, she's not doing very well, she can't be much good! Too new and expensive, she's doing well, she must be good... but does she charge high fees to pay for that snazzy car? You can't win! Annie decided, she wanted to look successful, so she leased the silver number, even if she was living on baked beans at the end of the month.

Parking right outside Damien's studio, so he could get a good look at the car, she had dressed in designer black, and the tightest Armani jeans. He clearly saw her arrive, as he was out of the door in a flash to greet her.
'Hi are you Damien?' She gushed 'I'm Annie.'
'Yes, that's me.' He said shaking her hand 'Pleased to meet you.'
Here was a tall young man in overalls with a natty cotton scarf, tucked into his shirt, his hair flopped onto his forehead, in that fashionable arty way. Guiding her towards the front door he said,
'Shall we go in?'
Damien guided her into his slightly chaotic office. Sitting opposite each other, Annie pulled out some plans she had borrowed, to discuss what she had in mind for the garden sculptures.
'Let's go through to the studio, so I can show you a pair of Lurchers I've just made for either side of an entrance… that will give you an idea of the sort of thing I can make.' He said. Having marvelled at the scale of the bronze Lurchers, Annie started wandering around the studio looking at other work in progress.
'This is an amazing space you've got here Damien.' She enthused 'Have you been here long?'
'No, no' he said, 'Just a few months, I moved here from Camberwell'
'So, from the smoke to a country village!' 'You were pretty lucky to find somewhere like this you know.'
I know, I know.' He was pleased with himself and continued 'It was a nightmare to buy though!'
'What do you mean?' Annie said, eyes ablaze
He continued 'Well the guy I was buying it from, was a double dealing little shit!' 'Oooh! Excuse my French!' He said covering his mouth and grinning.
'No problem.' Annie said waving her hand 'I had all sorts of problems buying my house.'
Damien didn't want to compare notes though. He had a story and wanted to tell it to this personable young lady in her skinny jeans.
'You see this guy had already sold this place to a friend… they were working some kind of scam.'
'What do you mean?' Questioned Annie
'Well, when I went to my solicitors to sign all the paperwork… that's when I found out he'd already sold it!'
'No!' 'You're kidding me!' Annie egged him on.

He was in his stride, playing to the gallery… he could dine out with this story, it had legs!
'So … Well I don't get it.' Annie looked quizzical and shrugging her shoulders, played the stupid girly card.
'Well apparently, it was in a pension fund, with his ex-wife… so if it was cheaper, he'd only have to give her half of the first price…''Not half of the price I paid this other guy, which my solicitor says was *a lot* more.' 'Do you see?'
'So… you mean…?' Annie was certainly going to coax it out of him
'The other guy was a friend.' 'They set it up between the two of them.'
'No!' '*The Rat*'! She said meaning it.
'People round here have told me…. this couple, they'd been married for a long time.' 'But now I see a middle-aged woman, popping in with food on trays… I mean can't he cook?'
'Well I never!' Annie mused.
'But, Damien, you were so lucky, this is just such a great place and I *love* your work!'
He beamed like a school boy getting his first star from his favourite teacher.
'I didn't realise you could get mortgages on places like this.' She queried rather nosily.
'Nah didn't have to.' He continued 'Ma… well she's always encouraged me, loves my work you know and well… she could do this for me.'
'You *lucky* boy!' Annie said.
They looked at a couple of other pieces currently being modelled in clay, then Annie decided it was time for off.
'Look you've been *amazingly* helpful Damien.' 'Now I know what you can do I'm going to do some drawings, talk to my client and get back to you.' 'Is that alright?' 'Oh, have you got a card I could have?'
He collected a brochure and card from his office as they made their way to the front door.
'Let me know if I can help with, well… anything.' He was putty in her hands.
'Will do and thanks once again.' She said as she dropped into the low-slung car seat.
The engine revved with a satisfying tone as she drove off, waving through the sun roof
'Bye bye byeee byeee…!' and she was gone.
Damien strolled back to his studio, immersed in the feel-good factor, he was positively glowing.

I heard Annie's car pull up outside my office and in a nanosecond, she was impatiently standing on the door bell. I rushed to open the door.
'He sung like a canary....!' She screamed. 'He told me everything.... Everything'!
'Oh my God' how amazing.' I gave her a big hug. 'Tell *me* everything; I want to know every detail.' I said

Over a pot of Earl Grey, Annie told me verbatim, the whole thing. I was so thrilled, I decided to telephone Mary Collins at Garston & Welland.
'Mary don't you think this is amazing?'
'Well you have to realise that this is called *hearsay*.' She said, 'There are no witnesses, but you can get your friend to sign an affidavit at a local solicitor, if she is prepared to do this?'
She really didn't sound enthused by Annie's amateur sleuth work. Annie had been in the kitchen washing up when I made the phone call. I put the phone down, disheartened to say the least.
'Hey what's up?' She queried 'What did she say?'
I explained about hearsay and the affidavit.
'Look, let's just get the affidavit done while it's all fresh in my mind.' 'I'll type it up tonight.' 'Your job is to make an appointment with a solicitor to get this thing signed.'
I felt pretty crushed by Mary's lukewarm response and was grateful to Annie for organising me. I really needed her motivation to get the material she had so cleverly squeezed out of Damien, accepted.
'Got it!' I said, 'I'll give you a call when I've got a date.'
Three days later we were in Simpkins Hunt & Gable's offices, a local solicitor a few streets away. Annie swore on the Bible and signed the affidavit in front of a solicitor. He read through the affidavit and said
'Do you mind me asking what this is all about?'
His eyes weren't quite on stalks, but he was clearly inquisitive. By now, I was used to explaining a complex storyline in an economical, coherent way. This time, his eyes were on stalks.
'This is very serious.' He said, 'You've got a case against Pensions & Mutual for a start.' 'As trustees they have a duty of care to you.' 'They should have written to *you* as an individual about this sale, not as a couple.' 'The law is very clear about that.'
'I've written to the Ombudsman.' I said 'But we're hoping a third party, that's this guy Damien Humphries, who has learned about all this by default.... I mean about the first sale, can help build my case.'

'I see.' He said, 'Well good luck.'

Annie was buoyant in her newly single state.

'You know this *will* come right girl.' She said, 'We just have to keep at it Alice.' 'No shirking, now!'

But I couldn't help but feel disheartened, this was turning into a marathon and I was flagging at the back without water. We returned to my office where we made several copies of the affidavit and posted one Recorded Delivery to Mary Collins. Here we go again, three steps forward, two steps back.

Pulling the Yellow pages from the top shelf again I thumbed through the headings, Painters & Decorators, Plumbers, Pooch parlours, here we are *again*... Private Investigators: I might as well stick a pin in a name for all the good the Panther was to me. What do I know? I'm just a photographer, snapping away, making rich people look more beautiful.

Chapter 16

WDFA

'Whatever you do, don't be late Barbara.' 'I really want someone here with me... These guys, they run close to the wire to get results and in one way that's a good thing, but it's also why I feel nervous on my own.'
'I'll be there.' She said, 'Don't worry, 10am tomorrow, right?'
'Right.' I say.
I am pinning all hopes on WDFA Investigators, even if they operate from a PO Box, I'm desperate. I want action. I want a sleuth who will get me results.
At 9am I am sifting paperwork, typing out contact sheets, pacing the office, being prepared like a Girl Guide. Except I have no idea what I am preparing for. Outside it is a grey drizzly day. Damp, damp, damp. The kind of day, that one glance at a travel ad with blue sea and white sand, will cause you to max out your credit card and just GO! Some hope I think. Finances are so tight. Solicitors squeezing my every last penny, to ensure they will see the blue sky and the white sand en famille. Its fat cats and starving dogs!
Alistair from WDFA is due at 10am, so when the doorbell rings at 9.55 I open the door expecting to see Barbara. Instead, I am greeted by a tall young man with dark glasses pushed up into his platinum bleached hair. He is wearing a black polo, black jeans and scuffed, pointy black shoes. Alarmingly, he has a fresh scar on his cheek.
'Hi I'm Alistair.' He says.
As I study his face, his scar pales into insignificance. He is sporting an unlikely deep tan, which if he had more teeth, would have been a dazzling combination. Calm, Alice Calm! His lips have clearly been in the wars and seem to have been blanket stitched. I also notice his nose is slightly wonky, presumably from a previous encounter. *Barbara, where are you?*

My face must have said it all, but I remained professional, as he gave me his card, WDFA Investigators. He followed me down the hall and into the office. If I had seen this guy in a thriller on TV I would have thought Wardrobe and Make Up had gone over the top. The only thing missing was a bulge under his arm for the holster, but wearing a polo that wouldn't make sense... what do I know?

I decide I am not going to indulge him and discuss his injuries, I just ignore them, as if this is what I expect an investigator from Central Casting to look like.

Barbara, where the bloody hell are you?

We sit opposite each other, and I explain my requirements. He tells me, work like this is not a problem.

'We tail people all the time.... we uncover fraud, record and video our suspects.'

He shifts stiffly in his chair. I think he has other injuries, but I will *not* be drawn.

'And... we will give you a full written report along with recordings as necessary.'

His pitch, which lacks the vocal clarity of someone with a full set of teeth, continues 'We've had years of experience and helped hundreds of people.' He pauses to suck back the saliva that is trying to escape the gaps in his dentistry. *Barbara, I so didn't want to do this on my own.* I lean back in my chair, feigning a relaxed position, but the truth of the matter is, I want to avoid the sprays of spittle coming my way, as he launches into the last part of his patter.

'We are a small firm and use ex police officers to assist us.' 'Anyone under surveillance will be followed by numerous people, so they never suspect were onto them.'

My mind boggles. Does this man think this is genius or what? Does he watch any TV? Yes, he must do, he's wearing the outfit. We talk money. He will need a substantial deposit and then stage payments as the investigation continues, with a final payment, before tapes / videos are handed over. He continues to sell the services of WDFA Investigators and I nod in the right places. I just need to believe this man. I need to recover my pension and must prove what has happened. I know the truth, but my solicitors aren't taking this seriously. They try to placate me with emotional guff like...

'He's the father of your children.'

'I do know that Messrs Garston & Welland, but what has that got to do with the price of fish, Mary Collins?'

And then, 'He could end up going to jail.'

Only cry on Fridays

'And Messrs Garston & Welland your point is?' 'This man has stolen my pension – he will leave me in penury in my old age, there will be no retirement, ever'. 'He has committed fraud'. 'What do you think I should do?' 'Send him flowers and a thank you card?'
Then they talk to me about a separate trial. I will need criminal solicitors. 'Divorce solicitors cannot deal with this' 'We will have to instruct….'
I see £ signs in their greedy, cash register eyes. I must get incontrovertible proof, so he will pay back what he's stolen or risk jail. My girl's father in jail? That's another one to think over when the first light is stealing into my fluffy pink bedroom, that is St Phillips Square. When I finally fall into the deepest sleep, just before the jangling alarm, these are the anxieties that fill my head.
He continues with his spiel, delivering want I want to hear. Like a fish dangling on a hook, waiting to be reeled in, this is the antithesis to Panther investigations and I continue to nod in the right places. *Calm Alice, calm again*. Barbara will come any minute. I just need moral support. The rain beats hard against my office window. Its greyer than ever out there. It could be evening it's so dark outside. I hear the Bendy bus lumbering down the road like an unwieldy, prehistoric animal. Its horn squeals expletives, to force lesser beings to reverse out of its path.
The doorbell! *At last!* It's twenty past ten, for heaven's sake! It's Barbara of course. In she blusters, waving her wet brolly everywhere. Profuse apologies! Then she mutters something about Mr Tucker and his allotment…… When she finally stops blithering she looks across the table at Alistair and I know I can't stop her. Oh God! Here we go…
'*My*, you've been in the wars! What on earth happened to you?'
He gives her a huge smile, so *not* attractive. But it was as if oxygen had been pumped into his veins. At last, someone who cares… he's thrilled. He launched into some story worthy of the TV drama he stole his outfit from. Our platinum blond, Alpha Male investigator is in his element. Barbara doesn't see my face grimace, she is all ears.
He gesticulates, his bloodshot eyes light up. Again, *not* attractive. He was in his (top of the range) Range Rover, tailing a criminal, when the accelerator failed, and he is hit by oncoming traffic. He spreads his arms widely (the crash scene). Then, brings his hands to his face, (the impact of oncoming traffic). I can smell the top of the range, leather upholstery. Barbara squeals 'That must have been terrifying?' 'You poor boy!'
Why doesn't he just say, he was done over by someone who didn't like being followed? It is only when he catches sight of my cheque book, he draws to

a close. Opening his black attaché case to write a receipt, I see a paying in book. On close of play, he's ready to hot foot to the bank. Like a lamb to the slaughter, I hand over my cheque and pray a little. Please God, let Alistair get me the results. I can't afford to lose this money. It's nearly the end of the month and terrifying brown envelopes will hit the mat again. I see him to the door. He assures me he will be in touch in no time with a progress report. It's still grey with heavy drizzle out there, but at least Barbara's day has been lightened up. I make us tea and then, ever efficient, open a file for the receipt and his business card. WDFA Investigators. I casually think WDFA must be the initials of the partners in the business. After all, his name is Alistair.

I turn the card over.

WDFA
We Don't Fuck About.

We nearly choke on our tea with laughter.

Chapter 17

Delays

I can smell cigar breath. Feel slobbery lips on my face. A knee rams into my upper right thigh. A hand pushes firmly into my left. His hot body weight drops on top of me. I have woken as my arms are now held above my head and pushed hard into the pillow. My wrists are held in as if in a clamp. I am dry. You are hard. I do not want this. You force yourself inside me to my gasps of 'NO NO!'

I wake in a cold sweat shouting 'NO!' My face, hair and hands are drenched with perspiration. It takes me a long, few seconds to come to, gather my senses. I swallow hard and burst into tears, as I realise I am in a safe place. The nightmare is a recurring one. Sitting up, I swap pillows as mine is soaked with the nightmare. The reassuring fluffy pink bedroom of St Phillips Place comes into focus. I *am* in a safe place. I will get you out of my head. Your scathing, demoralising words still haunt me. I will survive this. My heart pounds with the memory of what I have just been through, again. The reality is still with me. At least I know tomorrow morning there will be no bruises on my inner thighs, where your sharp knees have forced my legs apart. This was not a single episode. This was a smouldering occurrence, because I had the temerity to refuse your needs. How could I find it in me to respond to a man who, with his own self-serving rules dispensed belittlement like others might dispense love?

Punishment achieves compliance, believe me it does. It's the safest way to survive. Your cold contempt for every part of my existence was distressing, so I just withdrew, from what should have been the safe harbour of a loving marriage. Your continued recriminations would estrange me further, but then at the drop of a hat, I would be required to be responsive, on demand, like an object, just available. This intimacy was now, never an exchange of love, it was an overriding pressure for me to concede to your requirements, and in the depths of my sleep- aid induced sleep, you would display your power and control. In the morning you would be cheerful, singing in the shower even. Sometimes there would be a cup of tea on my bedside table.

This is where bewilderment sets in, the consternation and confusion. Even though I knew exactly what had happened in the night, my mind was baffled by the normality of the day. There was never any mention of, what I now concede was rape. Sometimes, I thought I had imagined it, but even if there weren't bruises, there were all the other tell-tale signs. And the day just got on its way, as normal. I was in despair, how could I let this happen? I felt helpless. It is easy to say, *move to another room, why don't you?* But I knew the repercussions would be untenable, in all sorts of insidious ways. At this stage my confidence had been undermined to such an extent, my defences were down, I couldn't cope with any more. I was right on the edge. Behaving like this, walking on eggshells is exhausting. Trying to second guess someone else's mood or reaction, staying one step ahead was soul destroying. All my energy and focus were on one person and it wasn't me. My needs were low down in the pecking order. *His* work was the most important, *his* financial situation took priority.

When my father died, he left me a small amount of money, I immediately put it in a building society saver account. Within days Steve was presenting me with his overdue invoices, from his current business. It took all the steely willpower I could muster, to refuse to pay them. I cited saving for next term's school fees and said the money should stay in a safe place, until we could see where we were financially at the end of the term. But the pleading and remonstrating didn't stop. Every day, like a dog worrying a bone he would go on and on, about how much it would help *us* if he, could just settle this account, that account. He simply couldn't countenance the fact I might have funds and he didn't. It meant the power balance had shifted and he couldn't handle it. His moods were blacker than ever, so I kept a low profile. Yes, a low profile in my own home. I would do nothing that might rock the boat. Quietly, I just went about my life like a mouse. Sometimes he would ignore me for weeks with a hostile silence and undisguised distain. His eyes could meet mine in such a way, I would be really frightened. His disparaging language, knew no bounds. His controlling ways overshadowed every cell in my body and were responsible for repelling me further. Should I not agree with him, I had mental health issues. Just like when I refused his advances, I should see a sex therapist....

Only cry on Fridays

'Because, *this* isn't normal!' He would scream.
Normal I would think, I wish everything *was* normal.
We might be in his office with our PA Irene and he would be *the* nicest man. But I hated the way he would seek to embarrass me, with his libidinous stroking of my buttocks. This at least Irene didn't notice, but then his arm would drape around my neck, letting his fingers reach my nipple area. I would shrug him off, to sit somewhere he couldn't get behind me. Back on our own, I would bravely remonstrate with him,
'Don't do that!' 'It's not professional.' 'It's not the time or the place.'
He asserted, 'It's only a bit of fun….' 'The trouble is there's never a time or place is there Alice?'
'You're just Frigid! '… 'Get some help, will you?'

By now the girls were at boarding school, (I'll come to that) so sadly we were on our own, night after night. One evening, his cutting words were so demoralising. They came thick and fast all evening, like an automatic weapon. My inadequacies were verbalised over and over. I cannot explain how every new outburst, was like a physical punch. I was virtually speechless with fear, I couldn't think straight. I remember putting my hands over my ears, to stop the ricochet of cruel words. In floods of tears I pleaded 'Stop it…. Stop it'.
I ran out of the room to head for bed. Now a gibbering wreck, the pain manifested itself in a terrifying way. I was physically sick and shaking, as I made my decision. I could not wake up to take anymore. Looking at myself in the bathroom mirror, I questioned who I was, how it come to this?
I found my over the counter sleep-aids and took what was left in the blister pack. I just wanted to close my eyes and then this pain would go away. I had some post- its in my bedside drawer, which were there if I needed to remind myself of something for the morning. I just scribbled a note to my girls.
I'm so, so sorry my darlings. I just couldn't cope any longer. All my love Mummy.
I put the post-it in the drawer of a small chest, where I kept my toiletries.

Deep in the night I woke desperate for the loo. My heart was thumping, as if it was going to break out of my chest. I remembered what I had done before I had gone to bed. Was my heart racing with anxiety or had the tablets caused this to happen? The thought of changing my mind at this stage was not an option. Immediately, I could see myself being berated,

screamed at, with warnings of mental health issues being flagged up to the girls…
'See, I told you all along!' he would say
I just lay there silently sobbing, thinking I can't wet the bed, I can't wet the bed. But when I moved my legs to the edge of the bed, they weren't working. They were like jelly, they were not going to support my weight. Irrationally, I kept thinking, I can't wet the bed. He muttered something in his sleep, so I waited for him to drift off again. As his breathing grew deeper and more regular, I dropped myself onto my knees and crawled round the bed to the bathroom and the blessed loo. I wondered if the sleep-aids have some sort of diuretic in them. I crawled back and somehow pulled myself back into bed. The next day I woke late. The shutters had been opened and on my bedside table were some roses from the garden. He always knew when he had taken me to the edge and would recoil fast, sensing there may be repercussions, typically turning on the charm offensive, leaving my mind *so* confused and troubled, that I didn't understand reality.

Now the safety of my flat, on a quiet Sunday, ironing and generally tidying up, carried me through to Monday morning at the office. As I came in through the front door, I could smell the coffee. Trish my PA was bright and breezy, sifting through the post, looking for handwritten envelopes, which usually signified enrolments. Numbers were at the half way point already, but typically once August set in, the world and his wife went on holiday and the phone wouldn't ring until September. I finished roughing out some ideas for a client, but my mind was racing through the Pension fraud. The part that annoyed me almost as much as the loss of funds, was that he thought I was *so* stupid, I would just accept the derisory sum as a *fait accompli* and I wouldn't question why our property had been sold for roughly half the market valuation. Can he really have underestimated my tenacity to get to the bottom of his treachery?

In over two months despite several voicemails, WDFA had not come back to me with any results. I picked up the phone and here we go again, another voicemail option. This time my message was in angry mode.
'If I don't have the recording and the report I have paid for, by the end of this week, I will be reporting WDFA to Trading Standards… without fail.'
My anger vented, I returned to the drawing board. Then Antonia phoned 'Hey, Mum, I've just seen an offer… a holiday in Hydra' 'It's a really good deal'… 'What do you think'? 'Shall we go?

We discussed dates and though money was tight, Trish convinced me a week away at this time of the year, when we were not manic, would stand me in good stead for the winter term. In five minutes, my mind was made up… I was on the plane already, soaking up, bone warming sun, listening to the lap of waves. But first I needed that recording.

A few days later, as I pushed open the front door of the office, there was a jiffy bag on the mat. I tore it open. There it was, a tape, no covering letter, just this tiny tape. Trish told me it was from a Dictaphone and we would have to get a Dictaphone to play it back. Grrh! The frustration! In five minutes, Trish was on her way to Dixon's to buy the requisite piece of equipment. I sat staring at the tape willing it to speak to me but had to hold my soul in patience for Trish's return. It seemed like a week, but she was back in under an hour. She was familiar with Dictaphones so loaded it up with ease. Switching it on, we waited with baited breath. Then, as if someone was speaking through bed socks…
'Time, three thirty-five.' 'I can see the Blue Merc outside Mrs Doulton's House.' 'It's been parked there for fifty-five minutes now.'
We looked at each other with incredulity.
'What the …??'
The sock continued 'All this time the bedroom curtains have been drawn.' 'Now the curtains are moving.'
This riveting information was followed by lots of interference and scratchy sounds for several minutes. Then…
'A man with greying hair is leaving the property.' 'Mike is taking a photo of him.'
'The same man is …. CRRRRRH…. ZEEEE…. Scratchy interference…
'The number plate …. Zzzzzeeee crrrrh…. TWK….
Then.
'Hello, are you Damien?'
Yeah…! Result I think.
'Can you tell me how you came to buy this property?'
What! The stupid man… About as undercover as a Giraffe wearing a Bowler hat. Then.
CRRRRRH… zeeeee squeeeeeeel Sadly we didn't hear Damien's reply. Then…
'No, man I'm just interested….'
Then it sounded as if the sock had gone into the washing machine. Eeeh Gods!

Alice Waite

'Just leave will...' CRREEEEE squeeeel
'Sorry mate no offe...... Zzzzz squeeeeel CRRRRRRRH!
The washing machine moved onto SPIN...!
If it hadn't been so funny, I would have been crying.

Chapter 18

Nadia

Returning from a much-needed holiday, Trish was excited to tell me, we only had two places left on our next set of courses. Hello, what happened? Normally August was as dead as a Dodo, I must go away more often. Antonia and I had had a great week together. We were both very tired, so with books in hand, we dozed and slept all day. Conversation came at lunch, over the ubiquitous Greek salad and then in the evening over supper. Of course, there was no conversation about the whole nightmare of the Pension fraud or anything else to do with the divorce. The girls were still staying, well and truly neutral and who can blame them. They loved us both and whilst I knew they were still cross with me for leaving, upsetting their beautiful applecart, they were starting to come to terms with the situation. Like it or not, their home was on the market and they knew this would eventually mean, all their stuff and by stuff, I mean childhood treasures, would have to be found new homes or go into store somewhere.

On my return there was a phone call from the Estate Agents. They usually gave me a weekly update on enquiries and viewings, so when Caroline from Threadwell's, made her Friday call, I expected to get the usual information. However, when I heard her voice, I detected something was up.
'This is really difficult Mrs Waite…' she hesitated
'What is Caroline'?
'Well, err… this isn't the first time we've had this feedback…umm'
'What feedback'?
'So, the people viewing last Wednesday….err… '. 'They commented …well, that the house was in rather a mess… Err' 'I don't know if you've been over recently… but….'
'Mess, what do you mean mess?' 'You need to tell me just what you mean, because as I'm sure you *are* aware, I have not been back to the house since I left.'

'Well, there's no easy way to say this, Mrs Waite' 'Err, …. the house certainly needs a spruce up, a tidy up… and it doesn't smell too fresh really.'
'Oh God' I said 'Really?'
'And one of the rooms, err... the Study, well it's impossible to get in…. it's well, it's filled with boxes.'
'Filled with boxes?' 'What on earth…'
I was exasperated with this news
'Look, I said 'I'll get my solicitor to write to him.' 'He's got to get a cleaner, because this will be hampering sales'
'You're absolutely right Mrs Waite.' 'Please let me know how you get on.'

Slumping in my chair, I put the phone down. My head in my hands, I remonstrate
'That ******* husband of mine.'
Long suffering Trish, made a soothing cup of coffee. I wish I was still on a sun bed in Hydra. I took some deep breaths and tried to visualise the turquoise water, gently lapping across the shingle.
Mary Collins said she would write to his solicitors, to insist he gets a cleaner in, as well as some semblance of order in the house. Another set of expensive correspondence ensued between Mary Collins and Mark Kenny. Mark Kenny, then must write to my husband, who would no doubt phone him with his view on the matter. Then, Mark Kenny must reply to Mary Collins, who in turn writes to me, enclosing Mark Kenny's letter. This lot probably totalled some £500+ vat. And to add insult to injury, my husband claims, he cannot afford a cleaner, but should I want to provide one….!
This is another delaying tactic. If the house looks unkempt it is less likely to sell and he can just sit tight. I know the smell Caroline so tentatively referred to. Think a greasy spoon café with old cigar smoke, and heaven knows what else on top of that. He was not prone to opening windows.
'Why waste money on heating, if you're going to let it all out of the window?' He would declare.
There probably hadn't been a breath of fresh air through that house since I left. The iniquity of asking me to provide a cleaner for him, so that he could leave even more detritus in his wake, filled me with anger. He was still sending me his gas and electricity bills, which I always returned. The nerve of the man!

Term started, and I did not provide him with a cleaner. He would be demanding a cook and gardener next. The one-month course was full, they were a lovely buzzy group, firing on all cylinders, lapping up the intensity of the work required. About eleven every morning, we would have coffee and biscuits. Everyone would help themselves, chatting twenty to the dozen. Over a period of at least four weeks, depending on the number of courses a student had enrolled upon, firm friendships were made, and I heard lots of stories about their lives. Many were returning to work after a family, others making complete career changes. Some beginning again after a relationship had gone wrong. These women hailed from all over the country and occasionally Europe, staying in flats around the city, loving the freedom they had suddenly found. They spent all day together in the studios and in lectures, as well as beavering away with copious homework, every evening. At the weekends, they would get together around their kitchen tables to work on their projects. Husbands had been known to turn up with the children in tow, only to be sent packing.

'Get on with it.... I've got my course work to do!'

Over the years, I have seen huge bouquets of flowers delivered, as well as champagne and chocolates. in an attempt to woo someone back to the fold. Once, a Security man delivered a pochette of diamonds, which were duly returned. I met so many savvy women determined, for all sorts of reasons, to become financially independent. So, while everyone was drinking their coffee, I quickly checked into the office for a minute and seeing a pile of unopened post on the desk, made the cardinal mistake of opening a letter from Garston & Welland. Normally I would wait until after 4.00pm when everyone had gone, but for some reason I opened the letter. Mary Collins was advising me, that not only was my husband on Legal Aid, but also, now on Job Seekers Allowance. Further, he was still claiming half the profits of my business, as he was technically a partner.

'Does this man have no pride?' I said to Trish

I took a deep breath. There was always something else, another twist, another problem. My eyes welled up with tears. Just then, there was a tentative knock on the office door and a head popped round.

'Hey, you're not going to get your coffee, are you?' 'Here you are.'

It was Nadia one of my lovely students, proffering a coffee.

'Oh sorry... have I barged in?' She said viewing my face, which was on the edge of crumpling.

'No no... it's OK.' I said in a wobbly voice. 'Thank you, coffee is just what I need.'

'You're not in a good place, are you?' She ventured.

'No really.... I'm fine, I'm fine.' I said putting on my best chirpy voice.

She looked at me as if to say, *you are joking, aren't you*? Then she slid back out of the office to the others.

At the end of the day, Nadia was the last one in the studios, packing up her files ready for the evening homework.
'Can you turn the lights for me out when you're ready, please Nadia?' I said.
'Of course,' she replied… 'But look, I couldn't help overhearing when I came in with the coffee this morning… I've been through a pretty shitty divorce myself and I do understand what you are going through.'
'That's kind Nadia, thank you.' I said, slightly taken aback. I had always tried to be professional with my students and not wear my heart on my sleeve. They were here on an intensive Media Course, not as relationship councillors.
She continued 'It's pretty lonely dealing with all this flak on your own.'
'I've got a great support network of girlfriends.' I said
She then proceeded to tell me her story. Nadia was a pretty woman, who always wore interesting clothes, all very Nadia, feminine and slightly Boho. Her hair was a soft brown, highlighted here and there. One day, it was loosely pinned up, the next it was falling onto her shoulders. She must have spent some time every morning, perfecting her makeup, because her eyes, a deep brown looked amazing with the kohl smudgy eyeliner. I sat on the stool beside her desk and listened for what must have been half an hour. It seemed her ex-husband was a Private Banker and every week flew to Zurich with client's cash in his briefcase, to deposit it in numbered accounts. Apparently, he also had one of these accounts himself. When it came to the division of their assets, he chose to ignore the Zurich account in the calculations. Sometime before, she had made a note of the account number and a few others belonging to *Names*, as he called them. Nadia then went on to describe her Mother.
'She is as a tough old boot' she said, who on hearing about the banker husband's double dealing, gave Nadia some very firm instructions.
'Send him a fax NOW.' She said, 'Tell him he's got twenty-four hours to agree to your settlement proposal, or you will spill the beans to the press and The Financial Services Authority.'
Nadia said she was scared and didn't want to do it, but her chain smoking Mother stood over her, until she sent the fax. Within the hour, the settlement was agreed.
'It takes a toughie, to give you the nerve sometimes.' She said
'I love the sound of your Mother.' 'She must have been a tower of strength?'

'She is just brilliant… and I owe her so much.'
'So, how far have you got with this divorce?' 'What's caused the problem I walked in on…?' 'I am sorry about that by the way, I didn't mean to intrude.'
'No, no don't worry.' 'You weren't to know.' 'I never usually open mail from my solicitor until the end of the day.' 'I don't know why I did.'
Slowly it all came out about the fraud, the affidavit which my solicitors were so dismissive of, calling it hearsay. The useless Private Investigators…. How I had to gather proper evidence to support my claim that the property was sold in a 'back to back' deal with his despicable friend, Rolo Hargreaves.
'I'll help you.' she said, 'You need a proper recording, with a transcript than can be signed like an affidavit.'
'Yes, I suppose I do.' I said, 'But honestly, I don't know where to go from here…" How to get such a thing.' 'These investigators have been completely useless.'
'You know, I've been in Am Dram for years, I'm sure we can dream something up.' 'We need a proper, secret recording machine…. not a Dictaphone.'
I looked at her as if she had just dropped from Mars.
'Are you sure about this?'
'I certainly am… it will be a lot of fun too. …count me in, I promise I will help.'
I asked her to sleep on it and said if she changed her mind, I would understand completely.
'Let's talk it through tomorrow.' She said, as she flung her bag over her shoulder and headed for the front door.

The next morning, I told Trish about Nadia's offer. She was all over it, like a rash.
'That's great!' 'I'll make some enquiries while you're teaching.' She said
I should just to remind everyone, yet again, there was no internet for research, no Smart Phones to record. Technically we were in prehistoric times, compared with the ease these things can happen now. So, Trish armed with the trusty Yellow Pages again, started searching for recording equipment. When the morning teaching was over, I came back into the office with my sandwich from the fridge and a cup of tea.
'You will never guess?' She said, full of excitement.
'Go on, what?' I replied starting on my lunch.
'I've found A Spy Shop in Bristol!'

'A what?' I nearly choked 'Is there such a thing?'
'There sure is, and what's more they will hire equipment out!'
Trish could hardly contain herself. This was so much more interesting than typing up my notes or invoices. She was in her element. She told me what was on offer and how the man in the shop apparently specialised in surveillance equipment. For our requirements… for complete clarity, he would recommend, a digital recorder. Why didn't the two sleuths I had hired, know about this? Why was my recording by WDFA muffled and full of screeching background noise? At the end of the day's teaching, I pulled Nadia to one side.
'Have you thought more about our chat last night?' I asked
'There's nothing to think about.' She said 'This needs to be done…. I'm in.'
Ushering her into the office, Trish, wide eyed and bushy tailed, had made a pot of tea. She poured everyone a cup and proudly explained about her findings.
'That's fabulous.' Nadia said waving her hands in the air, sliding herself onto my desk with her tea.
Sipping my tea, I said, 'Now we need to sort out dates…. because we can have a three-day hire.'
Trish butted in 'One to collect it, I will get on the train'…. 'One for the recording… and one to return it.'… 'Simple'!
'So, are you up for making an appointment to see this guy?' I queried again, not believing this was happening.
Nadia was in her stride
'I'll see if he can do next Wednesday after lunch.' She said
'Next Wednesday?' I questioned conscious of her commitment to the coursework.
'You've forgotten, that's our research afternoon.' I am pretty much up to speed on my research, honestly, so no problem.'
'If you're sure?' I said
'Yep, I'll phone him in the morning before lectures.'
OMG! It was going to happen! In the blink of an eye, it was going to happen, and I had a good feeling about our Am Dram Nadia.

The appointment time was set, then Nadia asked me to help with the storyline for her visit. I found some plans, from a shoot at a lovely old house that would fit the bill. We decided the story line would be that she wanted to commission sculpture, for a landing. On the following Tuesday, Trish was on the train to Bristol. She was back by early afternoon, so we could play with our new toy. We were as excited as children, with a new piece of gismo at Christmas. Following the instructions, we tested the digital recorder with the mic under several layers of clothing and played it back. Our voices were crystal clear, we were euphoric. Now it was down to Nadia to see what she could come up with.

I had a client appointment on Wednesday afternoon. Annie was on studio duty, helping the students with their research for their final project. I asked Nadia to leave me a voicemail, as I would have my mobile turned off, during my meeting.

As I pulled into my client's drive my mobile rang. It was Nadia.

'Just to let you know, I'm in a lay by and the mic is in place. I will turn it on in a second as I'm literally just outside the village…." Here goes, wish me luck!' 'Cue…Lights…. Action!'… 'Over and out.'

She was killing herself laughing. I was so excited at the prospect of Nadia playing sleuth, but reluctantly turned my phone off, before going to see my client, Jane Fuller

As I went through ideas with Jane, my mind kept flitting to Nadia and her appointment with Damien. After discussing several different options for the shoot, Jane said she wanted to talk about them with her daughter and would call me tomorrow. At last I was back in my car, and immediately turned my phone on. One voicemail…! Nadia's voice rang out loud and clear.

'If you want to give marks out of ten.' she pronounced 'Give me twenty!' Her voice was euphoric. I couldn't drive back fast enough.

Racing through the front door to my office, I caught a whiff of something exotic and sultry. As I opened my office door, there was a beaming Nadia, with the cloud of the exotic and sultry all around her. She was in a tobacco tweed jacket, blue flouncy skirt and brown boots. Under the jacket she wore a little chiffon number, in the palest blue, which revealed just enough cleavage…

'Don't keep me in suspense.' I yelled… 'Tell me, tell me all about it.' 'No play the recording first, then tell me!'

Nadia jumped up to give me a big hug.

'You will be thrilled.' She said, 'Just listen to this...'

Trish turned the recorder to play and I listened enthralled, with Nadia giving a running commentary.

'I am Nadia Jefferson.'

Alice Waite

She gave the time, date and address. So professional…She could be a real sleuth. WDFA could learn a lesson or two.
'I'm going in now.' She continued.
I heard the car door slam, footsteps and a background of bird song. Then a front door opened.
'Hello, are you Damien?' She said, 'I'm Nadia, we talked on the phone…' she trailed off.
'Hi, Nadia, pleased to meet you.'
This was the first time I had heard Damien's voice. It was friendly and quite posh. But I realised Nadia's voice had changed, it wasn't the one I knew, it was melodic and really sweet sounding, almost girlish. Am Dram Nadia was playing the part.
'Do come into my office.' He said, 'Perhaps we can discuss what you have in mind first?'…. 'Then I can show you some ongoing work, in my studio.'
'Sounds like a good plan.' Nadia enthused, as I heard doors open and close.
He offered Nadia a seat; she fished in her portfolio. Spreading the plans out on his work table, she leant towards him, pointing to the landing space.
'We've got a *great* ceiling height here.' She gushed…. 'Over three meters!'
'That's fantastic.' He said getting into the project.
'And… A huge window, so lots of natural light…'
She trailed her finger tips across the plan. Her lightly pinned up hair, fell onto her shoulder. As she gently whisked it back into place she smiled.
'Great possibilities don't you think?' …She almost purred

Damien placed a large photograph album on the table.
'I'm not really sure, what I am looking for.' She mused 'I need inspiration…'
'And
I hope you will be able to help me, this could be *such* a lovely project.'
'I'm sure I'll be able to.' He said.
Cleverly, Nadia had now put Damien in charge and in no time at all he had succumbed to her charms.
'Oh, look at this…' she said. I could hear pages turning…. '*This* is amazing…' tell me how you got the inspiration for this.' 'It's so clever.'….
Flattery, flattery, it will get you everywhere!
In my mind's eye, I imagined Damien's chest puffing up as he ventured, 'Well, I had been to Venice a few months before and … I think I was probably influenced …'
Nadia cut in 'Oh I love this…"Who would think to put a crown on a

Only cry on Fridays

Greyhound…?' 'That's *so* clever.' Damien 'So did you go to Art School?' She cooed.
'Yep.' He said, 'I did a few years you know and then a post grad at The Royal College.'
'Wow…! The Royal College of Art' …. 'So, you are up there with the great and the good?' …
Flattery, flattery again …. I bet, she was fluttering her eye lashes.
'No no….' He protested… just slightly 'Look, Nadia come and have a peek at the studio and my current work.' 'I think there might be something of interest.'
'I'd love to.' she said following him through some huge doors.
'Now, this one…' He started…. 'This one is based on Greek Mythology … The Chimera… you know from the Legend of Bellerophon?'
He stroked a lion like creature still in the making.
'You put me to shame Damien!' 'My education didn't stretch to Greek Mythology!'
Damien felt rather special and was about to embark on the whole legend of Bellerophon, when Nadia moved deeper into the studio, to look at a large bust on a tall stand.
'Oh My God, I just *love* this one!' She enthused 'Go on; tell this ignoramus, who am I looking at now?'
She stood back, hand on hip, pushing a few wisps of recalcitrant hair from her face.
'That…' He said 'It's … well its Pericles.'
'I love his beard, it's so tactile and yet it's clay!' 'And… that scary helmet!'
'Do you know Damien … this…. what's his name again…? Peri…?'
'Pericles!' Laughed Damien
'Well do you know, this Peri…?" 'He just might fit the bill….' 'He's so tall and has great presence.'
'Can I take a photo of him… would that be alright?'
'No problem.' He agreed
She rummaged in her bag for her camera and snap it was done.
'I love the way the overhead light catches his features.' She mused 'The light here is fantastic.'
'I love it.' He said, 'I'm very lucky.' 'When I was in Camberwell, I had so little natural light and of course parking was a nightmare.'
Nadia wandered around the studio entranced.
'So, you moved from Camberwell …?'

'Couldn't be more different.' He said, 'I mean, I can actually park outside… how's that for a novelty?'

'It's amazing!' She replied, 'I mean … just finding a place with all this light and space… never mind parking….!' She laughed. 'So…. Well, are there specialist Estate Agents, for properties like this?' Nadia was playing dippy designer, but Damien didn't notice, I think he was falling in love with her.

'Oh no!' He laughed 'I found it through a regular Estate Agent….' 'He just had a few commercial properties on his books… and well, when I saw this, I *just* knew.'

'I'm not surprised!' She said, 'Did you have to do much to it?'

'No… Not really.' 'The guy that had it before, left a skip load of rubbish….' 'But, I just had to deal with it.' 'I mean, I gave him the chance to clear it or pay for the skip, but he didn't clear it or pay for the skip!' 'He was a right pain.'

'Yeah, but to get somewhere like this….' 'Dealing with a skip load of rubbish isn't the end of the world, is it?' Nadia enquired

'Oh, that's the tip of the ice berg.' He continued

'Well buying *any* property isn't easy.' Nadia, cleverly tried to sprinkle some cold water on his story, but he wasn't having any of it.

'Well this guy, and he only lives down the road… he agreed the sale with me'

'You know we agreed a price and….'

'Do you mind me asking how much you would have to pay for something like this, Damien…?' 'I mean… sorry you don't have to tell me if you don't want to.' She said, in an embarrassed little girl kind of voice. Damien was not about to refuse such a pretty lady.

'£250,000' He said

'Well, you know, I don't think that is so bad… "Considering you've got parking!' She started laughing and he joined in. She was his new best friend.

'Anyway'… 'He so badly wanted to finish his story. 'This guy…'

'The one down the road?' She queried.

'Yes' he said, bursting to tell all now. 'This guy, well he'd only gone and sold it to his mate!'

'Hold on…' said Nadia 'I thought you said you had bought it off the man down the road?' Bless her; she was going to *make* him spell it out.

'It was a scam…!' 'He sold it to his mate at a reduced rate because this place was in a joint Pension fund, with his wife…. and they'd split up….'

Only cry on Fridays

'So, you mean…' Nadia played; I've got to think about this, it's too much for my pretty head.
Damien patiently explained 'It means, that his wife only got half the amount of the first sale… you know of the cheaper price!' (Duh)!
'That's terrible!' Nadia shook her head 'How could someone do that to his wife?'
'So, when I went to buy it …' Damien continued 'for £250,000 I discovered I was really buying it from his mate….' 'That way he got loads of money out of their Pension!'
'That's dreadful…' 'He must have had that planned, all the time he was negotiating with you.' (Careful Nadia you are sounding like you've really got a handle on this. Fortunately, Damien didn't seem to notice).
'Yeah. He's a rat alright.' 'I've had people snooping round here you know, asking all sorts of questions.' 'Wouldn't wonder if the Tax man isn't after him you know….'
'Yes… maybe.' Nadia ruminated
'But look Damien, I'm so glad it worked out for you in the end… it's such a great place.' 'Just put it all behind you.'
'Yes, I must.' He said, 'It's just I see him most days, you know he's still living in the village.'
'Hey…! Just looks the other way!' She laughed
She headed back to Pericles.
'So back to business….'! 'I think he's my man for the landing you know.' 'I'll show the pics to my client and see what he says … have you got a card?'… 'I'll give you a bell in a couple of weeks.' 'Would it be OK if I brought him over to meet you and of course to see Peri…eeerrrh?'
'Pericles!' Said Damien, laughing at this charming hare-brained woman.
'Pericles…! Got it!' She said

'Now which way did I come in? 'She said reinforcing her ditsy credentials. Damien guided her back through the double doors to the hallway and onto the forecourt where her car was parked.
'Great parking!' She laughed as she got into her car.
'Definitely!' He said smiling as she reversed into the road.
'I'll be in touch!' She shouted and with that drove off out of the village… Then into the mic 'This is Nadia Jeffries, mission completed at 3.25pm.'
'Over and out!'

'OMG! You've nailed it Nadia… that's amazing, just amazing!'

Alice Waite

I flung my arms around her. I was practically crying.
'You deserve an Oscar, for that performance.'
'At least a cup of tea.' Trish said rushing out to put the kettle on for a fresh pot.

Trish transcribed the recording, then Nadia duly accompanied me to a local solicitor, where she signed an affidavit, stating it was a true transcript of her recording.
Result!

Chapter 19

FSA Ombudsman

I couldn't wait to phone Mary Collins, I was so excited to tell her about the recording and how we had it backed up with an affidavit. She seemed a little more interested than before, so we put a date in the diary for a meeting. At this stage, I am half way through the Business section of the course, so heading into December, with another Christmas looming into sight. At 12.30 I took refuge in my office, with a plan to start tackling numerous lists, which never seemed to get any attention. The afternoon lectures were covered by a Life Coach, taking the session until 4.00pm. But first, I sift through a pile of post to see an envelope marked Financial Services Ombudsman. The Ombudsman's department have had the files for months and despite regular phone calls to try to elicit some response, I simply don't seem to get anywhere. All I have had, is a letter acknowledging receipt of my files. They are probably in some storage unit in Uxbridge, waiting for my number to come to the top of the list.

On headed paper, there is just one short paragraph. I cannot comprehend what I am reading. It seems The Financial Services Ombudsman, is unable to assist with my complaint against Pension & Mutual. Instead they advise, I should deal with The Financial Services, Pensions Ombudsman. All my files are being returned and they regret any inconvenience caused. They have taken five and a half months to decide this? I think I am going to combust with the frustration of it all. I didn't even know there was a specialist Pension Ombudsman. Why should I? I am just an ordinary mortal fighting a David & Goliath battle, with a major Financial Institution. My solicitor, even directed me to the FSA Ombudsman. Here we go again, two steps forward three steps back.

In due course, a large package arrives with all my files returned from the FSA. By now, I have received the forms from the Pension Ombudsman ready to accompany the files, but this time they will be sent with one extra piece of information, the icing on the cake, as far as I am concerned. The transcript of Nadia's Oscar nominated performance with Damien Humphries, accompanied by her affidavit. Every time I think of it, my heart skips a beat and I smile to myself, with the expectation that this will be a turning point.

At my meeting with Mary Collins, she suggests keeping the tape and affidavit in Garston& Welland's safe. After taking a few minutes to read the transcript, she looks up. Her face has incredulity written all over it.
'How did you get this?'
I have explained to her on the phone, but she clearly hasn't taken everything in.
'Spy shop…what spy shop?' She mutters, looking slightly bemused.
I continue with the details, while she shakes her head in disbelief. Suddenly, she looks at her watch and says we must get a move on.
'Why?' I ask, as she takes her jacket from the back of the chair. 'Where are we going?'
'Sorry, meant to say, but we rather got carried away, didn't we?' 'I have made an appointment for us with Margo Wilson.'
Putting her handbag over her arm she grabs her document trolley.
'Who?' I say buttoning up my coat, swiftly following behind her, out through the doors of reception, into a network of narrow streets.
'Margo is a fine barrister and you are going to need a barrister for the Final Hearing.'
'Final Hearing… we haven't had any hearing yet…' I protest.
I can see the £ signs like confetti, fluttering in front of my eyes. In less than five minutes we are heading into a courtyard marked St George's. Chambers. We navigate our way up some narrow stairs, to a reception that might be a library. Shelves and shelves of fine legal books, floor to ceiling. We sit on hard repro Chippendale chairs and wait. I cannot help myself, I deconstruct the interior, wondering how someone made the decision, to put those curtains with this upholstery and *that* wallpaper? I conclude someone's wife has been let loose with her paint swatches, the company credit card and unrecognisable flair. The result, is a dog's breakfast of green and gold, maroon and another shade of gold, with blue and another shade of maroon upholstery. I think I might go into cardiac arrest if we sit here much longer. Not only am I reeling with the thought of a barrister's costs, but the biggest assault to the senses I have seen in a long time. Fortunately,

and before I can quiz Mary on costs, Margo Wilson appears and introduces herself to me.

I guess she is probably in her fifties, as neat as a pin in a sharp navy suit. She obviously knows Mary well, presumably because Mary sends her clients, on a regular basis. We sit in an airy office, where I recognise the interior design skills of that wife yet again. Fortunately, tea arrives to divert my attention, so I concentrate hard as Mary starts to fill Margo in, on the whole saga. Mary, it now seems, is as proud as punch, as she tells Margo about the digital recording. Margo's eyes light up. She asks me for more detail.
'How *did* you manage this?'
I already like her, she's very friendly, not at all like I thought a barrister would be. It feels like we are all old friends, meeting for a cup of tea. In a very matter of fact of fact way, I describe the whole episode to her.
'That's just brilliant!' she says, 'But Mary, I think you should also go to talk to Damien Humphries, to see if you can persuade him, to sign a statement corroborating the transcript.'
Mary agrees. Nice little trip out of the office to the country, I think. Then inevitably, I start adding up the hours this will take. I am leaching fees every minute of every day. Every week, I try to calculate what work Mary will have done on my behalf, so I can add in the date, multiply by four, to get some idea, of my end of the month invoice. I am usually hopelessly out and sometimes alarmingly so.

I once had a change of career, young lawyer on one of my courses. She was changing direction because she couldn't cope with every minute of her day, having to be accounted for, that is charged to a client. From the second she was at her desk, someone had to be billed. When she started working on a client's file it would be recorded via a billing number on the computer. When a client telephoned, the billing code also came up on the computer. After learning this, my phone manner to my solicitors, became very economical with the small talk. All the pleasantries, such as
'Hello Mary, how are you…'
Were being logged at some hideous rate. Once I knew this, I was ever vigilant, to cut through chit chat, perhaps in a rather a brusque manner. All my queries were written down, with the necessary paper work to hand. There was never any
'Hold on I'll just find the file.'
To my peril, I knew that a few minutes here and there would mount up

into something significant at the end of the month, plus disbursements plus vat….

Mary had planned her visit to Damien, at the beginning of the following week, so I was anxious to hear what had happened. When I was going to telephone any of my lawyers, remember I am now on my fourth, not only was I prepared as I could be, but I would always put on my jacket, slip into heels kept under the desk, add a slick of red lipstick, then, stand up to make the call. This way I felt more powerful, more confident. I could stride up and down the office with my cordless phone, asking the right questions, noting down responses. Conversely, when I saw Garton & Welland's phone number appear on the screen, I would push my feet into those heels, under the desk, and then stand to take the call; it helped me to feel unbreachable, fearless and self assured. These are the games we play in denial of our true self because we need an indomitable spirit to carry on. Mary Collins advised me, Damien Humphries was angry he had been recorded and was going to consult his solicitor before he signed anything. Mary didn't seem concerned if he didn't sign the statement, she said we could always subpoena him to court if necessary. Wow! This is getting serious.

I only spent money, I absolutely had to, cutting corners, where ever I could, Christmas just had to be put on a credit card. Here I was, still in the flat at St Phillips Square, what happened to that, oh so neat, tick box divorce? Christmas was looming again and as the previous Christmas, the girls divided their time strategically between myself and their father. However, this year, I knew something was different. It seemed they weren't too panicky about their father being left alone for too long. Gradually, over a few days things were pieced together. It became clear that the lady who Damien Humphries had mentioned to Annie, the one who was popping trays of food over to my husband, was my neighbour's widowed mother. Dear reader, it appears, she had now become his soul mate. Then there was more intrigue. Over a long lunch on Boxing Day, Hettie said
'Mum, you know that Christmas card we get every year, from Canada… you know …and we don't know the Sarah and Matthew who send it…?
'Gosh yes, has it appeared again'?
For years we had received a card every Christmas, to Alice and Steve with love from Sarah and Matthew. No address, just a Canadian stamp to mystify us further. The only Sarah, we had known, years ago was married to a friend of ours George Robinson. She was a Health visitor and he

was the Sales Director for a contemporary glass company. We had got to know them well, as we regularly organised exhibition stands for George's company. We were not married then, in fact I was still a student, but my flat was not far from their house. George was away in London all week, which Sarah hated, but they couldn't afford to move to London and it was difficult with Sarah's job anyway. They were a few years older than us and with their own house, they seemed terribly grown up. We often went to supper there and I always teased Steve, Sarah had a bit of a thing for him. You do know, when you see the chemistry, eyes meeting eyes, and then the glancing away. I would tease him singing…

'And, here's to you Mrs Robinson… Jesus loves you more than you will know, Wo, wo, wo!'

This made him furious. Two or three times a week, Steve would come across to my flat from his parent's home, where he was still living. He would usually roll up about seven in the evening and we would make a meal together. On more than one occasion, he was late but when I asked why, he openly said 'I just popped in to see Sarah on the way.'

I couldn't get my head round this. He almost had to pass my door to get to Sarah and George's house.

'Why didn't you pick me up, I'd have liked to see her too?'

'Oh, it was just a spur of the moment thing.' He replied, sounding a little irritated.

'How is she?'

'Oh, a bit low you know, George is away so much…' 'I think he's in Berlin all next week and at the weekend.' 'Then he's off to some conference, in Prague…' he trailed off.

I was just twenty-one and Steve was my first serious boyfriend. Looking back now, I realise how unworldly I was, how innocent. At some point, the Robinsons moved to a much larger house in a nearby village. George was clearly doing well with his job, but it seemed to mean he was away from home even more. Who knows, if he chose to be away, rather than deal with the difficulties in their marriage? Supper at their house started to feel a bit strained. They barely spoke, conversation just didn't flow, their body language was different. We could sense an atmosphere within minutes of arriving; they were no longer the carefree young couple we had known. One weekend, Steve came over to the flat as usual and said, he had popped in to see Sarah who had announced she was pregnant.

'What a stupid thing to do.' I said, 'Having a baby won't mend a marriage.'

'And anyway, why didn't you collect me?' I remonstrated.

Alice Waite

He made some excuse about getting into the wrong lane on the by pass… and it was easier to carry on.
By the following year, I had moved to another Art College for my degree and we were making plans to get married. Sarah had a son; I don't remember what she called him. She and George divorced, and we lost touch with Sarah and then George, as he moved to London, but we heard on the grapevine that Sarah has moved to Canada.

So back to the mystery Christmas card, to Steve and Alice, with love Sarah and Matthew. The card had even appeared correctly addressed, after we moved to our current house.
'How does this person know we've moved?' I would query 'That's spooky!' But in the run up to Christmas, with cards arriving twenty to the dozen, the question would be shelved until the following year. Hettie continued 'That card. …. you know the one from Canada…'
'Yes, go on.' I said clearing the glasses from the table.
'This year it's only addressed to Dad and says
To Steve with love from Sarah and Matthew. I will always love you.'
'Goodnesss!' I said, looking for a clean tea towel.
'That's very strange, isn't it?'

Later that evening when the girls had gone back to their Father's, I had a long think about the only Sarah we had ever known. Could this be her? What was her son called? Why can't I remember? Then there was the change of address conundrum. There was something very odd about the whole thing. I remembered when our wedding invitations were sent out, to Sarah and George separately, Sarah declined. She wrote to my mother, something along the lines of; *given the circumstances, I won't be able to attend the wedding of Alice and Steve.* I thought at the time, she was probably referring to the fact George might be at the wedding, which she would find difficult. But maybe there were other circumstances? I was starting to put two and two together and coming up with some strange answers, especially when the Canadian penny dropped. Years ago, one of his *brilliant ideas* was exported to Canada and quite successfully. Yet somehow the funds never seemed to reach the bank account. In his Alpha Male way, he took charge of the business finances, whether I liked it or not. I had queried the Canadian payments, a couple of times and been rebuffed with,
'I'm dealing with it… leave it to me, will you?'

Generally, I got back into my box and more fool me, I did leave it to him. So, thinking out loud now. What if Sarah and Steve had a fling, and Matthew is Steve's son? Then did Sarah emigrate to Canada to start a new life? Someone must have informed her of our change of address and more to the point, who told her I had left Steve? Did the Canadian money find its way to Sarah? Maybe the girls have a half brother somewhere? I can't prove a thing. I have just built a shaky Jenga tower based on intuition and a Canadian Christmas card. This is a smoking gun.

Chapter 20

Run up to The First Hearing.

Mary Collins has sent me an information sheet, about how the divorce process works.
Every time I try to read it, I break into a cold sweat. It does not help that she refers to the proceedings as, The Trial. The very word trial immediately makes me feel guilty. I am in a complete panic, but Mary seems calm and quite matter of fact. One of the many reasons, for my apprehension is that, this hearing will be the first time I have seen my husband since I left home. He is still in my head and one of those intimidating icy stares from him, can turn me into jelly. I wish I could be behind a screen, for the whole proceedings.

The term Coercive Control, was not in the vocabulary of the divorce lawyers then, nor was Emotional Abuse. Thank heavens it is on the statue books now, because those of us, who have adapted our behaviour, to create a strategy for survival, know the toll this abuse takes. Even my solicitors, appeared to make light of the situations I had noted in my statement, rationalising as far as the courts were concerned, the term Unreasonable Behaviour, was our best way forward. The tactics of mind games, humiliation and gas lighting were going to be brushed under the carpet. I was unfamiliar with the term *gas lighting* until I saw it used in a one of the many self-help books I had been reading. This is a form of manipulation where the perpetrator deliberately creates a situation to destabilise their victim, by sowing seeds of doubt, using every day occurrences, so that memory and sanity are questioned. Thus, over a sustained period, the emotional manipulation takes its toll, undermining the sense of self-worth. As soon as I read about it, there was a huge sense of relief. I wasn't imagining things, I wasn't going mad, I was living with a master manipulator, the outside world saw as a charming, lovely man. Constant undermining, erodes self-confidence, until the belittling words,

have taken root in your brain. Take driving for instance. I hated driving with Steve as my passenger. He made me so nervous with his intakes of breath, then muttering expletives, causing me to make mistakes I would never normally have made. Sitting next to someone who not only perpetually judged, but also gave instructions was nerve wracking.
'Take the outside lane…. get past that fool, will you?'
Then at a roundabout,
'Go on … what's the matter with you?'…… 'You could have gone then… now we will have to wait ages, look at the traffic!' 'This is hopeless… what's the matter with you?' 'Pull in, I'll drive, or we will be late.'
It got to a point, where I was so bothered about my driving, I secretly booked some driving lessons to sharpen up my skills. The driving school was a little thrown when I explained I had a licence but just wanted *a refresher course* as I put it. A pleasant man sat in the passenger seat, as I drove him where instructed. He had a calm demeanour, putting me at ease straight away. When we pulled in to a parking space he said,
'What's the problem?' 'Who's been telling you, you can't drive my dear?'
The rest of the refresher course was cancelled.

The First Hearing was suddenly upon us.
'I'll pick you up at quarter to eight.' Barbara said, 'Because the traffic will be heavy at that time of the morning and we've got to park and everything.' She continued 'We don't want to get there, without time to collect ourselves…. You know, have a coffee, take some deep breaths.'
'I will have an early night.' I said, 'I hope I can sleep, it's all going around in my head, you know.'
'I'm so nervous Barbara, I've never been to court before.'
'See you on the doorstep then.'
'OK I'll be ready.'
'And don't worry, you hear me…?' 'Don't worry!'
'OK I'll try.' I said, 'Bye now.' I put the phone down.
By eight pm, I am running my bath. I haven't been able to eat much in the way of supper. My tummy feels like it is full of pebbles being churned, by a raging river. I pour lots of Lavender bath essence under the running water, inhale the calming scent, then apply a thick layer of a rejuvenating face pack. Sinking down into the deep hot water I close my eyes. My mind will not be quiet, it is a jumble of jabbing words, that make no sense at all. In my dressing gown, I drink Camomile tea and by nine thirty my head is on the pillow, attempting sleep.

Sleep, give me sleep. The alarm clock glows at two forty am. I punch the pillows, turn them over, spray with *Resume the Position*, in the hope the miracle of deep sleep will take place. The man at *Origins* said it works wonders for broken nights, I could do with a chat with him right now. I resume the position, amidst a deep lavender and vanilla mist. Five minutes later, I resume another position and another, until my nightie is a swirling loin cloth, around my legs. *God, please give me sleep….!*
I decide to try some yoga. Lie on your back Alice I tell myself. Arms either side, palms facing upwards and breathe in, to the count of six…… hold for three…. breathe out, slowly, slowly Alice, concentrate on the breath why don't you…? To the count of eight and r….e... l... a... x. And again! Breathe in, one, two, three, four, five. … How come I can drop off to sleep in the yoga class, but not in my own bed?

My mind is elsewhere. I am in a traffic jam and its ten to nine… The traffic is solid. I'm late for my trial. The judge bangs his gavel. I am charged with contempt of court and my solicitor has billed me for another £500 for the few minutes it took for the judge, to charge me. I race towards the court building, dishevelled, tears rolling down my face. Everyone is leaving. *He* is flanked by men in suits. Mary Collins is at the doors, she reverts to type. She always looked like a school mistress (one that needs to wash her hair.) Now she behaves like one, balling at me, as if I hadn't done my homework or I have come into school wearing lipstick. She is remonstrating with a bundle of paperwork in her hand. Suddenly, a gust of wind catches the papers. My divorce is flying across the ring road. Cars are beeping as Mary tries to retrieve them. Stop the beeping! Take care Mary, you will get run over….

The beeping stops with my hand on the alarm clock. Am I late? What *is* the time? Relieved I see it is only six thirty, I sit with my head in my hands for all of ten seconds, then with a swig of Rescue Remedy, head for the shower. I mustn't be late. I mustn't be late. This is the day. It is *the* day…. D. Day. All must be well with the world because the Today programme is on the air and John Humphrys gives a time check. The next news item follows….it would be so much more reassuring, if Sue Macgregor was at his side but now we must deal with Sarah Montague, who sounds like she is talking to the parents at Pony Club. I need a coffee. I must put some cold water on my heavy eyes.

My suit is pressed; my high heels have been given a new lease of life with black suede renovator. How I wish I had some serious facial renovator. The bags under my eyes are an attractive shade of blue black. Farrow & Ball would call it Terminal Tiredness. The lighting in this bathroom, is not helping, so I move into the kitchen, mirror in hand. Not much improvement. There's serious work to do, I can't let him see me looking so tired and exhausted, and I must to exude confidence, joie de vivre even. Every bit of my maquillage is applied with the utmost care, including an expensive make up primer which according to the sales girl…
'Will give you an amazing porcelain glow!'
Who could resist? Kerching! Sold! Then I am tutored, to PhD level, on the application of a new Concealer. In a well-honed, fake American accent, she said
'Now remember when we put on our Concealer… whad' do we do?'
She quizzed the idiot standing at her counter.
'We don't apply it in a strokey way, do we?' she continued. 'We don't rub it in… do we?'
'We, *pat and glide*…. *Pat and glide*…. using our ring finger, gently across the surface.'
'Err yes.' I said, '*Pat and glide*, got it.'
I was mesmerised '*Pat and glide*' was now like a mantra, the words cooed soothingly in my head. I looked at her perfect, frozen face. It must have been applied at 6am with a magnifying mirror. It *is* flawless, in a Barbie kind of way. Then we got on to the new lipstick. I asked for some advice. She started collecting possibilities from her display stand and the next minute, I was sitting for the world and his wife to see, precariously on a stool, at the side of the display. She pulled out some brushes from a black bag attached to her waist. This was the business. She had all the tools of the trade, like a handyman, in various containers strapped about her person. If there was a bomb alert, she would be ready to leave the building… no doubt grabbing some Porcelain Glow primer, on her way out. She brushed some Coral Rose onto my lips and held up a mirror for me to see. She was beaming.
'I think that's *great*, don't you?'
I was a bit nonplussed. It was very *nice,* but I felt like a Mummy, who was considering a perm.
'Not sure.' I said, not wanting to offend her.
She cleaned it off and selecting another brush from her kit.
'Let's try this one then.'

She twirled her brush across another lipstick that looked for all the world like a stick of cinnamon. She handed me the mirror and I viewed my cola stained lips. This time I had to be firm,
'Oh, not me at all.' I said
'Ohh… Ka. aaay!' She said thinking about the problem and perusing the display…. 'Whad d'ya have in mind… do you wanna take a look at the colours then…?'
'Well, it's like this.' I said quietly 'I am going to be in the divorce courts and think, well …maybe …'
She cut me off. In a nanosecond. She immediately got it, no soft, demure corals, no cola stains…
'Ah Ha!' 'Your goanna need a *Kick Ass Red!*' She shrieked, almost doing a dance on the spot. The world and his wife started to take notice, they shuffled closer. My stool was now centre stage. Intrigued, shoppers put down their carrier bags and watched intently as she selected *Bad Lady Red* from the display.
'This will do the job… this is the business!' She laughed, as she twirled a new brush around the Bad Lady Red lipstick. She applied it expertly and then handed me the mirror. This felt good. This felt strong. This said *'Don't* mess with me.'

I drink my coffee; Bad Lady lipstick will have to be applied last. I can't eat any breakfast. Those pebbles, are still churning around in my tummy and they won't mix well with Muesli. I start to get dressed. Pull in pants, the no VPL variety. This cheese wire corsetry, gives serious discomfort to some areas of the anatomy I'd rather not discuss. Unfortunately, the pull ins, funnel the excess to the higher waist. Note to self: Next time get the version that goes under the bust, then the funnel effect could be beneficial to diminishing breasts. On with the padded, moulded, smooth, uplifting bra. Double lashings of deo. Wait for it to dry as I drink the now, cool cup of coffee. Can't have white deo marks on my smart black top. Then, my suit trousers, then, the newly renovated suede high heels. God, they are great, but by the time I have finished faffing about, the balls of my feet are stinging. I check the time 7.20am. Opening the wardrobe, I pull out shoes, all over the floor, hoping to find the relief I need, some gel insoles, left in other killer heels. I pounce on the gel numbers and drop them into my shoes. I look at my hands…'
No!' I yell.
Black suede renovator is all over my hands. I scrub away at them; the black

marks stubbornly laugh at me. I find some spray bleach, but first cover my black top with a bath towel, then scrub my hands and to my relief, see the black stain disappearing down the plug hole. I look up into the mirror above the basin. Clearing it of steam, I see I have overdone the mascara. I look like a transvestite. It's now 7.35. I've ten minutes max, to sort this out. Cotton wool pads are soaked in eye makeup remover and I apply to both eyes, pressing firmly. After removing the pads, I am staring at a Panda. More pads, more remover. Please God, will this extraordinary waterproof, vertiginous stuff, leave my eye lashes? Eventually the Giraffe lashes, loosen their hold and I can see all the thickening spiky bits, have now stuck to the amazing porcelain glow, I had so carefully applied. I reach for a tissue; cover it in cleansing milk to wipe everything off. I must make a start on the whole thing again. This is now a race against the clock, but not one to be won, because the doorbell rings. Holding the intercom phone to my ear, I hear Barbara's voice.

'Come on lady… thought you were going to be on the doorstep?'

'Yep, yep… I'm on my way.' I say, grabbing my makeup bits and pieces.

Oh, I wish I had one of those professional tool kits, to wrap around my waist. Instead, I throw everything into an exploding makeup bag, I grab my keys and as I slam the front door behind me, glance at the bedroom floor. It looks like Russell and Bromley on the first day of the sale. Now I am tasked with doing the whole thing in the car, waiting for red traffic lights, to apply the tricky bits.

Sliding into the car, I notice the change. It is immaculate. There is even space for my feet. It is apple core and sweet wrapper free, it even smells clean. Barbara is wearing lipstick and a smart suit. Glancing down I see she has abandoned her, oh so soft comfy footwear, for the sort of pointy spikes, we all buy on a whim, to admire, mainly on the bedroom floor… for another day.

'Are you, all right?' She asks

I relate the mascara mess, the suede renovator hands, as I reconstruct my face on route.

'Pat and glide.' I mutter 'Pat and glide.'

'What's that?' She asks

'Oh nothing' I say……Nothing.'

Barbara is very business like as she contemplates the rush hour traffic. The supportive role she must play today, is a huge responsibility. She knows only too well, if she puts her arms around me or gives me a hug, it will

reduce me to pulp, so she treads a fine line, tip toeing around my feelings, whilst keeping me feeling strong.
'What ever you do'... she says, 'Don't cry'... 'You hear me Alice? ... don't cry'
'No, no I won't.' I reply, hoping I can keep it all together.

Barbara concentrates on the traffic and I worry about facing my husband across a court room. Truth be known, I am absolutely terrified, I can hardly string my words together. Reaching into my handbag to take some more Rescue Remedy, the litany of abuse that he has etched onto my mind is telling. Underneath this terrification, (I know there isn't such a word, but there should be) underneath, I am confident, justice will be done. We have proved fraud. We have an excellent case, I am assured. He can't claim half of my business; therefore, how can I be responsible for his unpaid tax? Today, I think we will blow him out of court. He will want to crawl under a stone and never come out again. And, wearing my heels, plus Bad Lady Red lipstick, I will stand on top of it.

We negotiate the one-way system, via several, badly signposted roundabouts and then I spot an ugly grey concrete building on the left, with Crown Court over the door. We are in the right-hand lane. I simply shut down, knowing that if we don't leave the roundabout here, we will be sucked out onto a dual carriageway, going somewhere, we do not want to be. I close my eyes as a cacophony of horns protest when Barbara makes a manic move, across the lanes to pop out of the right exit. It's a wonder we aren't in the wrecker's yard, instead we are navigating the ramps of a multi deck car park.

My heart is in my mouth. Barbara guides me to the lift and suddenly, we are in daylight heading for a café she has spotted. We are in plenty of time and I could kill for a good strong coffee. Barbara continues to take charge. She orders double espressos, which appear promptly at our table. My hands are shaking, and I take more Rescue Remedy, to wash down a couple of Kalms. I must have drunk enough Rescue Remedy, these last eighteen months to rescue the world. Barbara fixes my gaze.
'What ever you do, DON'T CRY!' She says firmly. 'You are strong, YOU MUST NOT CRY!'
'Hear me?' 'If you cry, you will look weak.' 'You are strong!' 'And remember; be confident in your solicitor.' 'You're paying proper money for these

people.' 'He's only got Legal Aid bods… usually they're the ones from the bottom of the pile, they get paid a pittance compared with the real ones.' '*You've* got the best… *you've* done nothing wrong…remember that.' 'It will be OK.'

I suck up her confident words, drink my espresso, my tummy is still in knots. Of course, I know I haven't done anything wrong and Mary Collins has been brilliant, strong, clear and decisive. She will guide me through. Then, after one last visit to the loo and a last slash of Bad Lady Red, I practice smiling to myself, tossing my head back in nonchalant abandon. 'It's OK Alice, it's OK'.

I am cool, I am strong…*Pat and Glide. Pat and Glide.*

Chapter 21

The First Hearing

We are now in the waiting area of the court, which has the ambience of a bus station. I know we are early, but Mary isn't here. I scan the rows of seats, no sign of him, either. There are several huddles of people with paperwork on laps in deep conference.

Its 8.50… No Mary, but also no sign of my husband. I start thinking he has pulled out, but surely my solicitor hasn't pulled out too? I take time to check the other passengers en route to who knows where. Women with hollow eyes, looking how I feel, hanging onto every word, the suits are advising. If I knew then, what I know now….

8.57. I am in panic. Self-doubt creeps in. I have got the wrong day… Is it next week? Where is my legal representation? We are due in court at 9am. My hopes focus on the idea that he has declined the humiliation and at the very last-minute, Mary will whisk in to tell me of a settlement, agreed at 8.30am. At 8.59 she walks in, bearing no such news. She starts talking of bargaining…. What is the minimum I would expect? I am completely thrown, this is the first time we have discussed such a thing. Barbara pipes in

'Why would Alice need to bargain?' 'She's done nothing wrong.'

This sudden, panicked, part conversation, puts me even more on edge. Too late for discussion: Ms Collins and her luggage trolley containing my destiny rise to the Clerks call.

'Waite v Waite.' He bellows.

This sentence is so sad, never mind what is to come. Mary is in her court suit, she is even wearing lipstick, but I wish she had thought to wash her hair. Where is the other party? Where is my husband? Mary pulls her case down a corridor and I follow in her wake, like a child trying to keep up with a bad-tempered Mummy. Barbara is not allowed in…

'Bye Barbara.' She squeezes my hand and says

'Stay strong darling.'

Only cry on Fridays

As I strut, (no VPL) tummy tucked in, shoulders back, feet killing, a door on my right opens, just sufficiently for me to catch a glance of the man I have been married to for thirty-one years. How is it, this man on Legal Aid has the use of a private room and is flanked by two suits? We turn right again, entering a room with a crusty man at the helm of a T shaped table. With great sensitivity, my husband and I, are placed exactly opposite each other. Our Legals are nearest the judge who now appears to have come to life and is shuffling papers. Sitting bolt upright, I look up the table towards the judge. My notebook and pen are ready to scribble furiously. Mary ignores me, I am but a pawn in the divorce solicitor's game. These are very early days, but I do not know this. With no comprehension of what is to come next, I am hopeful, matters may even be resolved today.

The judge mutters something, and quick as a rat's fart, the other side are on their feet, asserting this, spelling out that. They are demanding, eloquent, savvy and whip sharp. This is his Legal Aid team in action. Meanwhile, Mary, who in her office is an eloquent, confident woman, stands to speak. Her face is pink. Her hand is shaking as she holds her documents. She splutters an objection. She looks like a woman about to go down in quicksand. Without even looking, I can feel *his* eyes burning into my being. I keep looking ahead at the judge, but still can feel his glare. Out of the corner of my eye, I see he has his head tilted, trying to catch my attention. This is intimidation right in front of everyone and no one, not even Mary, is taking this on board. She appears to have enough of her own problems, for this to be of concern. I write furiously, so my shaking hand, cannot be detected. In twenty-five minutes Mary, barely utters a word. Their case seems to be taking precedence. Mary hasn't even raised the fraud issue. What about the fraud Mary? What about the frigging fraud …Speak, please speak!
'Sir' she says so nervously, she appears to be brave, for even uttering a word. 'There is another issue, I wish to bring to the courts attention.'
A clerk walks in and whispers to the judge. The Judge starts shuffling a new set of paperwork on his table. Another set of sorry souls are waiting their turn in this hideous game. The Judge looks at Mary and firmly asserts,
'Ms Collins, this case has over run its allocated time.'
'But Sir!'
'You should have booked more time if this case is too complex for 30 minutes.'

She rallies (at last)
'Sir I must protest….'
She is not eloquent, she is shaking. I want the ground to swallow me up with the humiliation. The Legal Aid suits and my husband are smirking, at her inept presentation. I am paying £265 per hour + vat for this desperate performance. I sit mortified and speechless, as she tries to recover her position. It doesn't help that she knows she has messed up, big time. It only serves to make her more jittery. The judge momentarily, (twenty seconds) shows a modicum of sympathy, to allow her to speak. But the words won't come out in any order that makes sense, she is bungling it. He loses his cool and rebukes her.
She has not made the issues clear, in our court documents.
Her statements are ambiguous.
Her grammar, lacking.
He cannot understand her position.
Mary's face has long turned from pink to red and her hair seems to be stuck to her head. She tries, in vain to issue a few sentences in her defence, but he's having none of it. He adjourns, asking for further information on the issues she's raised. (Or in reality, the issues she *hasn't* raised) This is a car crash. The files are closed and the Legal Aid suits, flanking my husband, glide out of the door, like they are in a Hollywood court scene. We, meanwhile gather up paperwork into the suitcase on wheels and follow meekly behind, tail between our legs. Another set of Legals and a woman with anxiety written all over her face, pass us in the corridor. By the time we reach the bus station waiting area, the next marriage is being overhauled by a Judge, who by now is thinking about his lunch and to be rid of us all, as quickly as possible.

I have now concluded, that Legals, and they are not going to like me for saying this, are rather like hairdressers. There are hairdressers that are brilliant at cutting but can't blow dry to save their life. You leave the hairdressers with a flat, bird's nest and know your own skills in this direction, are superior. Then, there are hairdressers that can't cut to save their life but can disguise the fact by a superior blow dry. You only know this, when you wash and dry your hair yourself, to find all sorts of stray bits that won't sit with the rest. The star hairdressers, with a full appointment book and waiting list to match, are those that are masters of both the cut and the blow dry and we all want that elusive talent.
Legals, it seems, fall into similar categories. There are those who couldn't

organise a return telephone call, whose paper work piles up on the floor, but they can get on their feet in court, speak coherently and give the other side, a run for their money. Then there are those, who are organised behind the scenes, they know the law. They are efficient and excellent at communicating with their clients. Believe me, these guys are *not* the ones you want representing you in court. Mary Collins falls into the latter category. Her disastrous appearance in court has left me shell shocked. Barbara has seen the exodus from the corridor and is on her feet to greet us. My face says it all. She puts her arm around me, a tear plops onto my notebook, without knowing, it I am crying.

'How did it go?'

She knows the answer but *must* ask. Mary jumps in

'The Judge's instructions for an extra length hearing are a great leap forward.' She says, 'And this will be to our advantage… next time.'

Were we in the same court room Mary? Have I missed something?

Next time?' I mutter

Mary, isn't going to hang around for the post-mortem. She is already making a move towards the double doors. Without a bye or leave, she is through the doors and on the way to the lift. I think she is running scared. At this stage, I lack the confidence to remonstrate with her. I need her onside. I am scared, if I make waves she won't do her best for me. Writing this now, I can see how skewed my perspective was at the time. Mary, has not been a star performer, she should have been hauled over the coals, for such a lack lustre court appearance. Arriving with only a minute to spare, her arguments were not thought through. She certainly was not organised and ready for court. I am dismayed by my inability to confront a professional, about the non-professional service they have provided and for which I am paying a very professional fee. I must not act out of pique. In short, at this late stage, I cannot take on my solicitor *and* my husband. I have enough stress to bear. The mind has a wonderful way of shutting down on the unpalatable issues we do not want to contemplate. This is because we will have to raise our voices, take a stand and sometimes this is a worse option, than the problem we are trying to solve.

For years in my marriage, I blocked out the unpalatable. I had three small children, a house to run and a business to keep on track. There was no head space left to deal with what was happening on a day to day basis. Like a slow burning fuse, I experienced undermining tactics, so subtle I was barely aware of them. Small put downs, that build up, layer by layer, until

they settle deep in the psyche. They fester in the mind, until the message is reinforced loud and clear. *You aren't good enough... Who would want to employ you? That's a rubbish idea.*
Like an ear worm with a fragment of music repeating itself maddingly, running through the mind, the incessant repetition lodges in the recesses of the brain. He got into my head, there's no way round it. Like a fourth child, he required endless attention. His business *always* took priority. He resented the time I spent working on my business and would deliberately interrupt my precious working hours (sans children) with some minutiae of his own, that required *immediate* attention. When he couldn't think of any plausible work-related request to interrupt me, he would come into my office, stand on the other side of the desk, to stare at me in an intimidating way. Such resentment, I was busy, and he was not. In the early days I would remonstrate with him, telling him to get on with his work and please leave me to concentrate. But slowly as his behaviour became more menacing, the control so insidious, I found I lacked the courage to speak out.

When I enrolled on an Open University Arts Foundation course, he hated the fact I might achieve another degree. This would mean my further education would surpass his, undermining his supposed superiority. His comment which I can remember to this day, encapsulates his sense of impending inferiority.
'*We are* all right as *we are*... there's no need for *you* to do another degree.'
He constantly questioned the amount of time I was spending on the course work. If I used any free time during the day he'd say,
'Why aren't you working?'
If I worked on assignments in the evening…
'Why are you leaving me alone, to do that stupid O.U. work?'
Eventually, there was so much pressure, I reluctantly gave it up, unable to cope with the daily recriminations and the disharmony, it was causing in our marriage. This was just one of many unconscious episodes of control I lived with. In my mind, I had given up the course, to keep an even keel in our marriage, whereas in reality, it was to keep him happy. However, a few years later, a friend persuaded me to enrol on a part time MA. This time I was prepared for the flak and worked on my dissertation, doggedly over two years to achieve my post graduate degree. When the graduation date was announced he sarcastically said,
'Don't tell me you are going to dress up in a mortar board and gown and go to the ceremony?'

Only cry on Fridays

But, I certainly was… and he was embarrassed into joining my girls, to see it happen. This was a rare brave moment of asserting myself. In front of our friends he would say how proud he was…
'Look what my amazing wife, has gone and done… an MA if you please!'
Behind closed doors, life couldn't be more different and the best way to survive it, was to pretend it wasn't happening. Over the years, I had trained my mind, to block the inner turmoil. This was not happening to me, in fact, within forty-eight hours, I could turn a situation around, convincing myself, *I* had caused the problem. *I* must have done something to upset him. *I* must be over reacting. *I've* got this all out of proportion, because here was Mr Nice Guy, making me a cup of tea, cutting some Roses from the garden to put at the side of the bed. These loving gestures, only added to my confusion, and I started to lose all sense of what was happening, I found myself relying on him to define reality. Something very damaging was going on inside me, but I couldn't vocalise it.

This man, holding court, at a drinks party, telling amusing stories, was *so* charming, had so much charisma. My self-confidence was diminished with every Jekyll and Hyde mood swing I was subjected to, behind closed doors. Little wonder, I lacked the inner strength to confront Mary Collins. Confrontation was rewarded with punishment. Dare to raise your voice, query a comment… then join the ranks of persona non-grata. The silent treatment could last for weeks.

'OFF DAY!' Screamed Barbara in the car 'You are kidding me!'
We were on our way into the city centre to find somewhere for lunch.
'What if she has an off day, on your most important …Final Hearing Day?'
Over lunch, I related the whole ghastly court scene. It felt even more hideous reliving it. Barbara, incredulous of Mary's incompetence, tells me, I must complain.
'You can't let this slide… you're paying for this bungling woman.' 'Alice, what's the matter with you?'
'I just can't take on any more battles right now.' I said meekly. 'I need her on side.' 'I'm all in…' My face crumpled, and then the tears started. I grabbed my paper napkin, to dry my eyes. Aware other people were looking in our direction, I tried in vain, to pull myself together, but couldn't speak. Barbara whispered
'OK, OK I get it…we won't talk about this anymore, you've had a pretty rough day, to say the least.'

She poured me another glass of wine, I pushed the rest of the food around my plate, but there was no appetite. On the way home, we talked about it some more, but all I wanted to do, was get into my flat to let the tears out. It was Friday after all. There would be time for recovery, before work on Monday morning.

Chapter 22

Hettie visits

Despite my original euphoria of having a transcript of the recording, after Mary's bungling efforts at the First Hearing, I am all in. Given Mary didn't manage to raise the Pension fraud at the Hearing, she reverts to type, becoming efficient as ever, with paperwork, letters, and copy letters flying backwards and forwards. One of the letters she copied me in on, advises my husband of the evidence we have against him, including the transcript and the fax he sent to David Elliot, arranging his commission payment on the second sale. Wearily I read the letter, all should be well then, I thought…?

A new project came in which was exciting but more importantly it meant I had to concentrate on something else. The commission was for a series of black and white images of Georgian houses. This was going to be a much-needed, creative distraction, to get my teeth into. This work came via one of the evening classes at the university. A couple attending the classes last year, now wanted a photographer for a book they were publishing. Exhausting as these evening classes are after a full day's work, they consistently bring in all sorts of projects and with more legal fees pending, I need every penny I can get.

Overwhelmed with the enormity of the divorce, despite the project, I was having difficulty concentrating. My mind was jumping around, from issue to another. There was no room for creativity. A friend sat me down and gave me some very good advice. She said,
'Imagine seeing all the problems, laid out on a table.' 'Then, visualise piling them all into an old trunk…then lock it.' She continued 'Now put it under the bed.' 'Only get the trunk out, when you have to deal with the problems…. otherwise leave it locked and inaccessible.' 'If you don't, your mind will never have any rest from all this awful divorce…. that way you

can concentrate on your work properly, without all this shit overtaking everything.'

With practice, I learned the technique. It was a godsend. I don't know how I would have survived without it, as day by day, the divorce grew legs.

My girls never wanted to discuss any part of the divorce, and rather strangely, never wanted to hear why I had left their father. As far as they were concerned, it was a case of we didn't get on any more. Understandably, they wanted to remain as neutral as possible. Even though they knew we were going into court, they never asked about the First Hearing, it was the proverbial elephant in the room. Hettie had now finished university and had moved back home with her father. They had always had a good relationship, but it meant she was back in the fold, and I can only imagine, she would be privy to all the letters flying back and forth from our solicitors. It was not going to be easy to remain as neutral as she would have liked. Living only ten miles away, it was hard she chose not to come to see me. I saw and heard more from her sisters, who were at universities miles away. There was now a huge gulf between us, as last time I saw her, she had made it clear where her sympathies lay. The poor Daddy syndrome, had done its job, he needed help. He was having a breakdown… He was seeing the doctor, he was having *internal investigations*. He was desperate, he was depressed…. and more to the point, broke. The cause of the depression and his breakdown, was more to do the fact the nearest dog to kick had walked. It didn't look too good did it, if your wife of thirty years just leaves…? Now his cries for help meant visits to the doctor and pills. There were apparently pills lined up on the kitchen work top every morning. (To spell out to all and sundry, how poorly he was). There had been discussions in hushed tones about the *internal procedures* he was about to suffer the indignity of undergoing.

'Well you know Grandma had some kind of rectal cancer… and well…'

But, I think that particular granny, died before you were born, and it wasn't rectal cancer that killed her. So, someone has been giving you all this *mis-information* to elicit sympathy…. so, you will worry, and have the utmost compassion for this consummate actor. I can only assume Daddy's *life-threatening* condition was also relayed to your sisters, to ensure he achieved, the necessary attention and understanding he craved. So, when the cancer turned out to be no more than a strangulated pile, some of your empathy momentarily evaporated, but not all. He is a man after all, incapable and in terminal mid- fifties decline. He currently has no one to

Only cry on Fridays

blame, no one to make him feel in control (she left). He only has himself for company, but he will suck people into his world, where all he needs, is an hour or two of their time.... And perhaps a few thousand pounds to tide him over.

I hadn't heard from Hettie for a couple of months, conveniently putting this down to poor mobile reception in the village, but it hurt none the less. Therefore, when I heard her voice on the landline at the office I was delighted.
'Mum it's me!'
'Hello sweetheart!' I said
She must have heard the surprise in my voice.
'I thought I'd pop over tonight.... are you going to be in?'
'Yes, I am, do you want to come over for supper?'
I immediately envisaged making a lovely meal, so we could chat endlessly and hopefully reconnect again.
'No, no, just...well, it will be quite late, about nine... if that's OK?'
A visit from Hettie, out of the blue? It was unusual to say the least, but I consoled myself, she had made the effort.

Later that evening, I heard her voice on the entry phone, so I buzzed her into the building. Waiting at my front door, she bounced up the last flight of stairs. She looks tiny, vulnerable and tired.
'How are you darling?' I said, giving her a big hug, but she seemed wooden and barely reciprocated. I put the kettle on for tea.
'Yes... OK, OK ...' she said.
She didn't seem OK. Her face was drawn.
There was a pause and I thought she was going to tell me she was unwell or....
'Mum' she suddenly blurted out. She looks pained as she continued 'Mum, on Saturday.... Err .... On Saturday....' she faltered ... 'Rolo came to see Dad.'
I don't know what she wants me to say. Should I just be casual, matter of fact and say,
'Oh, you mean the man that helped Daddy steal my pension?'
Or, 'Oh Rolo" How lovely of him to come to see Dad....how is he?' 'Was he looking well?'
Instead, I remain silent. She fixes my puzzled face. Now I am playing this hideous neutral game. The silence is deafening.

'Mum' she starts again 'I had just been over the road to see Martha and the front door was just on the latch, so they didn't hear me come in…' she broke off

What on earth is she going to say?

'Rolo and Dad were in the dining room…and Dad was saying he'd had enough… and all the trouble you've caused him…' Her voice was faltering again… 'And then he said, 'he just wanted to kill you.'

She came over and gave me a long overdue hug.

'Now look Hetts, we all say stupid things in the heat of the moment… Dad's under a lot of pressure with one thing and another.' (Here I am, playing the diplomatic card again.)

'No Mum…' She was serious now. 'Rolo said that wouldn't be a problem… and he could arrange things….' *'They mean it Mum!'*

Sinking down onto the sofa as my legs turned to jelly, my heart raced. There was a huge sense of foreboding in the pit of my stomach. If Rolo Hargreaves, was proffering his services, or rather those of the low life he kept company with, this was something I couldn't ignore. Much as I would l have liked to dismiss the story, I knew if this reprobate was involved, to save his own skin, I had to take this seriously.

'I went straight into them, Mum, and said you're in enough trouble as it is Dad, what you think you are saying!'

I took notice of the fact she had said he was in enough trouble. This has been the only time any of my girls, have acknowledged his culpability.

'They told me to get out…. mind my own business and to f*** off.'

'Mum, I'm scared.'

'Well I'm scared too.' I said

By now, we were both crying and consoled each other with more big hugs.

'You must check your tyres Mum… and your brakes, take extra care coming home in the evening…' she trailed off. The enormity of what she had related was sinking in.

'Oh my God Hetts, I'm going to have to report this.'

She gave me a look of incredulity, as if I had just slapped her face. It wasn't hard to read her mind. By reporting this conversation, I'd be putting her in the firing line. What did she think I would do, just look over my shoulder? Not walk alone at night?

'I must talk to my solicitor first thing tomorrow, it's the sensible thing to do.' 'I'll leave you a message, or you can phone me again, so I can tell you what's what…'

In her panic to safeguard me, she really hadn't thought this through. How

Only cry on Fridays

could she expect me to just be more aware and not take any action? I had to flag it up to Mary Collins. I took this threat extremely seriously, my husband and Rolo, were now like animals trapped in a corner with their claws out. I could see the repercussions for Hetts were intolerable. She was in a no-win situation, but at the same time, I felt extremely frightened and vulnerable. The fact Hetts had come to see me, confirmed she realised, this wasn't a flippant conversation she had overheard. We parted in a slightly detached way. She was in a state of disbelief but was also making me feel that *I* was the problem. In a matter of minutes, the whole ghastly episode had turned on its head. She pecked my cheek and quickly vanished down the stair well. I watched out of the window, as she climbed into her car in St Phillip's Square. She normally looked up for a last goodbye and a wave, but this time she simply drove off into the darkness. I took out a notepad to write down an account of everything Hettie had said.

That night, I hardly slept a wink. I was in a suspended state of shock, but so worried for Hettie. I must get onto Mary first thing, but first thing, took an age to arrive. When I did wake, everything from the night before, rushed into my head. Yes, I must take advice from Mary, she would know the best way forward. With my notebook in my bag, I headed to the office. Mary was the first person I had told and as I reiterated the events of the previous evening, I started to cry. Mary was quiet at the other end of the line and I heard her take a deep breath.
'We have to report this' she said
She tried to calm me down.' 'Look, there's probably lots of bravado and anger…'
'Just loose talk involved here.' 'I doubt it's a serious threat……..' 'Nevertheless, I must flag it up to the other side, that we have been made aware of the conversation and I will advise the police.'
'But Mary… my daughter is in an impossible situation… I don't know what to do.'
'Your daughter is a young woman of twenty-three… she made her choice to come to you.' 'She chose to tell you what she heard.' 'She is not a child, she is involved by her own volition.'……. 'She *chose* to tell you.' 'Am I right?'
'You didn't press her for this information?'
'Well no.'
'She came to you willingly?'
'Yes.'
'Then we have to take action.'

Alice Waite

'Yes.' I said reluctantly

The next morning, I received a copy of the letter Mary had sent to my husband's solicitor. Mary had recently started faxing me copies of letters to my husband, when she felt she needed approval. However, on this occasion she didn't. She was not going to waiver. The letter was clear and business like, but never the less compromised Hettie. She was right at the centre of the issue, I didn't know where to turn. Her sisters wouldn't thank me for embroiling her in this situation, but now I felt we were on a collision course. Any possibility of rekindling our relationship had well and truly diminished and I was frightened for my safety. Things were turning very nasty.

Rolo Hargreaves was low life, with a voice of molten honey, but there was a murky undercurrent to his charm. Rumour had it, that this Machiavellian, double dealing character, had only escaped a prison sentence for Vat fraud, because he had hired a brilliant QC. He was also known to mix with a less salubrious circle of people. He always knew 'A man that can…' And some of this circle clearly left a lot to be desired. Once when some clients had owed us money for several months, he suggested organising 'Men with dogs to…. just frighten them …. You know…'
'No, absolutely NO!' I said, 'This is not the way, we are tackling this problem.'

The whole episode with Hettie worried me so much. When I tried my visualisation techniques, this issue, would just not stay in that surreal, locked trunk under the bed. I phoned her mobile, but with poor reception in the village, as ever, it went straight to voicemail. I left her a couple of messages
'Not to worry darling, my solicitor had thought it best …. In view of everything to write to Daddy's solicitor and I hope you understand?'
But she didn't call back. I cannot imagine what the next day must have been like for her. She was in the lion's den. He would have screamed and shouted. Mr Bully, would have shown his true colours, intimidating his own daughter, until she did exactly what he wanted, because two days later I received, via his solicitors, a letter that devastated me. Composed in words that certainly weren't her own, Hettie had signed a letter, denying our conversation of just a couple of days before. The letter stated, I had imagined the whole thing, because I was jealous of her relationship with

her father. I couldn't believe what I was reading. I was bereft with his emotional blackmail of our daughter; how could he sink so low, to force Hettie to sign the letter?

I wrote her a letter, but never posted it. I knew I would only be throwing petrol onto the fire.
My darling Hettie, I am so sorry you have been caught up in all this mess…. I can only imagine, how brave you had to be, to warn me of the threats you heard. The manipulation involved for you to sign this letter, refuting everything you told me, is something I am more than familiar with, and I know your integrity has been tested to the extreme. I am distraught you have been put in this invidious position, but don't worry sweetheart, I know you will have gone through hell on earth before the letter was put in front of you to sign. I do understand, believe me, I won't hold it against you, because you and I know the truth of this matter. The conversation you heard, between Rolo Hargreaves and your father and then relayed to me that evening is very frightening. I am only grateful you told me. I feel safer for knowing, bless you for telling me.
All my love Mummy xx

I know the menacing and intimidating ways these things happen. I have signed documents under duress with a kitchen knife drawn from the knife block, the point tapped on the document, where I was required to sign. Or if I said *No* to any of his demands, the silent treatment would come into play when I would be ignored for days or weeks at a time. To become persona non-grata, undermines the spirit. Of course, he would chat away when we were with other people, or the girls were around. He presented so well to the outside world, but as soon as we were on our own again, he reverted to the cold silent person he had been a few hours before. Subtle, unseen punishments, for non-compliance are a hideous form of manipulation. The longer I held fast about something he wanted me to do, the nastier the repercussions would become. Driving the car recklessly was a favourite. He would delight in my terror, laughing, when I begged him to stop. Here, he was, in charge, over taking on bends while I was pleading for this man to drive in a safe manner.
'Please stop this… we have children to think about.' 'Slow down… slow down for God's sake….'
With an icy look of distain to his left and his foot hard on the accelerator,

my pleas were ignored. Eventually, the exhaustion of his behaviour would escalate into compliance, at the expense of self- respect. So, devastating as this letter of denial is Hettie, I do understand my darling. I do understand. To this day, we have never spoken of it.

After the post mortem on the letter, I didn't hear from Mary for a while. Then one morning, out of the blue her colleague telephoned.
'Mrs Waite, my name is Greg Midgley.' 'I have always worked alongside Mary Collins.' 'I am so sorry to tell you, Mary died last night.'
'Oh, my goodness.' I said, 'What on earth happened?'
'Mary had Cystic Fibrosis and her lungs just packed up I'm afraid.' 'We're all deeply shocked here, as you can imagine.'
Such a huge shock, I couldn't believe it. I had always thought Mary seemed a bit chesty and sometimes her breathing seemed laboured, but for her to die…. This was so unexpected. Greg Midgley went on to tell me, that as her number two, he would be taking on my case and was already familiar with everything on file.
OMG! This is now solicitor number five!

In due course a letter arrived from number five solicitor, Greg Midgley. He advised me that my husband's friend, Nat Selwyn, was claiming a third of our house in France. I stared at the letter in complete and utter disbelief. We had a property in rural France, which for years, we had been in the process of converting. As and when we could afford it, we had water connected, then electricity, but there was a long way to go, to make the house habitable. Over the past few years, we hadn't been able to do much renovation work at all. Now, Nat Selwyn seemed to be claiming one third of our major asset. I read on. Apparently, he had been lending my husband considerable sums of money for his business (of which I was a paper director) and my husband had smoothed the waters with Nat by telling him he could have a share in our French property. This was the first I had heard about it. I immediately called Greg.
'How can this be, Greg?' 'I haven't signed anything to give Nat Selwyn a third of our property!' 'What's going on?'
'Well, if this claim is upheld, it means you only have a third of this asset.' Greg advised
'And well... Your husband has given a valuation of the property, of which well one third is about what is owed to Nat Selwyn.'

'This is farcical… they are making it up as they go along.' 'How can it be upheld…?' 'Where's the paperwork?' 'This is crazy!'
'It's about the borrowing from this Nat Selwyn… it was to prop up the Company and you are a Director… so have responsibility to pay half those debts.'
'But, I never had anything to do with the wretched Company.' 'My husband wouldn't allow me to make any decisions, even if I was a Director on paper.'
Greg sighed 'I'm afraid that won't stand up in court.' 'As a Director, legally, it is your responsibility to make yourself aware of the financial position of the Company.'
I became cross 'You try that when your co Director won't speak to you for weeks, or just won't tell you anything about what's going on in the business….' 'It was very much his business, not mine.' 'I was shut out of the day to day running of things and when I put my head above the parapet to ask, I was told to mind my own business… *I'm* dealing with that!'
'That's most unfortunate Mrs Waite, but Company law does ….'
I cut in 'Yes I get it, I get it…. Sorry I didn't mean to interrupt you.' 'But hold on' I said, 'Where's the proof of these payments?'
Midgley said 'Nat Selwyn says he paid your husband in cash.'
Getting into sleuth mode I queried 'So how can he prove he's paid this money?' 'Let's see the bank statements, showing he withdrew cash.'
Why was it me, asking for proof of payment, why wasn't my solicitor, thinking of this basic question?
'I don't for one minute think the money was from the bank.' 'But let's ask the question, shall we?' 'And where is the evidence, I had agreed to give Nat one third of our property?'
Greg Midgley said he would request proof of the payments and also proof of transfer of ownership.

I put all this hell into the visual trunk, locked it firmly and kicked it under the bed.
I had to get on with my work. There were presentation drawings to produce as well as well as ideas for new projects. Spring was upon us, white Narcissi and deep blue Muscari were heralding its arrival in the little courtyard garden, outside my office, if I looked at this scene long enough, all was well with the world. In the meantime, Trish had taken a message from Alex, my landlord. He wanted to pop down for a chat later today, if convenient.

'No problem.' I said, 'Give him a call back please, let's say 4.30pm when all the students have gone.'
At 4.30 Alex was sitting in my office looking slightly nervous.
'I am so sorry to have to tell you this, but we won't be able to renew your lease this summer.' He said
'No, no, no!' I said, 'Why not Alex?' My heart was pounding, and I could feel my eyes welling up.
'Believe me, if it was possible we would, but well we find ourselves in a tricky situation.'
I sat in silence, waiting for him to elaborate further. I don't think he really wanted to, but the silence made it necessary to fill in the gaps.
'We have to sell our house and we've decided to move in here, until business picks up.' 'So ... we would convert this area into a kitchen / diner/ family room…. Straight out onto the garden for the children and well … we've also given Tom on the top floor notice, so that area can become bedrooms…' 'I'm so sorry Alice… we just have no choice I'm afraid.'
Tears were rolling down my cheeks, which I was embarrassed about. I tried to wipe them away with the back of my hand. I don't think for a moment Alex was expecting this reaction, but of course he wasn't privy to all the other things I was dealing with at the time.
I spluttered 'This is just the last straw, I'm sorry, I can see you have problems too Alex, but every day it seems there is another car crash in my life and I am all in….'
Trish put her arm around me and I tried to pull myself together.
'We've tried to give you as much notice as we can…' his voice was genuinely concerned. 'So, we are talking about the end of August.' He said
'It's just finding somewhere I can afford and in two years, I've started to become established here… it's such a great location.' I said
'Well of course, we will give you an excellent reference.' ' You've always paid your rent on time and been a great tenant.'
'Thank you.' I muttered
There really wasn't anymore to be said. He saw himself out and then I completely lost it. They say you will never be given more to bear than your shoulders can take. At that moment, I felt if anyone added so much as a feather, I would collapse in a heap. Trish made tea and promised to get the commercial register tomorrow, to start the trawl for another office and studio space.

Chapter 23

The letter

It's time to launch a shot across the bows. Let him know what an invidious position he is in. There is a weight of evidence against him and I'm going to spell it out, in no uncertain terms. He will put up his hands, beg for mercy and drop all this nonsense about Nat Selwyn, owning one third of our property in France. It's time to just divide everything in half, so we can all get on with our lives.

I illicit help from some of my girlfriends, then set a date for Annie, Dee, Barbara and Nadia to come over for some supper. Nadia is now firmly one of the clan. After her Oscar winning performance she has star status, I owe her so much. When we have cleared away the supper, with notepads to the ready, everyone sits around the table in the window of my flat, armed with Dictionaries and Thesaurus. Just a reminder, in these dark ages, there were no on-line dictionaries to guide us. Annie oversees taking notes. She sits poised in the wing chair, glasses on the end of her nose, in secretary mode.

I start…

'Dear Steve,
I am sure by now you are aware of the *wretched* situation you find yourself in.'
'I think we can do better than *wretched*' said Annie
'Yes maybe…' I say
We all start thumbing through our Dictionaries.
'What about *calamitous*? Dee suggested 'Or *contemptible*'! 'Or *deplorable*….'
'What about *atrocious*?' Shouted Barbara getting into her stride.
'I like *calamitous*… but no, perhaps we were better with *wretched*.' I said
'You know describing someone as a wretch, is pretty powerful, don't you think?'

'It suggests someone is a reprobate or deplorable.' Nadia reads from her dictionary.
'Ok let's stick with wretched for now.' I said… 'We can always come back to it.'
'So, were we're we?'

'Dear Steve
I am sure by now you are aware of the *wretched* situation you find yourself in.
You and your double-dealing friend, Rolo Hargreaves have …'

'Hold on Alice' said Dee 'Let's make this so eloquent, it's frightening … so *double dealing,* whilst it is accurate, doesn't cut it…it's more colloquial, do you agree?'
'Yep, you're right.' 'What do you suggest?'
'I like NEFARIOUS!' Barbara (our girl with the English degree) declared.
'*Nefarious… what* does that mean?' Dee asked.
'God, he's going to have to have a dictionary by his side to read this!' I said
Barbara filled everyone's glasses to the brim and continued
'*Nefarious* means, wicked or criminal.'
She said in her best school teacher voice. She just needed the chalk and blackboard to complete the picture.
'So' she continued taking the A4 sheet from Annie's hand

'Dear Steve
I am sure by now you are aware of the *wretched* situation you find yourself in.
You and your *nefarious* friend Rolo Hargreaves have perpetrated fraud …. Err….'
'To the detriment of my Pension fund.' She continued,
'I like!' I said
Annie started taking notes again on another sheet of paper.
'I have amassed sufficient evidence against you….' Barbara closed her eyes searching for inspiration.
'And you are deep in the *do do*!' Nadia burst in hysterically, spluttering her wine.

Everyone cracked up laughing. Nadia had to be patted firmly on the back to stop her choking.

'OK, OK let's start again' said Dee taking the page from Barbara, who was now lying on the sofa fanning herself and seemed incapable of uttering another word apart from
'Do do...!'
'Err hum...' Dee cleared her throat

'Dear Steve,
I am sure by now you are aware of the *wretched* situation you find yourself in. You and your *nefarious* friend Rolo Hargreaves have perpetrated fraud, to the detriment of my Pension fund. I have amassed sufficient evidence against you, for you to be charged with fraud, which typically attracts a five to seven-year prison sentence.'
'How do you know?' Annie said
'I don't darling, but that will do… he can do his own research, can't he?'
'So, Alice what evidence *do* we have?' Dee asked
'Well, of course, a tape-recorded conversation with Damien Humphries, the transcript of which is validated by an affidavit, by Nadia.' I said blowing Nadia a kiss. 'And …we can apparently subpoena the Damien boy, to court to validate the transcript.'

'*Poor poor* Damien' cooed Nadia 'such a darling, so innocent… he was adorable you know….' She was looking into the distance; she was back in his studio all over again.
'Nadia!' Annie butted in 'I didn't put you down as a cradle snatcher.... you *naughty* girl!'
'Well he did have rather nice hands'…Nadia said dreamily. 'You know strong hands.'
Barbara had now recovered from the 'Do do' moment and was back on her feet. 'Forget his hands… let's get on with this letter.' She instructed us. I expected to hear her say 'Now all get into line' next.
She recapped,

'Dear Steve
I am sure by now you are aware of the *wretched* situation you find yourself in.
You and your *nefarious* friend Rolo Hargreaves have perpetrated fraud, to the detriment of my Pension fund. I have amassed sufficient evidence against you, for you to be charged with fraud, which typically attracts a five to seven-year prison sentence'

Then I chipped in,
'My solicitors hold a tape recording of Damien Humphries telling us, he negotiated the sale of the property with you, and you alone, for a price of £250,00. Yet you had already sold the property, without my knowledge to Rolo Hargreaves for £110,000.' 'There is a signed affidavit by the person who made the recording, corroborating the transcript.'

'How is he sleeping at night?' Said Annie
'I think he's going to hell in a hand cart!' said Dee 'Did he really think he would just get away with it?'
'What *really* annoys me' I said, 'Is that he thinks I am *so* stupid, I would never find out!'
'Well he did *soooo* under estimate you, didn't he?' Nadia was on her third glass.
'Let's get something in about subpoenaing Damien into court… don't you think?' Suggested Dee.
'Yes, then it sounds like we mean business.' Annie said
'Let's get on with it… 'Said Barbara, now taking charge of this unruly class, of slightly inebriated teenage girls.
'Yes Miss!' We all trilled together
'So, we need to add the bit about the subpoena … Right?'
She placed her hand on her head, deep in thought and taking the reins again said
'So, ladies……'
'There is a signed affidavit by the person who made the recording, corroborating the transcript.' …'My legal team are prepared to subpoena Damien Humphries into court if necessary.'
'I love *my legal team*.' I enthused
'We need to mention the fax as well.' I said
'What fax?' Said Dee
'Well he sent a fax to the estate agent dealing with the sale in the first place, telling him he had already sold it… and well not to worry the property was to be sold again and he would get commission on the new sale!'
'He put that in writing?' Dee queried
'He sure did …. *And* signed it!'
'He *actually signed* it?' Said Dee 'He's *more* stupid than I thought!'
'Shall I send a copy of the fax?' I said
'Well nothing like rubbing salt into the wound.' Annie said… 'Don't you think?'

Only cry on Fridays

'I'll make sure it's attached.' I said

Barbara continued with her project….
'So, let's say …Of course you also signed a fax to…. Err….What was the name of the Estate Agent Alice?'
'David Elliot.' I replied Barbara continued 'Of course you also signed a fax to David Elliot, which confirms your *culpability* in this whole corrupt affair.' 'I enclose a copy for further reading.
'Yes, *culpability*.' said Annie 'it's so powerful.'
Dee had been quietly sitting with her glass of wine thumbing through her thesaurus
'I like *felonious*… but better still what about *malfeasance*?' She ventured
Nadia burst in… 'What the f*** does *malfeasance* mean?'
'Well' Barbara continued, *'Malfeasance means,* wrong doing or… misconduct.'
'Just perfect then' said Nadia 'So how do we weave *malfeasance* into this letter Barbara?'
Barbara was back in front of her class again …
'We could say…. without doubt your malfeasance and that of your reprobate accomplice, will be investigated by the court.'
'Whoop whoop!' Yelled Nadia 'You've got it Barbara, you've got it.'
The room broke into cheers and
'Yeah… yeah!' 'Brilliant stuff.'
'Love reprobate!' Said Annie
Annie poured more wine into the now, empty glasses.
'Is there more in the fridge darling?' She enquired
'There certainly is.' I said, 'And you know …. I think we are nearly there!' Taking a sip of the ice-cold Sauvignon Blanc. 'But I would like to say something along the lines of…He should be ashamed of himself…. You know … bringing this awful situation on his family'
It was now 11.30 in the evening and as much to do with the Sauvignon, as tiredness, words were failing me. Barbara came in …
'I think we should say he's *morally unprincipled.'* … 'So…. *Your morally unprincipled* behaviour has brought dishonour on this family and no amount of remorse, will discharge you of this stigma.'
'Genius!' I said
Annie moved across to the dining table to make a final copy, minus all the arrows and scribbles. Everyone else clinked glasses and drunk the last

of the wine. When she had checked a few things with Barbara, she passed the final copy across.

Barbara stood in front of her gals to read the evening's work to everyone.

'Dear Steve
I am sure by now you are aware of the *wretched* situation you find yourself in. You and your *nefarious* friend Rolo Hargreaves, have perpetrated fraud, to the detriment of my Pension fund. I have amassed sufficient evidence against you, for you to be charged with fraud, which typically attracts a five to seven-year prison sentence
My solicitors, hold a tape recording of Damien Humphries telling us he negotiated the sale of the property with you, and you alone, for a price of £250,000. Yet, you had already sold the property, without my knowledge to Rolo Hargreaves for £110,000. There is a signed affidavit by the person who made the recording, corroborating the transcript. My legal team are prepared to subpoena Damien Humphries into court if necessary.
Of course, you also signed a fax to David Elliot, which confirms your *culpability* in this whole corrupt affair. I enclose a copy for further reading. Without doubt your *malfeasance* and that of your r*eprobate* accomplice, will be investigated by the court. Your *moral turpitude* has brought dishonour on this family and no amount of remorse, will discharge you of this stigma'

'OMG! I love moral turpitude….'Annie said, 'What does that mean, exactly Barbara?'
'Well, an act of behaviour that gravely violates accepted standards.' Barbara lectured
That's so scary.' Annie said
'Imagine opening that letter in the morning' said Dee 'He will be rushing to the loo...'
'You'll see the skid marks from Mars!' Said Nadia

'You bet!' 'Oh girls… thank you so much, you've been just brilliant.' I said
It was now past midnight, and everyone had work in the morning. My dear girlfriends, grabbed their coats to make their way down the four flights of stairs, as quietly as possible. Given the consumption of Sauvignon Blanc… the exodus was not *so* quiet. There were a lot of rather loud 'Shhhishes' and giggles from Nadia who was firmly bundled into a taxi.

The following day, Trish typed up the final draft.
'Flipping heck' she said as we went through the scruffy wine stained pages from the evening before.
'Do you think you should get Greg Midgley to cast his eyes across this first?'
'No way' I replied, 'He will charge me £500 to counsel me against it!' 'I am up to here with unnecessary costs and bad advice.' I remonstrated, waving my hands in the air.
'Let's get it typed, signed, then send this Exocet missile in the post, Recorded delivery, today.'

Duly, the war head was fired. How I would have loved to have been a fly on the wall when the missile arrived. Only then, did I fax Greg a copy. Needless to say, he wasn't pleased I had taken it upon myself *to send such a strong letter* as he politely put I. However, I did think I could hear some approval in his voice, even slight amusement, because I had said, what needed to be said, and wasn't mincing my words. I bet he would have loved to be able to send a similar, plain speaking letter. A few days later we received a complaint from my husband's solicitor about the contents of letter. When I read the missive, I just shrugged my shoulders, trusting the contents had hit the spot. After all, every syllable was true. The facts had simply been clarified in a cogent manner, to be sure he understood his position.

Meanwhile, mindful I had to find new premises I was checking the Commercial Property Register as it was updated weekly. I viewed several office spaces but drew a blank, as many had shared kitchens, loos and entrance hall space, plus it was essential to have a room large enough for lectures. My rental budget was extremely tight, because as well as rent there were Business rates, plus the usual utilities to add into the equation. After long searches through the Register, I eventually found something that might work for me, so I made an appointment to view this rather run-down property, five minutes' walk from the town centre. It was in Edgar Place and had just about everything I required. The Estate Agent, sent a young woman to show me around and judging by her gasps at the disrepair, it must have been first time she had ever been inside. There was a huge, double height entrance hall with stone walls and a rough concrete floor. Then, a large ground floor office, a kitchen and cloakroom area, which were all in the most awful state of repair. On the first floor there was another office, giving way to a large, light and airy studio space, with a raised platform at one end. The room had two lovely Georgian windows and three and a half meter ceilings. I was told in its glory days, it had been a recording studio, for some now long defunct pop groups, but it hadn't been used in years. Judging by the state of the place, those boy band members were all probably accountants with grey hair by now.

The property was perfect, apart from its serious state of dilapidation. On the ground floor, I could see the lower levels of stone were a darker colour and damp to the touch. The kitchen and cloakrooms would have to be replaced. Then upstairs, the walk-through office space lacked a ceiling, it was open to the rafters with bits of hessian stapled to a few laths. There was a serious shortage of power points and some were so old, they were defunct round pin sockets. I took some measurements, so I could draw up plans to be sure the space would work. The rent was the same as my Garrton Street premises, but now I had to estimate how much the renovation would cost and whether my overdraft would cover it, until money started coming in, for the autumn term. This renovation on my tight budget was going to be a serious challenge. After long and protracted negotiations through a solicitor, Janet Gibson, (yes, another set of legal fees) I managed to secure the first three months, rent free in lieu of all the renovation works I about to embark upon. From the day the lease was signed, I had twelve weeks to lick this huge space into shape.

Chapter 24

The Package

Mid-morning and I am in the office, knee deep in work. Client work, prepping for the next set of courses, collating paperwork, on the phone, dealing with well…. so much.
The doorbell rang, and the postman proffered a huge Jiffy bag which I signed for. I saw it was from The Pension Ombudsman and on opening the package, saw a mass of tabulated paperwork. The covering letter advised, I am being provided with copies of all Pension & Mutual's files, relating to my complaint. A cursory look through the contents fuelled a yawn. My eyes glazed over sheet after sheet of copy files. Stuffing everything back into the bag, I put it on one side. I have a living to earn, rent to find, problems to solve and this pile of paperwork was not going to bring in a bean. It was completely overwhelming. I am not a lawyer, not even a Para-legal, but here I am trying to cope with the legal technicalities of my claim. I couldn't afford a solicitor to investigate the fraud and I knew I was floundering. I felt all in. The big guys from Pension and Mutual were writing me intimidating letters, advising, they would only deal with my Solicitors and in short just telling me to GO AWAY. I was tired, tired, tired with the stress of it all. My divorce was painful enough; I hadn't the energy to deal with this as well. Emotionally drained, the situation with my girls only exacerbated my feelings of guilt and failure. Maybe I just should have stayed in my marriage. Buttoned up and shut up, not made waves. Every time I berated myself and considered this option, I knew it was an unrealistic one. I could not have lived through anymore of those sunless Sunday afternoons and his games of power and control. Insulated by sheer optimism, I had made an incalculable leap into the abyss and although terrified daily by my actions, put my trust in life, drummed up my self-esteem to work all hours God gave, to get my business on its feet.

Wonderful things happened to me. Opportunities I would never have dreamt of, came out of the blue and I lapped it up. For the first time ever in my life, I was beavering for myself, not a free loading, task master, called my husband. The power and control were now in my hands and while after all these years it was confusing, it was also liberating. My bank balance, I knew to the last penny. There were no surprise unpaid invoices to haunt me. Girls, we are talking pre-online banking here. These were the days when you waited for your statement, (yes paper) to be posted out at the end of the month. So, I saved every card receipt, entered them into my accounts ledger, keeping a running total, so I was ahead of every bank statement, with a true picture of my finances and I revelled in it. If, I spent a small fortune (for me) on a cashmere sweater and lived on baked beans for the rest of the month, that was my choice. I didn't have to compensate for other people's choices, mistakes or rank fecklessness, in my calculations. Being in control of my own life made me feel dizzy.

Birthdays were now joyous affairs, rather than a date I dreaded. I loved organising a gathering in a favourite wine bar or restaurant. My girlfriends were an amazing female network of genuine support and love. We all had our own lives but knew we could pick up the phone at any time and there would be a shoulder to cry on. I know it sounds odd now, but in my old life, I used to dread birthdays. Instead of the day being a celebration of life; from the moment I woke up, it was as if a black cloud had descended. Of course, if the girls were at home it would different. They at least were in a genuine 'Happy Birthday Mummy' mood. On our own, his mood would be morose, and I knew just what to expect of the day, when he had disappeared down stairs, particularly early. With a heavy heart, I'd make my way down to the kitchen. There would be no lights on. No card on the table, I knew where he would be. He had taken himself off to his workshop and the rest of the day would follow the usual pattern. Eventually he would return to see all the cards from friends and the girls. Jealous of all the kind thoughts and love from others, he felt guilty for not partaking in the niceties of life. He would tell me, he *meant* to get a card, but well he forgot, when he was in town, and he really didn't know what to get me anyway.... 'And it's ridiculous at our age, expecting presents... we're not children for heaven's sake.'
Funny, he behaved just like a little child, when unwrapping *his* birthday presents.

Sometimes though, there was a present and I would have a *normal* birthday.

There would be dinner out and some joie de vivre about the day. The trouble with living with someone with such unpredictable mood swings and such a perverse sense of what was acceptable, I never knew from one hour to the next what to expect. Walking on eggshells doesn't begin to describe my day to day. One birthday I came down to the breakfast table, to find a small box, beautifully wrapped and tied with ribbons. I wondered what it could be. Jewellery or maybe perfume I thought but decided to wait for his return from the workshop before opening it. He came back to make coffee.

'Haven't you opened your present? He said in a pleasant voice.

'Well, no I was waiting until you came back.' I replied.

He had a big grin on his face and seemed rather pleased with himself, making me more curious than ever. Perhaps it was that antique brooch, I had pointed out ages ago... I started peeling off the wrapping. There was a layer of tissue under the heavier paper. My optimism quickly evaporated, as a red box came into view. I was now looking at a box of *Solpadine*. (Paracetamol & Codeine tablets) In large letters the strap line declared *The Power to take the Pain Away*.

He saw my face crumple and trying to recover the situation, he burst out laughing.

'Ha! I thought this would be useful... for all those migraines you get!'

What kind of person would...? How sick can you get? Did he expect me to take the lot? *The Power to take the Pain Away* seemed like something I could well consider.

The jiffy bag lay there gathering dust, an incongruous sight, on the antique walnut desk I had brought from home. One Saturday morning, I had come into the office to see if a much-needed cheque had arrived. I skimmed through the anonymous pile of post. There were certainly bills there, but no cheque. Dismayed, and feeling pretty low, I put the kettle on to make coffee. It seemed I had problem, upon problem, piling up and my exhaustion was instrumental in compounding my feelings of utter hopelessness and depression. Completely overwhelmed by my situation, I felt powerless to deal with it. Could someone please sort it all out? If only there was a fairy godmother to wave a wand, so that I would be on the other side of this awful pain. It's all very well having supportive girlfriends, but I felt I was stretching their support to breaking limit. There was always another twist, another turn to my situation, that I needed to voice. They were always there for me, but I was worried, compassion fatigue would set in. There were so many times I had picked up the phone, desperate to talk to someone, and decided against it. I was living in a soap opera and although everyone phoned not only to give me their support, they wanted a synopsis of the latest episode. With disbelief, I realised I was the star in this shabby drama. Surely it was happening to someone else, surely, I would wake up from the nightmare and all this agony, that had overtaken my life would evaporate?

Sitting down with my coffee, I emptied the contents of the jiffy bag onto my desk. Unenthusiastically, I leafed through Pension & Mutual's copy paperwork. So much of it was familiar. Copies of letters sent to me, my financial advisor, pension statements. Letters from Conveyancing solicitors to Pension & Mutual's legal department, land registry details…... idly I sipped my coffee.
Then, I came across a series of documents I had not seen before. Internal memos, emails and faxes from one Pension & Mutual department to another. The coffee went cold. With incredulity, I read and reread these pages. I had unearthed a seam of pure gold from this sad package, which been waiting on my desk to be excavated, for weeks.
An email from John Marshall, Director of Public Relations to the Pensions Department.
A letter from the Pensions Department, to the Property Investment Company.
Working through a couple of inches of internal files, page by page, I was riveted. It was like a novel, I couldn't stop reading. All the time, behind the scenes, culpability was being aired. Every department was anxiously passing the buck back to another. Meanwhile Pension & Mutual were writing patronising letters to me, insisting they had behaved impeccably, following every letter of Pension law…. And, unsaid, please just stop bothering us, little woman. My heart was pounding with excitement. The contents of this innocent jiffy bag proved their guilt in every respect. A huge weight lifted from my shoulders. I was particularly excited to read an internal memo from Public Relations.
'This woman has opened a can of worms for us and she's threatening to go to the Press.' 'This will be a PR nightmare.' 'No one is to speak to her on the phone.' 'Every letter has to be passed by me.'

Perfectly used to talking to myself by now, I was muttering
'Think you can scare me Pension & Mutual, well think again!' 'You can't

Only cry on Fridays

bat me away.' 'This irritating wasp, will be back and back again, until you put up your hands to surrender.' 'I am the demanding mistress, who won't take no for an answer....'

Soon every surface was covered with piles of paperwork. I highlighted important passages, bright pink post-its labelled specific sections. Each section, was then organised into manila files. The floor was the only surface left. I literally screamed with joy as each indictment leapt from the pages. I was now tip toeing from space to space, as the documents started to cover the whole floor. When I eventually looked up it was nearly dark outside. Hours had gone by. I realised I was hungry, but I didn't care. I put the kettle on again and staved off hunger with a couple of biscuits and a yogurt, I found in the fridge.
Euphoric with my jiffy bag and its riveting contents, how could I have ignored it for so long? The dear brown jiffy bag, had been sitting in my office unloved and, yet its contents had the ability to turn my world around.
As I walked home my mind was working overtime. I had to present my case to the Pension Ombudsman. All the correspondence had to be analysed so that I can make a salient case. The thought was daunting. I had never tackled anything like this before. If only a solicitor would take up the case for me, but I didn't have the funds, so there was no choice. This was David and Goliath, but with these internal files, I felt I had a chance. That night, I hardly slept a wink. My mind was in overdrive, this could be a turning point. Next morning, I was back in the office at 8am writing wodges of notes, cross referencing documents to correspondence from Pension & Mutual. Every time I found another nougat of gold, I danced on the spot, punching the air. Inside, at last I was smiling.

Chapter 25

Move to Edgar Place

The first day I had the keys to Edgar Place, I walked to the new premises with a folio of drawings under my arm, to meet the builder and electrician. Wandering around, I was nervous of this huge undertaking, but I simply had to shut my eyes, not waiver and get on with it. Now tied into a seven-year lease, I just had to make this work.

Desperate to save every penny, I begged for free assistance with the less skilled jobs, for example, enlisting the help of my girlfriends with the painting. My ethos had to be, pay others to do the work I couldn't possibly do myself, such as put up a ceiling, remove a stage, rewire, fit a new kitchen…the list was huge and grew daily, as new areas of concern were uncovered, such as a floor that had to be strengthened, rotten window frames… and more.

Over an exceptionally hot summer, I worked solidly, to bring Edgar Place up to scratch. I decided the stone walls, should be painted. The stone was not real stone, more, grey rubble, held together with concrete. Not only would the paint lighten the whole atmosphere, but I could apply a damp proofing solution to the lower layers before the paint. Brushing down the bare stone walls, proved an arduous task. I would emerge from the building in the early evening, ashen faced, prematurely grey and barely able to speak. I soon learnt a disposable shower hat and a mask were essential kit. When this lovely job was complete, the next was to seal all the stone work to stop any dust mixing with the paint. Then two coats of undercoat were to be applied, followed by two coats of top coat. Writing this now, it seems nothing, but the sheer size of the task with a double height entrance hall and a three-metre-high lecture room, meant I had to put out an S.O.S. to all my girlfriends for help.

The trouble with painting stone is that, unlike a smooth wall, that can be painted with relative ease, stone, has so many surfaces, nooks and crannies to cover, the paint cannot be applied in the usual way. Stone, I soon discovered, must almost have the paint punched into the surface, with a large fat brush. My right arm soon became incredibly toned, as I punched litre after litre into the textured surface.

In the evenings, straight from work, my girlfriends turned up in their suits, with carrier bags of old clothes and a selection of CD's. We used the first-floor office, as base camp to change and store anything we wanted to keep clean. As they trooped in, I could see they were already tired after a day's work, so the kettle was on for a caffeine hit, then biscuits were proffered to keep everyone going. The ancient CD player boomed with the beat of Tamela Motown, then one by one, they emerged onto the landing in a riotous selection of outfits.

Annie appeared to *'I heard it through the grapevine...'*
She sashayed down the stairs singing *'Honey, honey, yeah' 'I heard it through the grapevine... "Not much longer would you be mine...." 'Honey honey...'*
She wore flip flops, with a full boiler suit, already suitably covered with paint and a beanie to protect her hair.

Dee always wore some ancient pyjamas and a peaked cap, whereas Nadia went for some old sports- wear that had shrunk in the wash. With perfect timing, The Temptations boomed throughout the building. Nadia, ever the consummate actress, stood on the landing leaning over the balustrade singing to her audience below.

'Papa was a rolling stone ...' 'Where ever he laid his hat was his home' 'and when he died.... All he left us was, alone...Hey Momma'!
She quickly dipped back into the office, to return with a paint roller, now employed as her mic. As she posed on the steps, playing to the gallery, she let rip just in time to repeat the chorus again.

'Papa was a rolling stone "Where ever he lay his hat was his home... and when he died, all he left us was, alone....' 'Hey Momma'!
To shrieks of laughter from below, she danced down the stairs.

As the heat wave intensified, Nadia's shrunken kit was reduced to a skimpy vest and Lycra shorts. As she was the tallest, she was given the ceilings to paint, so to keep the spatters from her hair she donned a frilly shower hat along with swimming goggles. We were a sight for sore eyes, but in no time at all, were at work, painting every bare surface. When every pair of hands counted, Barbara was conspicuous by her absence.

'So, what's up with Barbara?' Dee shouted down from her step ladder.
I looked across from the other side of the hall.

Alice Waite

'Something about her allotment required watering….'
But she's on holiday….' Nadia yelled from the top of her ladder. 'The schools broke up ages ago… she could water that bloody allotment anytime.'
Annie popped her head around the corner, from what we now called the main studio.
'It must be a big allotment…' 'I mean, does she supply Waitrose or something?'
Everyone burst out laughing.

Evening after evening, this army of painters trooped in, the tasks were pretty much the same… just paint ladies! With my deadline looming closer and closer, we painted as if to save our lives. Most evenings the girls put in four or more hours of work. I don't know how I would have managed without them. Some evenings, we were as many as six women of a certain age, filling, sanding and painting, reliving our youth singing along to music ingrained in our brains, when life was less complicated.

Tonight, The Stones, Little Red Rooster bellowed from the CD player. With such high ceilings, the acoustics were amazing, the sound bouncing off the bare walls and floors. Adjacent to the forecourt, at the front of the building, was an Indian take away. From 7pm we were tantalised with the most delicious cooking smells, wafting from their open window. By 10pm everyone was not only shattered but starving, so after perusing The Mogul's menu, we would pass our order through the window to Nish. In the time it took to throw our paint brushes into a waiting bucket of water and wash our hands, our order would be delivered. Much to the amusement of the Mogul's chefs, on these unusually balmy evenings, we sat outside next to the overflowing skip. Paint speckled in our random outfits, we used a couple of make shift trestle tables, to eat from the foil containers. Indian takeaways, never tasted so good.

A couple of weeks in, a friend offered her student son Mitch, plus his friend, Art to help. They were in need of some funds for their Gap year and although I couldn't pay them much, they worked incredibly hard for two or three weeks. When it came to painting the double height, entrance hall ceiling, I realised we would have to hire a tower. I duly ordered one from a hire company, who turned up the next morning. When I opened the front door, to the delivery man, he plonked a pile of metal work on the concrete floor and asked for my signature.

'Is this the tower?' I said
'Yep' the man replied
'You will be err… putting it up for us….' 'Won't you?'
'That's not what we do my dear' he said, 'that's up to you to sort out.'
With that, he was in his van, reversing off the forecourt. Looking at the pile of metal parts on the floor with complete dismay, I was overwhelmed with the task ahead. How was I supposed to know how to build a tower from this chaotic heap of scrap metal in front of me? With only daughters, we didn't ever do Lego. Jenga was the nearest we ever came to tower building and I certainly didn't want this tower, to be built like any of our crazy Jenga efforts. Mitch and Art however, weren't at all fazed by the task and set about constructing the tower like pros. Bear in mind, as they were building; they had to climb up a layer to construct the layer above. As I watched their progress, conscious of the concrete floor below, my heart was in my mouth. Eventually the tower was built to its maximum height. They then proceeded to climb down with the utmost ease, like monkeys, their long arms dropping their body weight below them, layer by layer, until they reached floor level.

The heat wave continued. Even with every door and window open, the air just didn't move, it felt like a warm damp blanket, wrapped about our paint spattered bodies. To give you some idea of the enormity of this project, over the twelve weeks we used a hundred litres of paint. Every time I went back to the Decorator's Centre, the man behind the counter looked at me with disbelief as I requested
'Just another ten litres of Cover Matt please.'
I was dreaming about paint and breathing paint fumes all day, so I had constant headaches. One evening, after everyone had left, I had closed all the doors and windows and started to change from my painting clothes, when in the quietness, I heard a loud scratching noise. At first, I couldn't quite understand where the sound was coming from, but moving quietly from room to room, I finally located the noise to the entrance hall. The scratching, now loud scraping, appeared to be coming from some wooden boxing, which I assumed had been built to cover a metal soil pipe from the floor above. Bravely I banged on the boxing and all went quiet. I consoled myself it must be a (very large) mouse or…. I didn't want to contemplate an alternative.

Slowly, everything began to come together. The furniture was moved from

Garrton Street, just before my lease came to an end. Then, there had to be a massive clear up. All the old paint cans were forced into an overflowing skip, that had been sitting on the forecourt from the start. Before the Sea grass carpet could be fitted, the floors had to be cleaned, before the Roman blinds could be fitted, the windows cleaned, the newly refurbished cloakrooms and kitchen cleaned. In an ideal world, I would have employed an industrial cleaning firm, but I was on the wire financially, so I had little room to manoeuvre. With the builder and electrician paid there was still the Solicitor as well as the next quarter's rent and, of course, more Solicitors' fees for the divorce still in progress. Requests for money were coming in from all sides.

'I need to rally the troops Trish.' I need so much help to get this place together.' I said.

Trish, now camping at her newly installed desk on the first floor, set about producing a postcard.... Oh, how easy it would have been if everyone was on email...

'Calling all Scrubbers'
Alice needs your help at 7pm Friday 25th
Dress code: Bring your Marigolds. Wear your lipstick and Jimmy Choo's
Scrubbing and cleaning to some great music.
Followed by Supper courtesy of the Mogul Tandoori
Bring a bottle
RSVP Alice
On the reverse was an image of a perilously high heeled, Jimmy Choo in hot pink.

The next day the phone started ringing, and by Friday, twelve wonderful Scrubbers, wearing their Marigolds, were trouping through the door, chattering twenty to the dozen. The mood was light hearted, but everyone knew that tonight, was an Ajax and Flash evening, accompanied by Scissor Sisters booming from the CD player. Annie wore a turban with a pink nylon overall. Lucy forgot her kit, so wore a bin bag with her Marigolds. Dee had a wrap over flowery pinny, tied over her jeans, with red high heels below. Nadia stuck with the Lycra kit, but with fishnets and heels. By 10pm everywhere was as sparking, as bare concrete floors could be.

We were ready to sit down for that Tandoori on the trestle tables outside. As I called to pass our order to Nish, through the window, I felt a plop of rain on my head. Within seconds there was a rumble of thunder, lightning

Only cry on Fridays

lit the night sky and the heavens opened. We quickly retreated, dragging the tables and stools indoors to the hall. While everyone was slightly relieved that the heat wave had broken, mores the pity we were unable to enjoy our meal outside. Rain came down like stair rods, bouncing from the floor. This was a *proper* storm. Sitting inside with plastic cups of wine, waiting for Nish to bring our order, we watched the sky light up, with sheet lightening. The noise of the rain on the metal skip was intense, but through it all, I heard, plop, plop sounds from the first- floor office. I sprang from my stool and made a dash upstairs. The office ceiling had several, large wet patches and water was steadily dropping onto the floor. 'Help! Buckets, bring buckets' I yelled.
Everyone jumped to attention, grabbing every conceivable vessel to hand. We had just finished organising buckets, bowls and containers, when we heard the doorbell. On the other side of the rain splattered glass, there stood a beaming Nish, under a huge red umbrella with our much-anticipated evening meal.

When I was negotiating the lease, Mrs Lynton-Davies the owner, insisted on a Full Building Repairing lease. With no experience of negotiating such things, I was advised by my solicitor, Janet Gibson, handling the lease, not to agree to this. My chance of finding alternative accommodation was now slim, as I had exhausted every possibility in the Commercial Property Register. Nervous that Mrs Lynton- Davies would back out, I could see with the building probably 200 years old, this was good advice. Janet pointed out, if a chimney crashed onto the roof or indeed the roof required repair, I would be liable. With numerous letters on the subject going back and forth, time was running out. This was brinkmanship in the extreme. Eventually, Mrs Lynton- Davies, agreed to an internal repairing lease, which seemed more manageable.That night, with buckets placed all around the office floor, I now understood why my solicitor was so insistent I should not agree to the Full Repairing Lease. When we eventually sat down for that long-awaited takeaway, we raised a glass to Janet Gibson. My first call in the morning would be to Mrs Lynton- Davies.

Two days later, Mrs Lynton- Davies's builder, Brian appeared with ladders to inspect the roof.
'I told her last year, this roof couldn't be patched up again… it needs replacing.'
My heart skipped a beat.

'Replacing?' I said
'There's no other way.' Brian said, 'The roofing felt is shot… years old you see.'
This bill could have been mine, if Janet Gibson hadn't been so insistent. What's more according to the builder, my landlady knew about the roof problem when we were negotiating. Phew…!

By the beginning of September, we were completely ship shape and ready to go. Bookings were coming in thick and fast.

Chapter 26

Hugo Steele

The new term started with a flourish. The economy was good, and the autumn courses were full, with a waiting list for cancellations. The large first floor studio came into its own, when one of the local glossies suggested I held a Reader's Event on their behalf. With around twenty-five readers sitting in front of me wine glass in hand, I talked through my portfolio of my work. How I achieved a certain effect, why I chose a particular shutter speed, the creativity of long exposures, motion blur photography and many more components of the courses. Then after questions and answers, everyone left with a prospectus to peruse. This was a brilliant way of promoting the courses and always showed a good return.
Some Saturday mornings, I would wander in to catch up paper work. This was no hard ship, I just loved my new premises and, in the peace, and quiet I could concentrate. First things first… coffee! I put the kettle on and then went into the loo. I hadn't put the light on, as there was sufficient in the lobby area and on one's own, who closes the door? I caught sight of something dark within the loo itself. I immediately thought someone hadn't flushed it properly, but a second glance told me otherwise. I quickly put on the light and then slammed the lid shut. There was a rat half submerged in the water. I stood on the lid and flushed the loo, so many times. All the time between the cistern filling and the next flush I was saying
'Please God, be gone…. Be gone… Help!'
After what must have been twenty consecutive flushes, I timidly lifted the lid. All clear!
I put a note on Trish's desk to call Environmental Health first thing on Monday morning.

Walking back to my flat in the autumn evening light, Freshers from the university were parading the streets dressed as Romans. With bed sheets wrapped about their patchily, fake tanned bodies, crowns of greenery perched on unruly locks, they ambled through the streets, bottles of beer in hand, to congregate around the fountain at St Phillip's Place. This was the third set of toga clad Freshers I had witnessed, which meant unbelievably, I was now starting my third year in Andrew's flat. By midnight, some joker will have put Fairy liquid into the fountain and in no time, the gushing water, will be a riot of foam, whipped up by the wind into streams of bubbles, floating through the night sky. Sitting at my table in the window, I started to open the post. As usual, I felt sick and nervy when I saw an envelope marked Garston & Welland. With a glass of wine in hand I opened the fat envelope. Greg Midgley was advising me, Nat Selwyn was going to be joined to our divorce proceedings, to recover the money, he had lent to my husband. Further he was lodging a claim against our property in France and would be calling on my daughters to give evidence supporting his claim, that I had agreed to give him a third share of the property. Greg Midgley really made my weekend. I read on, he advised there was a strong possibility my daughters could be called to give evidence against me. Why do solicitors post bombshells like this on a Friday? Are they so emotionally dislocated? I now have this hideous situation hanging over my head for the rest of the weekend. I am falling apart... I need to talk to someone about this. I decide to call Antonia. From the background noise I gather she is in a bar somewhere.

'Hello Mum, how are you?'

'Antonia, I need to talk to you.'

'I'm at a party at the mo.... can we talk tomorrow?'

'Can you go somewhere quiet please, I do need a word.'

I know I am not making myself popular, prizing her away from a buzzy student party.

'What's up Mum?' She enquires from a very slightly less noisy place.

'I have this letter from my solicitors, which says that Nat may call you and your sisters to testify you knew about Nat having a share of Ferme Thenon.'

'Oh, that's horrible of him' she sighed. 'But we *did* know about it... you must have known too?'

I was horrified she believed this.

'How did *you* know?' I said, 'Who told you?'

'Well I don't know *how* we knew... we just did.'

'Well, I didn't tell you! That's for sure, *because I didn't know!*'

'The *only* person who would have told you would be Daddy.' 'This is a ploy

Only cry on Fridays

between Nat and Daddy to make sure I don't get any money out of this house.' 'It's another example of his double-dealing ways.'
I heard a sigh at the end of the line. One minute she was having fun with her friends, the next involved with a divorce she didn't want any part of.
'Mum, I can't deal with this stuff right now.'
I ignored her plea to be allowed back to the party, I had to make sure she knew the facts.
'When did you ever hear me say anything about Nat having a share of our house?' *'When?'* I persisted
'Well...... I don't know' she said quietly
I didn't like putting her on the spot like this, but I also couldn't stand by to watch a serious asset disappear from my life, because of my husband's feckless business dealings.
'That's the point.' I said, 'The only person who would have fed you this information would be Dad.' 'This is all because he owes Nat money... it's nothing to do with me...' 'Do you see?'
Trying to remain neutral she said, 'I just don't remember who told me Mum.'
'Well Nat has nothing signed... no paperwork to prove this...' I said
She cut in. 'Well if there isn't paperwork... I don't suppose it will stand up in court anyway, will it?'
'In theory no'... 'That's why he wants to pull you girls into the equation to bolster his case.'
'Oh gosh Mum. Can we talk about this tomorrow... do you think?'
Antonia was all but pleading to let this go and get back to her friends.
'Alright, alright.' I said, 'Will you ring me when you have surfaced tomorrow?'
A delighted voice replied 'Yes, yes after lunch maybe.'
Clearly this was going to be a late night.

Sunday came and went without a word from Antonia. On Monday, I managed a lunch time call to Greg Midgley.
'Greg, how can this be possible?' 'I haven't signed any document giving this man one third of our property... it's a nonsense!'
'Maybe' he replied, 'but he seems pretty sure of his ground and well... he's saying he will bring your daughters into court to testify.'
My stomach churned at the prospect of the girls being dragged into this mess.
'This property is worth so much more than we paid for it... we've been

improving it, getting all the utilities in place over the last ten or so years....
And it has a lot of land.'
'Maybe we should get a valuation?' He said, 'Let's see what sort of figures we are talking about.'
'How much will that cost'?' I said, forever thinking of costs.
'I'll get a quote.' he muttered

The following week, I heard that a London based Estate Agent, with connections in the area, (what does that mean?) would be prepared to arrange a visit, to give a valuation for £500 + vat. Greg Midgley advised we should agree to this and reluctantly I gave the go ahead. About a month later, the valuation arrived in the post. I was completely thrown. The valuation was around the price we had paid ten years beforehand. I remonstrated with Greg on the phone.
'Who is this person?' 'They can have absolutely zilch local knowledge.' 'Ferme Thenon is unique because there is a dearth of similar properties for sale in this area.'
'On the surface it doesn't appear this is the case, but believe me, we explored so many farm houses for sale and with every one of them there are problems... such as... it may be jointly owned by a family and one brother doesn't want to sell...' 'Or there are legal disputes about the access... or someone else owns the land the house is built upon...' 'This person they employed hasn't done any research... this is rubbish.'
'Well on a positive note' he replied, 'Should Nat Selwyn get his third it won't be much, will it!
'How can you think like that?' I argued. 'Don't you see if his third isn't enough to repay the money my husband has borrowed, I will be asked to pay him the balance out of my third...!'
I could almost hear the cogs in his small brain, ticking over.
'Oh yes... see what you mean... mm.'
Eeeh Gods, they say pay peanuts and you get monkeys, but I am paying Tropical Rain Forests and I have an Orang-utan! (Sorry Orang-utans... no offence)
We have a second hearing scheduled for January, I can't change solicitors again.

I resolved to take things into my own hands, as I had done several times before in the last three years. I dug out my old notebooks from years ago to find my notes of some of the Estate agents in the area. Oh, for something called the internet…! Why I hadn't thought to instruct them to value it… I don't know. My mind was in overload, swimming with every nuance of the divorce, the issues with the girls coming into court, running a business, keeping my head above water… My French wasn't the greatest but with a crib sheet in front of me I talked to several agents. I put the phone on loud speaker so that Trish could take notes as well as help me when I struggled with vocabulary or even just understanding them. Oh, for Google translate….!

'Hello, my name is Alice Waite, I have a property in your area I wish to market'.
'Oh yes, where is it?'
'Just south of Thenon …in the valley… it's called Ferme Thenon.' 'Do you know it?'
'Oh yes, yes, it used to belong to the du Croix family.'
'Yes, that's right… it's has sixty hectares.'
'Well, I can view it tomorrow on my way into the office if you like…'
'What about getting a key?'
'Ah yes.' 'If you go to Café Feddon, you know in the Market Square?'
'Yes, yes I know it.'
'They have a key.' 'Madame Feddon's son has been doing some work on the house… I will let her know you are coming.'
'Right, I will get the key and call you back tomorrow.' 'My name is Bernard Correze by the way.'
'Thank you so much Mr Correze… look forward to hearing from you.'

Bernard Correze was particularly interested in marketing the property, within two weeks I received the sales particulars for Ferme Thenon. With his detailed local knowledge, the asking price was significantly higher than the valuation figure, and more in line with my thoughts. I knew this was risky, because if Nat Selwyn's stance about owning one third of the property, was somehow upheld in court, he would be a happy man, but at least I would have a significantly larger amount of this asset to go forward with. I didn't tell Midgley about any of this. My thinking was, let's see what happens. If there is a buyer, we can discuss it then. They say to be self- employed you must be a risk taker… It seems this is absolutely right!

Midgley was now preparing for the Second Hearing and suggested a meeting with my barrister, Margo Wilson the following week. I was shown into her office at St George's Chambers. A tea tray with pretty bone china cups arrived within no time at all. While we waited for Midgley, Margo and I talked about the untimely death of Mary Collins, but when we were about to embark on the second cup I said

'Can someone give Greg Midgley's office a call… just in case he's err, forgotten?'

A secretary was instructed and a few minutes later, advised us 'He's on his way.'

Knowing Garston and Welland's office was less than five minutes away and he was now twenty minutes late, I prickled.

In a few minutes, Midgley, with bundles of files under his arms blustered through the door.

'Apologies… so sorry I was delayed by a phone call.'

(We don't believe you Greg, you will be telling us it was The Lord Chief Justice next.)

At last, the meeting could get started. Margo requires sight of the valuation of Ferme Thenon, so Midgley tries to oblige but it seems necessary to re-file the bundles on his lap. Some loose paperwork fell to the floor, so he had to get on his hands and knees trying to recover everything from under his chair. Margo's antique desk is clearly off limits as a surface for filing, as it has a brass galley around the edge. We wait in an agonised silence for the right piece of paperwork to surface. A few minutes in, Margo Wilson pronounced

'You know, the way your husband has behaved, with fraud and now is trying to gain an extra third of Ferme Thenon for his cohort…' She paused 'I think you need a Rottweiler to cross question them in court…. And … well, I am not that person!'

You could have knocked me down with the proverbial feather.

I spoke before I had put my brain into gear.

'Don't desert me Margo…'

She must have seen the complete panic in my eyes. The thought of being in the hands of Midgley and Midgley alone filled me with horror.

'No, no' she said, 'I mean to pass you on to my colleague Hugo Steele QC…… that is if you agree?'

The words QC sounded grand but filled me with even more horror as I heard Kerching, kerching…ringing loudly in the background.

'Hugo, is so *terribly* experienced with this kind of thing and yes I could deal with your case, but the duplicitous and mendacious behaviour we are

Only cry on Fridays

dealing with here… well… requires someone with experience prosecuting people like this.' She said nervously.
Before I could say anything, she continued
'I have taken the liberty of speaking to Hugo about your case…. But of course, *you are* free to use a QC from another Chambers and I would happily furnish you with the names of people with similar experience.'
'No' I said, lamb to the slaughter, 'if you think Hugo Steele is our man, why not pass the files across?'
During all this exchange, Midgely hadn't uttered a word. His paper work now appeared to be in order, he looked up.
'Oh …Mr…. Steele' he said in awe.
Margo picked up her telephone to ask Hugo Steele to join us and requested more tea. Hugo bounced into Margo's office. Probably in his early fifties he was dapper in a well cut, dark navy-blue suit, greying in that distinguished way, with tortoise shell rimmed glasses on the end of his nose. I would just like to say that Midgley with beads of perspiration on his forehead and his crumpled suit, was also greying but in an extinguished kind of way.

Clearly, already well versed in my case, Hugo Steele set about asking lots of questions as well as giving instructions to Midgley.
'I will need this… I will need that.' 'Fax them through to me when you get back to the office.'
There was no lee way for Midgley to have the possibility another appointment when he returned to the office. This was going to happen on Steele's terms and not Midgley's. Similarly, I was given a list of documents to send across to the Chambers. In the big picture, I am grateful for Margo Wilson's candour and her suggestion that Hugo Steele QC was my best way forward. Not many professionals in a similar situation, would have had the integrity to admit the case was too complex for their experience. Steele discussed the Second Hearing and what to expect, giving Midgley very precise instructions on what to file. Midgley scribbled away as if his life depended on it. Then turning to me, Steele said,
'There's no need for me to be at the Second Hearing, this is just about disclosure and it will save you money.'
Delighted at the prospect of someone in the legal profession talking about saving me money, I marvelled at his confidence in Midgley and thought I must have misread the man. As Midgley and I walked down the stairs together, I sensed his nerves as I asked him if he had come across Hugo Steele in court before.

'Err… Yes', he said, 'He's very thorough, a man for detail you know' ….
'And Steele by name… Steely by nature is how I would sum him up.'
I surmised they had certainly met in court before, and probably not in the best circumstances.

As soon as I returned to the office, I set about the task of photocopying all my bank statements and numerous other documents Hugo had requested. He had also asked me to chase up the Pension's Ombudsman, who had, had the Determination of my case pending, for months and months. I spoke to a solicitor, Jenny Hale at the Ombudsman's office, who was aware of my case but said they were still waiting for responses from Pension and Mutual's Legal team. She promised to chase them up again, as they were nearing the time limit for a response. Over the next few months, we spoke on a regular basis. She was not only very professional, but also kind; and knew how important the Ombudsman's Determination was to my divorce proceedings. Meanwhile Hugo Steele was a hard task master. He was regularly on the phone asking for information, but I didn't mind in the least. He was on top of every detail and this gave me huge confidence. I worried about the costs accruing, but he seemed to be prepared to wait until the marital home was sold before he put in his invoice. Another task for me was to talk with the Estate Agent about the condition of The Rectory, with a view to Midgley writing a letter to get the property ship shape for a re-launch, next spring.

Chapter 27

New Year

Another Christmas at St Phillip's Square loomed. Please God let this be the last one here. A girl friend was staying with her son and daughter in law nearby for Christmas and asked if I would like to spend New Year at their home in Derbyshire.
'We could pick you up on the 28th and then drive up with us, we'd love to have you.' Jane said on the phone one evening.
Knowing they were big New Year people, I queried
'Are you having a party…or…?'
'No darling, just a quiet one this year, nothing planned.' 'Lionel's back is playing up and all that standing around won't do him any good.'
With a Second Hearing coming up in the New Year, I was not really feeling in a party mood, so the idea of a glass of champagne by the fireside, was appealing.
'Sounds great.' I said, 'I'll bring some bubbly and nice things to eat.'

Over the years, Jane had confided in me about her troubled marriage, but with no real career, she would be hard pushed to go it alone. Lionel was autocratic, bombastic and *always* right. He was an accountant, who could manage everyone's money, but his own. They had down sized several times to pay HMRC and other unspecified debts. Jane made no more than pin money as a teaching assistant at a local prep school, so had to refer to Lionel about literally any purchase for the house outside her remit. And the answer was always 'No.' She told me that once, his temper was so frayed, he grabbed her by the throat and nearly throttled her, as her grown up sons stood by, presumably too scared to challenge their father. I suspect there had been more of this behaviour, but she wasn't going to share it with me, because the first thing I said when she told me of the throttling incident was

'You have to get out.' 'You have to leave Jane.... His behaviour is outrageous... completely unacceptable.'
Jane could make excuses until the cows came home.
'I think I annoyed him.'
I'm sorry that's no excuse.... He could have killed you.'
'But, I think he's worried about the business....'
'So that makes this acceptable, does it?'

The incident was swept under the carpet, but I worried what life was really like on a day to day basis, especially now the boys had left home. Christmas came and went with all the usual difficulties of who was to be where and when, suffice to say we were getting used to it. Except this year, we were one down as Cesca, my youngest daughter, had deemed she was staying with her boyfriend's family.
Meantime, I was looking forward to my time in the Peak District and packed warm things for some bracing walks. Jane and Lionel, collected me late in the afternoon of the 29th, then we drove back to their house in Derbyshire. Sharing the back seat with Booty, the golden Labrador, I relaxed, as Lionel huffed and puffed at the traffic, until we were on empty country roads. On arrival, the house was cold, as Lionel had apparently insisted it was wasteful to leave the heating on, even low, over the period they were away.
'What about burst pipes?' I said
'Well there aren't any are there.' Mr Know-All quipped.
Duly the heating was clicked on low. Jane asked Lionel to light the fire, but looking at his watch (it was eight thirty) he deemed
'It's not worth it now.'
We ate our supper wearing extra layers, but my feet were like blocks of ice. The next day, with thoughts we might go for a good walk with Booty and maybe a pub lunch, Lionel announced he needed to go into the office for some reason, so that left Jane and I on our own. Great, I thought. But, Jane started thumbing through an Ikea catalogue and wondered if I could help her plan some storage under the open plan stair case. Honestly, I know I can draw up scale plans, (evening classes, years ago) but *pleeeese, please* just give me a break! Jane, we all know it's never going to happen. Lionel will just say *No* as usual.
For instance, I have lost track of the times I have been to a friend's house for supper, and like a lamb to the slaughter, pitched up all bright eyed and

bushy tailed with a bunch of flowers and a bottle, to be confronted with surveyor's plans for a kitchen extension and ...

'We were just wondering if you could…well look at these plans for us?'

So, back to the Ikea catalogue. A tape measure was produced along with an A4 pad, so I could plan the storage. Jane said she hoped Lionel would be back by lunch time with the Estate, so perhaps we could drive across this afternoon, to collect it all. The thought of a late afternoon, trawling Ikea, was not my idea of a break in the Peak district, but hey ho, I am certainly paying for my B& B. Mercifully, Lionel did not appear until nearly 5pm. Although he maintained he had been in the office all day, I could smell drink on his breath. Jane, still excited at the prospect of the trip to Ikea, asked for the keys to the estate.

'What for?' Lionel quizzed

Alice has worked out the storage I wanted…you know for under the stairs, so we were going to Ikea to pick it up.'

'IKEA!' He stormed 'you are bloody joking Jane, tell me you *are* joking?'

Jane, embarrassed at Lionel's tone, blustered

'This is a good time, around now, it will be quiet while people are getting meals…' she tapered off

'And, don't we get a meal Jane?'

'Ahh' she said, 'I thought we could get a take out tonight.'

'I don't want a bloody take out' he yelled 'I've been at work all day.'

(Yes right, I thought, more like the pub…)

'So, what *are* we having tonight?' He boomed

Job done! Lionel's rules must be obeyed. Jane, flushed, walked into the kitchen to stare at an empty fridge. She did seem disorganised on the meals front.

'I have a casserole in the freezer' she said and err……'

Her voice was drowned out as Lionel hit the remote and the television boomed into life. So, while I was spared a trip to Ikea, I had to witness Lionel's abusive behaviour towards Jane. I know she was embarrassed and if anything brought up short, because someone else had observed her day to day life with Lionel. This was her norm. Only when she saw the look on my face, as Lionel boomed his instructions to her, did she notice his attitude towards her, wasn't reasonable behaviour.

We ate, with me providing most of the conversation. Jane looked crestfallen, her spirit was broken. All she wanted to do for heaven's sake, was to buy a

Alice Waite

couple of Billy bookcases, so she could neatly organise her sewing things, as in this last down size, she had lost her built in storage cupboards.

The following day, we walked Booty in nearby fields, picked up some groceries and headed back to prepare some lunch. Jane took a phone call and rather strangely I thought wandered upstairs to continue the conversation. I could hear every syllable of the call, as she stood on the landing.
''Yes, yes, looking forward to it' 'Can we bring anything?' ……..
'No problem, we've got plenty of glasses, what about plates?'
'Great! Disposable are the way forward … I agree.' 'But look… err… we've got someone staying with us now ……And err … I wondered if…'
'Oh, I see… … yes, yes, I do understand, our dining table is the same, even with the extension leaves….'….. 'Yes, it's going to be fun and of course we will bring bubbly and some wine….' 'OK …of course, yes, bye now.'
Jane came down the stairs, our eyes met as I looked up from my magazine. I waited for her to say something, but instead she bustled into the kitchen, throwing on her apron, she started peeling carrots to make soup.
'Jane?' I said
She didn't turn around, but just muttered 'Yes.'
'Jane is there a problem?' ' I couldn't help overhearing…'
She turned, her face was flushed.
'It's just that, well …we have been invited to friends for New Year…. and err… I thought you would be able to join us…. but, well…'
'I think I've got the picture.' I said 'But I don't understand… I asked you…. I *know* I asked you, if you had plans for New Year's Eve and you said no… something about Lionel's back and standing and…'
Jane cut in 'I know…. err, this is such a muddle… I didn't know this do was… a sit down do… I…' 'But look, we will back not long after midnight and I will make sure there is bubbly for you and some nice food of course.'
'So, you *will* be going…?' I said
'The trouble is' she said not looking at me 'the trouble is, these people… they're business friends of Lionel's and …. well it would be difficult to pull out now.'
'So how did you think this was going to work Jane?'
'I'm sorry… I should have checked on the arrangements ages ago… I meant to, but….'
She started chopping furiously as I walked away to call National Rail on

my mobile. I would have loved to have just left there and then, but there were no direct trains, until the following morning.
'You really don't have to leave' she said when I had finished my call.
A few years ago, I would have been the person who would have tried to smooth the waters with … *don't worry... these things happen... no problem... You go along, I'll just get an early night...* But fast forward to a new assertive me, who has had to learn to fight her corner, speak out when something is wrong and had ensured absolute clarity about New Year's Eve, before accepting the invitation.
'But Jane' I reiterated 'I asked you specifically about your plans for tonight...'
'Do you really think it is OK to stay in on my own with a bottle of bubbly on New Year's Eve when the plan was to have some company?'
Inexplicably, she blurted out 'But you won't be on your own …!' 'Booty will be here!'

I turned to go upstairs.
She called after me 'Don't be like that Alice.'
Tears prickling my eyes, I packed most of my things into the case. How has this happened? Jane hadn't really answered my questions, she was in denial about the whole situation, but it didn't really matter now. We are where we are, as they say. Could I blame Lionel? I wanted to. Jane was browbeaten for sure and it seemed she had let this arrangement happen, then drift, not wanting to confront the practicalities. With the Second Hearing in less than two weeks, I was feeling vulnerable and fragile. Even though Jane knew every nuance of my predicament via her weekly update, it seemed she had no comprehension of the emotional turmoil I was in. I needed solid support, not the anxiety of feeling surplus to requirements, the inconvenient guest.

Jane and I had known each other since our children were young and even though we had moved to opposite ends of the country, kept in touch by phone on a regular basis. Our calls could easily last an hour catching up with each other's news, although Jane would often cut a call short, because 'I've just seen Lionel's car pull up... must get on'
If, mid flow I had continued chatting away, I would hear Lionel in the background booming,
'On that bloody phone again...!'
Apologising Jane would swiftly bring the call to a halt
'Sorry... sorry... must go now Alice, catch up soon...'

Other times if she stuck it out, Lionel would start talking to her, asking questions which most definitely, in his book required immediate answers.
'Where are my glasses?' ......'*I said* Jane... where are my bloody glasses?'
Then, right next to the handset he boomed
'My glasses... where are they, woman?'
Thus, our phone call would be quickly curtailed until another time. Here was Lionel controlling Jane's social exchanges, his needs and rights paramount to hers. By truncating her phone calls, constantly displaying irritation when he was not given 100% attention, she was intimidated into furtive calls when he was out or cutting a call short, when she saw him return. So long as Lionel was in charge, Jane's social interaction became limited by intimidation. When we lived nearer each other, she was always concerned about getting home before he did.
'He likes to see the lights on .... You know... when he pulls into the drive.'
'Can't you leave them on when you go out?' I would ask.
'Well... he'll go mad if I have left the lights on when I'm not there...' she responded rather meekly. In short it was better if Lionel wasn't aware she had been out, unless necessary.

I have also known difficulties with telephone calls. For instance, Steve would come to sit in the same room when he knew I was making a call to a girlfriend. Pretending to read a newspaper, there would be clucking and sighing as he listened to my side of the exchange. It made me feel uncomfortable and self- conscious with someone listening in to our female chatter. Having someone eves dropping on my phone calls had the same effect as Jane with Lionel, and I would cut the conversation short.
Steve's office shared with our part time PA was in the Coach House across the driveway. I had gained a false sense of phone security when he was over there, happily breaking up my day with the odd social call to my girlfriends, at the same time as keeping an eye on the drive, to ensure he was out of the way. One day when the girls were at home on holiday, I heard giggling from Hettie's bedroom. The door was open, so I walked in to find all three of them around her radio. I could hear the voice of Irene our PA chatting away to Emily her daughter, emanating from the speakers.
'What on earth?' I said
'Mum... it's Irene....' Cesca laughed
'Well I can hear that.' I said fascinated 'How on earth...?'
'Sssh! Listen to Emily she's got a new boyfriend...'
Quickly gathering my sense of scruples, I insisted the radio was turned

off, whereupon they explained they often listened in to Irene when they were at home.

'How? I don't understand.' I said

'Easy peasy Mum....cordless phones transmit using FM.... so we just tune into FM radio, twiddle around a bit and BINGO!'

Intrigued and horrified at the same time, the penny started to drop. There had been the odd instance when Steve had said something and as ever, questioning my own recollection of events, thought well, I must have told him about that. And of course, if I had queried how he knew, he would insist I *had* told him and to get a grip.

'Your memory these days... It's worrying Alice.'

So, when I thought Steve was safely in another part of the house or in his office allowing me to have private conversations, in fact he could police my social calls. I shuddered at what I might have said about him to my girlfriends. Anxiously trying to recall conversations, worried as to how he might react if he had heard my true feelings. After that, I would only make calls when he was out. As soon as reasonably priced mobile phones became available I signed up for one. They were as heavy as bricks and with a limited battery life, but I didn't care.

Jane, now clearly trying to make amends for the predicament she had placed herself in, suggested we drive to Buxton to have a look around. The rest of the afternoon was filled with stilted conversation as we wandered through Buxton, pressing our noses against the windows of shops, most of which remained closed between Christmas and New Year. After supper, I made my excuses, taking myself off for a bath and an early night. In the morning, I rung for a taxi thinking my departure would be easier this way. When the cab beeped outside, Jane said

'Why have you called a cab'...? 'I was going to take you to the station....'

'No worries Jane.' I said picking up my case.

'Here, she said, running from the kitchen… your Champagne!'

Wearily I said 'Jane, I don't want to carry that on the train… you enjoy it.' We both had tears in our eyes as we hugged goodbye. I felt so low, this whole episode had been a disaster. I was cross with Jane for being Lionel's doormat, putting up with his behaviour, cow towing to his every need and by the look of it, letting him arrange New Year's Eve. Jane had been an exemplary wife and mother, but as is usual in those circumstances, when the children have flown the nest, women like Jane, find themselves economically disadvantaged. Her *little job* as Lionel liked to put it, wouldn't keep a flea in groceries. They have no power, no up to date skills for the marketplace and lack confidence outside the home. Leaving an abusive marriage takes so much more courage than any professional woman with earning capacity will ever know. I heard someone from a Women's Refuge comment once, that the women who walk out of an abusive relationship, with their kids and only the family allowance book to their name, are beyond brave.

If there's one thing I hope I have instilled into my girls, is that marriage is not a meal ticket for life. They must have their own bank account and career, no matter how hard it is to juggle childcare. Even if initially the cost of childcare breaks even with their salary, it means they keep abreast in their profession. They do not have to start again on the bottom rung of the ladder and more importantly they have choices.

A few hours later, I was carrying my suitcase up the stairs to my flat. By now it was 3pm. Waitrose was closing in an hour, so I raced around the corner to find some food for the next couple of days. The fresh veg shelves looked like there was a siege I wasn't aware of. Bits of cauliflower stalk, sad bags of salad right on their sell by date, were all that was on offer, bar apples and oranges. The chill cabinets weren't much different apart from Cheddar. All the usual lovely cheeses had disappeared. I bought a few things from the freezer section, some wine and made my way to the check out. The whole place was like the Marie Celeste.

That night, from my bed I heard fireworks zooming and crackling in the sky. I looked at my alarm clock, it was indeed midnight. Please God, let next year see an end to this hideous business.
Jane phoned about a week later asking *if I was alright?*
'It's just that I haven't heard from you......'
I told her I was wrapped up in the Second Hearing, which was true. I know she wanted to hear the next episode, but I wasn't going to enlighten her. She didn't call to wish me luck or indeed for a further episode in the whole ghastly saga.

Chapter 28

Second Hearing

Annie has offered to accompany me to the Second Hearing. After long discussions, we decide to take the train and get a taxi at the other end, rather then risk the whole ring road, multiple roundabout, nightmare. We deem this will be more relaxing, so agree to meet at The Green Man, ten minutes walk from the station, for an early bite of lunch.
Annie, looks slick and smart in her black designer suit, sporting an enormous brooch, more like a piece of sculpture, on the lapel. I wear my Margaret Howell double breasted pin stripe suit with a pretty, linen voile scarf, to soften the look, and of course we are both in heels. The Green Man is a favourite Gastro pub, warm and welcoming, always with fresh flowers on the table. We have spent many happy evenings here, celebrating birthdays and the like. Today, looking out onto a winter garden, with the first snowdrops in view, I am not in a party kind of mood. Instead, I feel like I am having an out of body experience. I can see all the chairs and tables, the fireplace, Jim at the bar, but I am floating above. I can see into the adjoining room the tables now facing each other, with a bad-tempered judge at the top table. There are no flowers on these tables, just bundles of files. Greg Midgley is as ever, refilling his bundles.
Nervously, I check my watch. What if the train is late? What if the train is cancelled? Why on earth would we go on the train…? Annie clicks her fingers in front of my eyes. Startled, tears roll down my cheeks.
'Hey sweetheart, I didn't mean to make you jump' she says, 'You were miles away!'
Annie didn't know, clicking fingers in front of my eyes was something he used to do,
when I had shut down, gone to another place, peaceful and without stress. The disconcerting, hard clicking of fingers, right in front of my eyes, was an artless rebuke, like a bludgeon to intercept any fleeting moments of peace I might have surreptitiously stolen. He couldn't bear not to be in

control of everything, even my mind. I once heard Joss Stone sing *'I gave you my heart, you wanted my mind... your love is the choking kind.'* Whoever wrote those lines had been in the same place. How could I love and hate someone at the same time?

Annie persuaded me to choose from the menu, which I did to oblige her, but honestly, felt sick with nerves. I console myself *this* hearing can't go as badly as the last one, after all Hugo Steele seems to have licked Midgley into shape with his endless *to do* lists, but I have learned to expect nothing from Legals.

Our food arrives. I try to eat my Spinach and Squash tart but fail miserably. To ensure clear heads, we stick to sparkling water, which doesn't exactly fill us with joie de vivre. I know my face, tells it all. I have been in this Lion's den before, I have no illusions. Prior to the First Hearing, I was full of confidence. As far as I was concerned our case was strong. We had evidence to prove fraud, but sadly Mary was struck dumb and well, just failed to mention it. I check my watch again. Annie looked across at me 'It's ten minutes later than the last time you checked' she says. 'Keep calm, I'm on the case. Calm girl!' 'We've plenty of time before we have to leave.' Voicing my concerns about the trains running late or heaven forbid being cancelled. Annie reached across the table to squeeze my hand.
'Look here, remember all that's in the plan.' 'Even catching the train, we decided upon, we will be a good hour or so, early and worst-case scenario... *every* train is cancelled...we get a taxi.'
After a double espresso I make for the cloakroom. Checking my face in the mirror, I despair. Who is this tired fifty-six-year-old woman? How did she get here? The Touché Éclat protests...'Honey I can't work miracles!'
We walk to the station. Yes, we forgot about that *only ten minutes walk to the station,* in heels.... At least we can sit on the train, then a taxi. But no, we can't. The train is rammed, so we stand most of the way. There is a queue for the taxis, but we are still in plenty of time when our cab pulls up outside that familiar, grey concrete, brutal accolade to the sixties, called The Crown Court.

My heart thumps, I swallow hard. My tummy churns. I know where the lifts are, the floor we require, how to check in with the man at the door... I survey the ghastly waiting area. We are early, very early so there is no sign of Greg Midgley or indeed the other side. As per The First Hearing, they have probably booked another private room. Oh, to be on Legal Aid…! Annie chats away, which keeps me sane, until Midgley appears with his trolley of documents. He comes straight over, and I introduce him to Annie. Immediately he starts rummaging in his filing system like a dog after a bone. He smells of ciggies and is already perspiring. His court suit seems to be his every day office suit, probably his only suit, looking at the state of it, I think he may even sleep in it. Annie and I are cat walk models besides this car crash of couture. I watch him continue to dig for the bone, I dare not ask just what it is, he is so keen to find it, I just want to see his tail wag, so I know he has found …. whatever it is. Please God, let this rummaging be his way of dealing with nerves, but why should he be nervous, surely, he's been here a thousand times before? Suddenly, I hear our names being called. Annie gives me a strong hug and says to Midgley, 'Just look after her, will you?'

He smiles nervously 'I'll do my best.'

We walk down the corridor to Court Room three. We are followed by the other side that yet again, have appeared out of their rabbit hole. I am sure everyone can hear my heart thumping like a drum, as I take the seat, Midgley indicates, which just as before, is opposite my husband. My mouth is dry, the kind of dryness experienced after an anaesthetic, where saliva is missing and the tongue sticks to every surface. Annie has put a bottle of water in my bag and although luke warm I am immensely grateful.

We start. The other side lead the proceedings, demanding this, remonstrating about that. Midgley stands to add his ten penth worth. At least his voice is not quaking like Mary's had been, God rest her soul. Immaculate in navy suits and Gittanne blue shirts, *they* demand I am still responsible for half the mortgage payments. Crumpled and perspiring, *we* point out the house won't sell while it is in such an unkempt state. There are arguments about, how I should pay his tax, share the profits of my business.

We point out that the partnership has been dissolved. They demand to see documentary proof. Midgley's filing system fails to find it.

The judge is *not* happy. The documents must be filed by the end of the day. *They* demand they are owed half the value of my business. *We* say we have had an independent valuation, which says the business relies solely on me and is therefore worthless to any buyer. Midgley's filing system fails to find it. The judge is *not* happy. The documents must be filed by the end of the day. *We* say there has been pension fraud. At last, we can produce something from Midgley's chaotic filing, now in bundles around Midgley's feet. *They* say, the fact our pension property was sold on, ten days after the original sale, is just a coincidence. The judge asks for the land registry documents to show the sale dates.

Midgley doesn't even look in his bundles. He apologies to the judge and says they will be filed into court by the end of the day. The judge is not happy. A plop of perspiration from Midgley's forehead drops onto the paperwork in front of him. His hands are so sweaty he can flick through his documents without having to lick his fingers. (Oh joy)! He produces the affidavit confirming the transcript of Nadia's recording. *They* say recordings are inadmissible. *We* say *we* will subpoena Damien Humphries into court to verify. The judge confirms this is possible.

The judge sums up. He is clearly irritated by Midgley's inefficiency.

He has neglected to produce three important documents. The Navy suits smirk. Why didn't Midgley check Hugo Steele's to do list? It's not that difficult. Read the list, find the document, tick. The Judge reiterates his requirements. He looks at Midgley as if he's something unsavoury, stuck to his shoe. Then, he wants clarification on the whole Pension issue. The judge stands. We all stand. The Judge leaves the court. The smart Navy suits representing *him* are putting their documents away. The perspiring crumpled person who is representing *me* is scrabbling on the floor collecting up his bundles.

The navy suits have gone. Five minutes later, at last, we are on our feet pulling the filing system of sorts along behind us.

Annie is on her feet to greet us at the end of the corridor.

'I thought they had locked you up!' She said

'No' I said' we were just delayed with…. *A packing issue*'

Annie's face looked quizzical.

'I'll explain over a glass of wine.' I said

Greg Midgley's face lit up. Did he really think I was so pleased with his presence in court, I was inviting him for a glass of wine?

'Greg what happened to the documents Hugo Steele listed you should bring?'

As we walked towards the lifts, he muttered something about 'No problem I am going back to the office to file them now.'

'But why weren't they here… in court?' I remonstrated 'We looked idiots.'

Only cry on Fridays

The lift doors opened to a reveal sea of faces all ready to go home. Someone said
'Just room for one more!'
Midgley seized his chance and ramming a few knees with his filing trolley, barged across the threshold into the lift. As the doors were closing he was heard to say
'Must get back to the office to file those doc…….'
Mercifully, for him, the lift doors closed on the crumpled suit and his woefully inadequate filing system.

Annie and I wandered further down the road to Hotel du Vin. We made straight for the bar. Plonking ourselves down in some ancient leather armchairs was the signal for the young man behind the bar to be at our sides with a drinks list. We ordered large glasses of ice cold Sauvignon, slid our feet out of those heels and took a deep breath. Annie had held her soul in patience long enough.
'I want to hear all about it.' 'What's this about having to file documents now?'
Our wine arrived, and I gave her a full debrief. She was as concerned as I was, about Midgley's shambolic performance.
'At least he spoke.' I said, feeling the tension melting away with every sip of wine.
'Eeeh Gods!' Annie said, 'Now you are grateful your solicitor actually spoke in court….' 'Unbelievable!'
'I know, but last time, at the First Hearing, Mary Collins….'
'The one who died?' Annie interjected.
'Yes, the one who died… well she was so nervous she was quaking, her voice was small and wobbly… Annie *that* performance was dire.'
'So Midgley's was an improvement?'
'Well let's put it like this… Mary would have got zero out of ten if she had put in that performance at Court School!'
Annie laughed 'Do they even have Court School?'
'I've no idea.' I said, 'But she would have zero and a detention' …!
'And Midgley?' She cut in
'Well maybe one point five out of ten!' 'And a detention!'
'Plus, lines' said Annie getting into the mood.
'Yes' …'. I must be mo….re…. orjernised' 'I mu…ssst… priss my suit!'
The empty glasses were responsible for Midgley's punishments becoming

more draconian by the minute. We ordered refills and talked until we could smell wafts of cooking from the adjacent restaurant.

'Come on, we are going to eat... 'I said 'Let's see if they have a table… my treat.'

Chapter 29

Life continues

Hugo Steele telephoned for more information, this time about credit cards. He can't see a payment leaving the bank for an amount paid on my Barclaycard.
'How was this large payment made?' He queried
Pulling out my file of statements I can see my notes written against the statement he is concerned about. With relief I can clarify.
'Ah yes… this is when I went on holiday with four girl friends.' 'I paid for the villa and the car hire on my card….' 'So …. Instead of getting everyone to make their cheques out to me, which would take time to clear through the bank, I asked everyone to write their cheques to Barclaycard and well… I just sent the payment due, that way.' 'That's OK, isn't it?' 'I can get everyone to write to verify this, if you would like'
'I see' Hugo replied, 'I don't think verification will be necessary at this stage.'
He was over every detail, and I was thrilled by his efficiency. When I went to his chambers, he would walk in, laptop under his arm, followed by minions carrying numerous lever arch files. They were well drilled and knew exactly in which order to place them along the conference table. I wished Greg Midgley could have witnessed this feat of organisation. He was allowed to join us for some of our sessions, but, more often than not, Hugo would fax him a *to do* list.
We could be in the depths of discussion, when Hugo would reach for a file, find the correct tab, ask a question, and make notes, before placing the bulging file back in position on the table. Never once, did I see him open his laptop. It seemed to me, that as a man of a certain age, he probably hadn't a clue what to do with it, if he had switched it on. I think it accompanied him, more as a trophy, a symbol that he was in this new world of gleaming silver, information technology.

Meanwhile, work hummed along. The bank increased my overdraft, which helped me through the lean summer months. I expanded the courses to include a module on garden photography, involving some nearby National Trust properties. The garden photography courses were a moderate success, but in the meantime the Media and Photography modules, went from strength to strength.

One afternoon, the French estate agent, Bernard Correze came on the telephone, or rather his English speaking, secretary did. There was interest in Ferme Thenon and they required sight of the plans showing the boundary of the land. Fortunately, I had taken copies of all the documents in our possession, as well as the details of the Notaries who dealt with the sale. The details were faxed through, while Trish photocopied the plans, posting them express that night. Within a few days, I had a firm offer, a little below the asking price. Ever the risk taker, I said I would only accept the asking price. I knew, even if smart London Estate agents didn't, the real value of our property. The following afternoon, the offer was improved to the asking price. The couple who wanted to buy Ferme Thenon were American, working at a Paris university. This was to be their summer bolt hole and a project for their eventual retirement. Now I had to tell Greg Midgley what I had done, so he could advise the other side.

'Greg, I have had an offer for the French property.'
'How...?' 'I didn't know it was on the market' he blustered.
'Ah well, I just put it with an agent to see what would happen'.... 'And guess what they are offering what I said it was worth!'
'Oh, my word' he said.... 'Well, this changes so much... I must let your husband's solicitor know.'
'I'll phone Hugo Steele' I said, 'In fact why don't you, in case he's got an opinion as to how we proceed, especially with the Nat Selwyn involvement.'
'Will do' he said nervously
I put the phone down, wondering if he felt comfortable telephoning Steele and indeed was up to speed with his to do list.

As spring turned to summer, the rat problem in the building was getting worse. We had been supplied with poison by environmental health. Little blue pellets in a red tray. Every day, as soon as I stepped into the entrance hall, I walked over to inspect the tray neatly concealed under a storage heater. Today there were little blue pellets all around the floor. Someone (and possibly friends and family) had been up for a midnight feast.

Only cry on Fridays

Walking towards the kitchen, I spotted sawdust and bits of wood on the floor. To my horror, I then saw a hole at the base of the wooden boxing, I had thought was neatly concealing a metal soil pipe. To think, I had been bravely banging this boxing, believing ratty was in a metal pipe within, when all along, he was but a whisker away. The hole was clearly the result of gnawing. Quickly scanning the floors for droppings or worse, from any revellers from the night before, I cleared up the mess and wedged a tray against the hole. As far as defences were concerned this was a bit of a joke, but at least the tray, looking casually placed, hiding the damage from the students, due in at any moment.

I enlisted the help of Dennis, our handyman, who agreed to come in at 4.30pm when the coast was clear. At 4.30pm bags of cement, wire netting and other unspecified defences were dragged into the entrance hall. Dennis, always relishing a challenge, decided the wooden floor next to the chewed boxing, must be removed to see what was happening underneath. A strong, stocky man, he now had new young assistant, Calvin, who looked like he had never seen a green vegetable in his life. Tea and copious biscuits were proffered as soon they came through the door. I've learnt over the years to get the best out from workmen, nothing does the trick better than mugs of tea and a generous supply of biscuits. As soon as they levered the boards away, Dennis could be heard sucking through his teeth.
'Wow!' He said, 'Wow come and look here Cal.'
Calvin duly knelt down to examine the space below the boards.
'It stinks!' Calvin told the world in no uncertain terms.
Rushing down the stairs I said
'What's there…. what!'
'A load of rat's droppings for a start.'
Dennis pontificated, hands on hips.
'And what's more…' he said shining the beam of his torch into the recesses
'It's a proper run … you can see the entrance holes… you know tunnels.'
'What do we do?' I asked in panic.
Dennis was on the case.
'Cal, start mixing the cement' instructed Dennis with urgency.
Calvin, now experiencing the sugar rush from a plateful of Jammy Dodgers set to with buckets of water, and the cement mix.
Dennis decided 'To be belt and braces… we're going to reinforce the concrete with wire netting.' He said, rolling the netting out on the floor.
In an hour or so they were finished, including neatly patching up the

gnawed hole, as well as re-laying the floor boards. Job done! Thank you, Dennis and Calvin. If only that was the end of it.

Two days later there were a few blue bottles circulating. A few days further on, it was in fact a Saturday, I opened the front door to a cloud of blue bottles. I knew I had to find the body. I had come into the office because I had work to do, but this situation was one I couldn't ignore. I started moving furniture, but to no avail. I sprayed fly killer around, until the floor looked like I had spilt a bag of raisins. Near the ground floor studio there was a trolley of books waiting to be returned to the shelves. Casually moving it to one side, I saw a sight that still haunts me today. There lay the source of the flies. Lunch alert… if you are about to eat, you might want to skip to the next page.

There was a badly decomposed body of a large rat, hardly visible because it was covered in writhing maggots and more flies ready to leave home. Moving away quickly, I wretched. I just knew I couldn't deal with it. Standing there on my own I had to get some help. I ran upstairs to the office to call Environmental Health's Emergency line.

'You are through to Environmental Health Emergency line' 'My name is Karen; how may I help?'

'Yes, hello' I said, 'Err… Your department came a couple of weeks ago, with trays of rat poison… you know the red trays with blue pellets?'

'Yes….' Karen replied hesitantly.

'Well some of the poison was eaten and now…'

Karen cut in 'We don't remove bodies, Madam!'

'Oh' I replied rather weakly 'Is there no help… I mean this body is decomposing and…. maggots and….'

Karen reverted back to her script 'We *don't* remove bodies Madam.'

Now, I'm sure Karen, you would rather be at home potting your Begonias on a Saturday morning, not dealing with woman discussing decomposing bodies of rats, but you could just show a little empathy.

Instead she said, 'is there anything else I can help you with Madam?'

'Well if you can't help with the ……'

'Thank you for calling Environmental Health Emergency line.'

Click, the line purred. Karen was gone.

What to do? The students would be back on Monday morning, I had to deal with this body. I knew it wasn't a case of just picking it up…. Another lunch alert… Excuse me if you *are* eating, but the only way to describe

what was required is.... scraping up the body with all the maggots still enjoying the feast. Sorry, this still makes me wretch, even now. Standing there staring into space, I caught sight of a postcard from a friend on my pin board. It was a black and white pen drawing of a Corinthian Capital. Beside it she had written,
'I saw this card and thought of you'
Someone strong, ordered, and withstanding the chaos around them.
Such an up lift! Thank you, Ellie. Never underestimate how helpful a few kind words to a friend in need of support, can be. Go on, you know someone who is having a tough time, send a post card (not a lazy email) so she can keep it in her bag or prop up in the kitchen, to read and re-read again. As I came back down the stairs from the office, I didn't feel particularly strong or able to cope with the chaos of Ratty's demise. Not only could I now smell Ratty, but another wave of maggots had hatched and had taken to the air.

Now, I don't do damsel mode. These days I am apparently a strong, capable woman. But in the past, I have not been so strong, dealing with a vortex of emotions and living in a twisted, controlling environment, where I have questioned my own instincts. I even created reasons for not leaving, which served to keep me prisoner longer, but when there was nothing left to cushion me from the reality of my situation, I knew there was no choice. So much has happened to me since I left and if I could have passed all those problems over to a (*capable*) solicitor, I would have jumped at the chance. However, because I had to take the reigns, dealing with every nuance of this car crash of a divorce, I *have* become a stronger woman, competent enough to deal with everything from Pension Fraud, to third party claims against our property in France. Sadly, these experiences have not made me strong enough to deal with Ratty.
I wandered around with more fly spay, as if the action would make the body evaporate. The smell of the spray was becoming overbearing, so I opened the front door to let some air in. As I did so, Guy from the office next door, wandered across the forecourt, keys in hand. He saw the flies making a dozy escape and I think he also saw the look of panic on my face.
'Everything alright Alice?'
Damsel mode kicked in. 'No not really.' I said in a small voice.
'What's up?'
'Well.... There's a dead rat and ... it's just awful... "I can't ...'

Guy cut in 'Come on let's have a look.' He said, as he made his way towards the front door.

'It's pretty grim' I said in an apologetic voice.

Surveying the problem, he said in quite a matter of fact way,

'Our dog Ludo, he's a Jack Russell… brings them in all the time…' 'Have you got some rubber gloves, you don't mind losing and a bin bag and…'

'Would you?' I heard the grateful damsel mutter.

'No problem' Guy dropped his jacket on the bench and rolled up his sleeves.

I went into the kitchen for rubber gloves, bin bags and the dustpan. I certainly didn't mind anything being consigned to the bin. I didn't care if the rubber gloves were made by Armani if someone was going to be kind enough to deal with this for me.

Guy set to work. There was a lot of scraping until finally the body, gloves and dustpan were consigned to double bin bags. I was ready with a bucket of heavily disinfected water, more rubber gloves and now the brush belonging to the binned dustpan, to scrub away until there was no sign of Ratty's passing. Rushing to the cupboard where we kept spare bottles of wine from Reader's evenings, I thanked Guy profusely, sending him off on his Saturday morning business with a couple of bottles under his arm. I was going to leave the front door open, to clear the air, but Guy popped his head round to say, I should keep it closed, as he had seen friends of Ratty on the forecourt before now.

Commenting 'Well you wouldn't want to invite them in, would you?'

Oh heavens. They were coming up through the floor, up the loo, and now Guy tells me they could be brazen enough to use the front door. Two hours had passed since I arrived to produce some visuals. It was time to get to the drawing board.

Chapter 30

The Determination

Alarmingly, we have reached mid- summer. After a busy term, the studios, now devoid of students, allow me a peaceful respite to collect myself. Greg Midgley tells me, he has just telephoned my husband's solicitor, Mark Kenny to advise, we have had an offer on Ferme Thenon. It seems that Kenny has a meeting planned with my husband for this afternoon, so they will be able to discuss the way forward then. Midgley, apparently has been assertive, rather proudly telling me, he has made it clear to Mark Kenny; the sale *must* go through. The proceeds of the sale will be allocated to a client's account, until such time, Nat Selwyn can produce evidence, he owns one third of Ferme Thenon. I know these are instructions from Hugo Steele, but nevertheless I am pleased Midgley has at last grasped the nettle and started working for me.

That afternoon, I was walking into town to collect some printing, when I saw a dark grey Passat driving towards me. I knew immediately. I knew without doubt, when it started to reduce speed and I knew with all certainty, when the window wound down. I also knew, I had to keep walking, eyes straight ahead, head held high, shoulders back, tummy in. I saw him lean out of the window but kept walking. Mercifully the traffic behind him meant he had to drive on, but I was nervous he would either turn around or indeed be waiting for me back at the studios. He was on the road home, so must have been to see Mark Kenny and therefore will have had the news about the buyers for Ferme Thenon. He will be *so* angry and spitting tacks, he hasn't been consulted. He will be furious I have found a buyer, proving his self- serving, derisory valuation completely wrong. (yes, I know too many adjectives, bear with me dear reader, but why use one when two will hit the spot?) Inside I was smiling. Something was going my way for once. I had proved the upmarket London estate agent's valuation to be wrong. I had proved my husband's valuation to be wrong.

Alice Waite

Midgley was at last, taking notice of what I knew to be true. When I had disputed the valuation figures, he simply shrugged his shoulders, pointing out, the smart London Estate agent's valuation was in line with the figure my husband was purporting. Also, he never actually said, he didn't believe me, when I told him, I knew nothing of Nat Selwyn's alleged share in our property, he simply didn't comment. Slowly the scales were lifting from his eyes and under Hugo Steele's tutelage, he had become more assertive when dealing with the super slick Mark Kenny.

Hugo Steele asked me to pressurise the Pension Service's Ombudsman for his determination, so I telephoned Jenny Hale again.
'We've had a response from Pension & Mutual' she said, 'And the Ombudsman is considering *his* response.' 'I hope it won't be too long now, my dear.' 'I know you have waited such a long time and how important this is to you.'
'Thank you, Jenny,' (we were on first name terms, by now)' I really appreciate your help.'
'How long can this take?' I sigh, after I had put down the phone.
Trish, supportive as ever, put a mug of Earl Grey in front of me.
'Thanks Trish, you are a darling.'

With very few hitches, the sale of Ferme Thenon went through, and the funds were deposited with Garston and Welland in a client's account. However, there hadn't been a single offer on The Rectory. The agents tell me the drive is overgrown with weeds, paint is peeling on the window frames and the interior is a disaster. Viewers are unable to gain access to the Study because it is still rammed with boxes.
'Boxes of what?' I demand
'I'm sorry, I really don't know.' Mary from the estate agents is embarrassed. She clearly doesn't want to get involved in any marital dispute but hints they may take the property off their books if things don't improve. The deterioration of our home is only to his advantage. He can sit in his castle, it seems indefinitely. The price has been reduced several times but there are no takers for a house in need of so much tlc. I feel completely impotent. If only I could reclaim this old friend, make it spick and span, smelling of polish, with bunches of flowers everywhere, to convey this house is loved. The trouble is, I had long fallen out of love with The Rectory, it held too many sad memories and the only flowers that ever came into the house, were those I had extravagantly bought myself. There would always be a

reckoning, when I came back from the supermarket, having added flowers to the tab. But somehow, I didn't care; they lifted my spirits and gave me so much pleasure. He just didn't *do flowers* as he would say (unless they were free, that is, from the garden). So, Wedding Anniversaries, Birthdays and Valentine's Day usually went unmarked, certainly with flowers.

One Valentine's Day, I had made the effort as usual. His favourite chocolate covered cherries and a lovely card. I can hear you saying, *but why?* The ridiculous thing is, for some reason, we keep trying, reaching out in the face of rejection. There is some crazy, non sensical hope, that suddenly he will change. He will love me, if I do this for him. It will all be just like it was years ago. So, at breakfast I produced the chocolates and card. He produced nothing, other than embarrassed vitriol that brought tears to my eyes.
'Stupid over commercialised guff...!' he ranted.
That day I had a meeting in London and then I was seeing a girlfriend for a late lunch. I gathered my things, drove to the station, tears in my eyes, tail between my legs. My heart was heavy, but I must put on a brave face for my meeting. Inside I am shot to ribbons. I resolve not to buy him anything, ever, again and therefore I cannot be upset when he does not reciprocate.

After my meeting I head to meet Lisa at Harvey Nichol's fifth floor cafe. We've known each other for such a long time, more than twenty years, but only manage to meet about twice a year. She is waiting for me, gazing at the menu.
'Hey!' She says standing up.
We give each other big hugs and sit down.
'You look great.' I say, 'Love the jacket.'
'How are you?' She enquires.
We compare notes for a few minutes then order our lunch. Two healthy super food salads, but we succumb to a bowl of hand cut chips between us. Lisa is divorced but couple of years ago met John, a pharmacist at Tango classes. She tells me he is lovely, and things are going well. Tentatively, she asks me how things are at home.
'Well, you know... nothing really changes, same old, same old.'
She notices my eyes well up.
'Hey, when are you going to bite the bullet...? Get out I mean, you have to!' 'Alice this behaviour of his .... He isn't right in the head.'
I hadn't said anything about the verbal haranguing, I had taken this

Alice Waite

morning. Valentine's day or not, this behaviour was typical, if I was going to be out for the day, apparently having a nice time... read, leaving him at home, having a miserable time. Usually, there would not only be the nasty missive to see me on my way, but punishment when I returned. The punishment might take the form of a filthy grease laden kitchen, the sink filled with frying pans. Maybe, coffee has been spilt on the floor and walked around, the cat hasn't been fed or maybe she's thrown up a fur ball or worse. Or the whole house is in darkness, there's no sign of a meal, not even a jacket potato in the oven, he's *gone out...* and all the above. So, I always returned home with a heavy heart. Lisa was right, I had to get out, but how to organise a new life? How do I make the jump? She said, I would know, there would be a moment when I couldn't go on any longer. Then, commenting on all the red paper hearts fluttering from the ceiling, we talked of Valentine's day. John had organised dinner for them this evening and had bought her a large bottle of her favourite scent.

'I am guessing by your silence' she enquired 'nothing has been planned for you this evening?'

'No, it was all a bit shouty this morning.' I told her 'It's guilt as much as anything.'

'You poor love' she comforted.

By now we were on our coffee, when a young woman leant over my shoulder. I could see from her uniform she was Harvey Nic's staff.

'Excuse me, sorry to interrupt' she said. 'Are you Alice Waite?'

I must have looked quizzical, but replied

'Err yes I am.'

'One moment' she said and then disappeared making her way through all the tables.

'What was all that about?' Lisa said

'Don't ask me!' I replied finishing a last sip of wine.

Two minutes later, the young lady was back, proffering a huge bouquet of flowers.

'There must be some mistake.' I said

'Not if you are Alice Waite' she beamed leaving the flowers in my arms.

I now had the attention of the whole restaurant. I could hear people saying 'Amazing!' 'What a lucky woman!' 'Wow! Someone's got a super Valentine!' 'Imagine that' 'How fabulous' 'Lucky lady'

I didn't feel like a lucky lady at all. I wanted to stand on the table and tell the world what was going on. I felt sick and knew exactly what was going on. Tears welled up. The onlookers thought I was crying with happiness.

There were nudges at the tables either side of us. Then, wistful speculation from the table on the left.

'I think she's overwhelmed, don't you?'

Sure, these were the most stunning flowers, but they had been sent for the wrong reason. Steve knew I was having lunch with Lisa at Harvey Nichols café, so he had cleverly managed to stage this very public display of affection, by calling their flower department, spending a huge amount of money to prove to Lisa and the world what a lovely, lovely man he was. He might as well have signed the card Jekyll and Hyde.

I wanted to leave this evidence of his divisive behaviour behind in the cafe, or send them back, but knew the repercussions when I arrived home, would be dire. Disguised as loving behaviour, mind games like this are toxic and we start to question ourselves yet again. Did I over react? Look what he's organised for me... they were probably planned all along and he just wanted to surprise me. But then, why was he so nasty this morning? My mind goes into overload, with a jumble of conflicting thoughts, that ricochet around my head until Lisa declares,

'This man is poisonous!' *'Don't begin to believe* he's sent theses flowers as a token of love Alice.'

Perversely, it was that huge bouquet of flowers that played a major part in my decision to leave. But also, it takes a good friend to be unapologetically honest, to tell it how it is.

'Alice, I don't want us to meet up in another six months and you are still going through this hell.' 'You *have, have* to leave!' She remonstrated in a rather too loud and forceful way. Now the tables either side of us *were* confused.

So yes, there are always flowers in the office and on my table in St Phillip's Square.

I don't care how tight money is, buying flowers is about cherishing myself. I buy them because I want to, and I can, without recourse to anyone else with another agenda.

It's the Friday of a Bank holiday weekend. At 4pm I have just turned the key in the office door when the phone started to ring. Part of me wants to let the call go to voice mail, but instead I unlock the office door to take the call. It was Jenny Hale from the Pension's Ombudsman.

'Hello Alice, I have a determination I want to fax through to you.' 'Please make sure there is plenty of paper in your fax… I'll send it through now.' Excited, I loaded extra paper into the fax machine and within seconds, it whirred into life. As the sheets poured out of the printer, I tried to read them, but they were coming thick and fast and I was at pains to keep everything in order. I refilled the paper holder, but more and more sheets followed so quickly, they were falling onto the floor, because I was still attempting to read some of the contents. I refilled the paper holder again. I couldn't believe just how long this Determination was.

Worried the ink would run out, I stared in disbelief as I saw page forty-eight hit the floor. The fax machine sighed with relief. As I picked up the last page I read,

'I also note Mr Waite's evidence is not entirely on all fours with Mr Damien Humphries
evidence……'
'Although Mr Waite suggests Mr Humphries' evidence cannot be relied on, I see no reason to doubt what Mr Humphries says. He is in no way an interested party, unlike Mr Waite who also seeks to claim from Pension & Mutual. …'

'Yes, yes, yes and yes again!' I yelled, jumping up and down on the spot. I wanted to organise fireworks, champagne and a big party! Carefully gathering up all the sheets I placed them in order on my desk. By now it was gone five o'clock. I wanted to call Jenny Hale to thank her. I picked up the phone and dialled her direct line.

'This is the Office of the Pension Ombudsman. Our hours are….'
I thought I must call Hugo Steele.
'St George's Chambers' 'Please leave a message after …'
Oh! I so wanted to tell Hugo about this amazing news. Maybe Greg Midgley might still be at his desk. I dialled only to hear 'Garston & Welland Solicitors' 'Please leave a message….'
Carefully placing all the sheets in a file to take back to the flat, I phoned my closest girlfriends, who were, like me, over the moon this ghastly saga was on its way out, with the culprits to be hung, drawn and quartered … well at least on paper! I spent the whole evening reading and re-reading the forty-eight pages. Glass of wine in hand I pace up and down in my little sitting room reading out loud. I telephoned Andrew with the news and he immediately invited me down stairs to his apartment to chew the cud with more wine.

'Darling!' He said as he opened his door. 'This is amazing!' He gave me a reassuring bear hug. This bear hug didn't reduce me to tears as previous hugs might have done at more vulnerable times. I was euphoric. A huge weight had suddenly been lifted off my shoulders, I felt I could fly. We danced and danced around his grand Drawing Room to something on Radio 2. Andrew, never really needing an excuse, opened some bubbly. We clinked glasses and sank down into deep damask sofas.

The Determination was damming, dealing with every aspect of the fraud, clearly and concisely. Pension & Mutual were also deemed to be at fault, not have written to me as an individual about the sale and further, because they did not have a system in place to ensure a change of address, noted at one office was also relayed to all other departments. They were going to be fined, but without delay must refund the missing funds to my Pension Fund with interest. Further, they were to send me a cheque for £250 by way of an apology. £250! That wouldn't pay Greg Midgley for an hour! Apparently, by statute, this was the maximum The Ombudsman could ask for.

The following morning, I bounced along to the photocopiers to have two copies made. I then sent one to Greg Midgley and the other to Hugo Steele both were sent by recorded delivery. I knew I had to hold my soul in patience until everyone was back in the office on Tuesday. All weekend I was smiling inside. At last, an independent legal opinion had determined that fraud had taken place. What more could I want? Well, just the house sold, so that I could move on. Andrew had said the night before
'Alice, I've loved having you here, I will miss you when you find yourself that country cottage you always talk about.'
'Well you will be the first over to dinner.' I said 'You've been my Guardian Angel for the past four years…. I'll never forget all your kindness Andrew.'

When I spoke to Hugo Steele on Tuesday he was thrilled with The Determination.
'You have to understand.' He said, 'The Ombudsman is one of the most respected legal opinions in the country.' 'This Determination is very important to us.' 'Your husband cannot continue saying that the second sale was just a coincidence.' 'I'm afraid he's dead meat.'
Duly, a cheque for £250 came through from Pensions & Mutual. It was paper clipped to a compliment slip, there was no apology. I immediately bought myself a smart new handbag which I have to this day.

Chapter 31

War Cabinet

Midgley tells me, Mark Kenny has been sent a copy of The Determination. I would have loved to have been a fly on the wall when that information was passed on to his client. We have a date set for the Final Hearing. At a meeting with Hugo Steele, I enquire if we know which Judge will be sitting on the day. Steele buzzes his Clerk to enquire.
'I'm just inquisitive… you know, the kind of person we are dealing with and well… if it affects the way we present our case.' I said
Steele looked quizzically across the conference table.
'It's not something I would have thought of.' He said, 'We have an excellent case and will be presenting the facts' 'This Determination helps us enormously… the Judge could refer the fraud issue to the Crown Prosecution Service.' 'And as for Selwyn signing an affidavit, telling the world he gave your husband cash by the bucket load… I can't think what he was thinking of?'
The Clerk buzzed through 'Judge Mc Pherson will be sitting on the 15th Sir.'
'What's he like?' I said
'He's actually very nice.' Steele said, 'and pro women.'
'That's good news then.' I muttered
We trawled through more and more detail. I didn't mind at all. This was a man who was going to be so thoroughly prepared, he would be able to recite half a dozen lever arch files to Judge Mc Pherson, if required. I was so glad Greg Midgley had been down-graded to gofer and photocopying slave. Not what he had imagined for himself when he left Law School, I'm sure.
The big stumbling block now was the sale of The Rectory. Antonia, ever the diplomat had said,
'It wasn't looking very tidy Mum.' Which I think must have been a huge understatement, judging by the estate agent's comments. Hettie was still

living there, but, just post student life, was no domestic Goddess… and why should she clean up after her father?

Back at Edgar Place, I pushed all the student tables together in the main studio, to form my own conference table. Taking a leaf out of Steele's book, I organised all my files along the length of the table. Pension fraud, my business, the sale of Ferme Thenon, the sale of The Rectory, Nat Selwyn's claim and all the subheadings pertaining to each of these. The moment Hugo Steele telephoned requesting more information, I was on the case. Steele and I got on well, because he knew if he asked me for something, I would have it in the post the same day. Whereas Midgley, would probably still be looking for whatever was requested, several days later.
By now I knew my files inside out and backwards. It felt empowering to have all the facts at my fingertips and what's more, I had done all the legwork to produce the information myself. I felt a stronger now, than I had for years. I was regaining control of my life, that had been so hopelessly constrained by others. Constantly visualising the cottage, I wanted to spend the rest of my life in, the safe-haven I craved, I knew my goal was getting closer, but didn't want to pre-empt anything. We still had to get through the Final Hearing and who knows what boulders were about to be thrown in the road in front of us? The last three years or so had been a time of confusion, hope, then despair. The acrimonious battle I had found myself fighting, certainly wasn't planned. I simply wanted my freedom and to regain my self esteem, but he wasn't letting me go with ease. He had chosen to try at every turn, to make my bid for independence, as difficult as possible. After all, he had been humiliated. His wife of over thirty years had walked out of a beautiful home, without not much more than a suitcase. How did that look? What questions must have been asked?

His rancour knew no bounds. Rallying reprobates like Rolo Hargreaves and Nat Selwyn to his aid was an insult to my intelligence. Did he really think I would just roll over and say?
'Oh golly, did Holden Street only achieve such a low price'? 'That's a shame isn't it'?
And, 'Of course Nat should have a third of our French house… I won't even get it valued.' 'I'll just accept the derisory valuation you have suggested and take a third of that, so you and Nat can keep the property.'
This man really didn't know me at all. His compelling desire to change and control me was paramount in everything he did. He wanted a submissive

wife, who wouldn't question his authority or indeed his wisdom. He told me about his school days. How the big boys had beaten him up when he oversaw the biscuit stall, they stole the biscuits and walked away laughing. He soon realised if he wasn't going to be one of the boys, he could be king pin with a group of girls. As little girls, we are taught subliminally and by observation what our role will be. We think it perfectly normal Mummy should refer to Daddy about, being late back if she meets her friends, or could she buy something.... because she has no funds to call her own. Once rather naughtily at a parent's evening, I stole a glance at another child's exercise book sitting on her desk. There were the usual creative writing essays like, *'what we did at the weekend'* and 'my house'. Reading the latter, I discovered that Daddy shouted at Mummy because she wanted to buy some new cushions and he said she wasn't allowed to. That little girl now knew her Mummy *must* refer to Daddy.

I can only imagine these little girls in *his* gang, flattered, he wanted to be with them, hung on his every word, until they were eating out of his hand. Then he grew up wanting to replicate the days when he was in control and no one questioned his charming, twisted ways. Of course, in the early years, we did have happy times and I think, an evenly balanced relationship. Looking back, the shift came after the birth of Antonia. A first baby is a shock to any relationship. No one can prepare you for that train hurtling down the track. Naively, I had planned to hire a nanny and just get back to work as normal. However, the moment Antonia's huge brown eyes met mine, my life plans changed. I did go back to work but, on a morning, only basis, to have the afternoons, bath time and bedtime with Antonia. When Hettie came along, Antonia was at Nursery in the mornings, so I had the two of them for the afternoons. Slowly my work life balance shifted to be more and more available for the girls. I would try to catch up with work in the evenings and fit a day's work into a morning, to keep on top of everything. It seemed strange then, but I didn't question, why I worked in the evenings, while he read the paper. Why I was up with the girls at night, because apparently, he needed his sleep, yet we were both at work the next morning. I just took on the pre-programmed caring role, because although I loved my work and gained a huge amount of creative satisfaction from it, my priority had become my girls. By the age of thirty-three I had three daughters, five and under.

Cesca was slightly premature, so I had to leave her in hospital for a while;

until they were satisfied her lungs were functioning properly. While she was there, I would be at the hospital for 6am to feed her, drive home to get Antonia and Hettie ready for school and nursery, and then drive them there. I would manage to get home for a quick cup of coffee, then back to the hospital for the 10am feed. Returning, via Nursery to pick up Hettie, I would then drive home to give her lunch. In the afternoon, we had a mother's help, Janine, who would take Hettie to the park while I drove back to the hospital for the 2pm feed. Then I would collect Antonia from school at 3.30pm, drive home to organise tea for the two of them. Steve would usually be back for bath and bed time assisted by Janine, while I drove back to the hospital to feed Cesca at 6pm. I would then return to the hospital for the 10pm feed, leaving any milk I had managed to express for her, for the night time feeds. I usually fell into bed before midnight, but if Antonia or Hettie woke in the night; to hear Steve tell me he needed his sleep, was beyond the pale.

The support I so badly needed just evaporated. He became the fourth child, demanding more and more attention, seemingly unable to cope with any aspect of the business on his own. Every evening there were lists of queries he wanted help with. But when *I* wanted just the practical help of holding a brand new Cesca because, Hettie had woken in the night, he would cold heartedly refuse. I have memories of taking Cesca down stairs in the small hours to breast feed and Hettie sitting on the sofa beside me with her teddy and a book. To be jealous of the attention your wife is giving to your children, is a very sad state of affairs. Young children require and demand so much time and love, so as a mother your own life takes a back seat. How immature and selfish can a father be, demanding more and more from a wife, already overwhelmed with caring responsibilities? At first the dynamics of jealousy are barely noticeable. There might be some bad-tempered behaviour or demands for attention while I was reading one of the girls a story. I was so busy with three little girls and just loved being a mother. Trying to appease a grown man, who cannot countenance anyone else might be as important, is exhausting. Falling into the trap of trying to be all things to all people impacted on my self esteem. I lost sight of myself and was made to feel guilty if I couldn't fulfil everyone's expectations, whether it was produce a fancy-dress costume, food for a dinner party, or deal with work related matters. There was a disconnection. Alice Waite had disappeared under a mountain of domestic and caring duties.

Alice Waite

Job Description

The applicant must be dedicated to the service of others. Anyone not prepared to be fully committed three hundred and sixty-five days of the year and twenty-four hours of the day, should not apply. Further, there is no sickness benefit, in fact sickness is not allowed. Anyone who takes to their beds for however brief an occasion, will be asked *to get a grip, get up and function as normal.* Still interested? Then you could be the kind of woman that I am looking for.
In a nutshell the requirements are:

- Work all hours that God sends
- When the children are small, get up at night and work the next day.
- Shop for the household, pay for it, unload it.
- Cook every meal, clear up and empty the dishwasher.
- Clear up constantly after others.
- Know where every mortal thing they neglect to put away, can be found.
- Wash all clothes and bed linen.
- Iron all the clothes and linen, hang up, fold and put everything away.
- Empty over flowing bins, wash floors, clean windows, silver, brass. Clean bathrooms, Hoover, polish and dust.
- Deal with everything and pay for everything relevant to the children.
- Make appointments for the dentist and optician and take three children there.
- Pay for school trips and clothes, including the girl's allowances.

Still interested? Well read on, there's more...

- Work for my Company, design two collections a year, advise on packaging, Company policy, exhibition stands, trade literature.

- Expect most of your advice to be ignored, as I push this business off a cliff.
- Expect your self- esteem and self-confidence to be knocked on a regular basis, because I am a bit of a bully to work for ... but I am sure you will find me amusing.
- There is no remuneration for the above but *be grateful for a roof over your head* is what I say.
- There is no holiday pay or indeed holidays, unless you can fund and organise them yourself (which will mean paying for me to come as well.)
- I should also mention that like holidays, there are no social arrangements outside the job.... unless you organise them and pay for them yourself.
- The other part of this contract involves you running an entirely separate company, which I call *your little job*. You will offer a full Media Design Service, plan and organise courses and lectures and travel to London to deliver them.
- As this business *does* seem to earn money; you will be required to pay for all the household expenses, school fees, food, gas, electricity, community charges and children's expenses.
- Finally, at the end of thirty years service, you will be required to sign away everything you have worked for through industrious endeavour. That is, what you had hoped to leave your children. Not only a property in France but also a home in which you have put your whole life and considerable love and effort.
- You will also be required to raid your pension fund to cover Tax I have neglected to pay.
- Further, expect to be blamed for *absolutely everything*.

As this is an enviable position and the last employee stayed in the contract for over thirty years. It will obviously attract numerous applicants, so apply at your earliest opportunity.

Please Note
We are *not* an equal opportunities employer.
We are *not* investors in people.

In one way, he liked it when, for a short time, I was financially dependent on him. He could control my life, handing out just enough money to buy, say, the groceries. With his never-ending stream of demands a light inside me dimmed and finally extinguished. As I became less involved in the business, I lost confidence, feeling completely powerless. I had no autonomy over my own life. On the other hand, he was angry, because the family, were dependant on him, he was the main breadwinner. Being King Pin came at a price, here was responsibility he couldn't handle. As the girls grew older and were all at school, I started working again. Much to his chagrin, some clients started asking for me to be at meetings. Slowly my confidence grew.

Year's latter when Antonia was taking her common entrance exam, she wanted to make her first choice, a top girl's boarding school. At the time, she was mad about Chalet School stories and Mallory Towers and much as I tried to put her off the idea, she was so keen to embark on the adventure of boarding school life. We were rather lax, letting her make this her first choice, as frankly we didn't think she would make the grade. Antonia sailed through her exam, leaving us with the dilemma as to how to proceed. Firstly, I didn't want my girls to board. I loved catching up with their day every evening, around the kitchen table and secondly, we hadn't budgeted for this level of fees. To cut a long story short, with much cajoling from Antonia and pressure from Steve, we signed Antonia in.
'You can't deny Antonia an opportunity like this, just because *you* want to have the girls at home.' 'It's selfish of you.' 'You *have* to put Antonia first…. This isn't about *you*…'
With that, I conceded she should go and suddenly all the wheels were set in motion. Somehow we pulled the first terms fees together. Antonia's trunk was packed and off she went. I was tearful all the way home, but Antonia really took to boarding school life. Within no time at all, Hettie wanted to board, then Cesca, until I had an eerily empty house. I know they had a brilliant education and I certainly didn't want to hold them back. Such mixed emotions. I was naïve enough to assume he had the girl's best interest at heart but there was another agenda. The reality of Steve's concern for their education was soon clarified when he said
'At last, I've got you back to myself!'

From there on in, we were on our own every day and every evening. This is when the destructive behaviour escalated. There was no one to see, no one to comment. I marked the days off on the calendar, waiting for the next Exeat weekend, when normal jolly behaviour would resume. For the first year, I wrote to them every day. (Oh, for email) In winter, I put hot water bottles in their beds to keep them aired. Inside I was crying.

Chapter 32

Final Hearing

Mini dilemma: In the big picture of the day to come, yes, this is a mini dilemma, but it is useful to occupy one's mind with trivia by way of saving the mind from combusting into flames and the owner of this mind going into meltdown. So, the dilemma is, shall I get a taxi to the station? It's less than ten minutes' walk away, but who knows if it will be raining tomorrow? I can't risk drizzle. Drizzle equals flat hair, but also dewy make up. I can't risk a bad hair day, I need every ounce of confidence I can muster, so I resolve to spray dewy illuminating finish onto my face. Then there are the heels to think of…Yes, a taxi is a *must have* and I book one for tomorrow morning.
I review my suit hanging on the outside of the wardrobe, fresh from the dry cleaners. My new shirt hangs at the side of it, my heels with 'Party Feet' jelly insoles sit on the floor, but I know this is going to be no party.

Sitting on a platform bench with seven minutes to spare, scanning The Times, I catch sight of a familiar face from Garrton Street days, which I do not want to acknowledge. My tummy is churning. I am not in the mood to make pleasantries. I bury my head in my paper staring at, not reading, Anatole Kaletsky's economic forecast, when the train arrives. Note, Garrton Street man has boarded several carriages away and with relief I see Lucy waving from a door in the opposite direction.
I open the door and she greets me with a strong hug. It's so what I need, but it is with the risk of turning me to pulp. She senses this, pulls back, guiding me to her seat, plus one she has reserved for me with her coat. Without a care in the world she has left her hand bag gaping open on the table. She does not perceive any problems, like stolen credit cards and if the worst happened… so what? If her wallet was stolen, or credit cards abused, someone will pick up the tab. Run out of petrol? …. Max will be on his way to the rescue. Lost the house keys? … Ditto. This works when a marriage

is a comfort blanket of love, for its own sake. There is no hidden agenda behind the kindness. Still, I think, it wouldn't hurt to get your act together, would it Lucy? The difference is she's not shouldering all the responsibility for her life as I am. Someone else is there to love and support her, whatever the circumstances. I've effectively been in *just take care of yourself* mode for years because there wasn't ever going to be a knight in shining armour to do battle on my behalf.

Steve and I were walking back to the car one evening, after a meal, I crossed the road to look in a shop window. He was looking into an Estate Agents, perusing the properties. A group of men, who were the worse for wear, turned the corner on my side of the road and heading in my direction shouted out,
'Hello darling fancy coming back to my place?'
In seconds they surrounded me, and one was wrapping his arm around my shoulder.
I shouted 'Get off, GET OFF. Leave me alone….!'
In hindsight it was probably all just high jinks, but nevertheless, at the time I found it alarming, given there were at least five of them and who knows what might have happened. Throughout the altercation my husband stayed on the opposite side of the road glued to the spot. He did not even remonstrate, he simply watched as I extricated myself from the flailing arms of my assailant. I quickly crossed the road to where he was standing. By now, I was crying.
'Why didn't you come over to help me?' 'I was really frightened.'
He looked completely unmoved. Shrugging his shoulders, he said,
'There's no point in us *both* getting into a spot of bother.'
He was just not prepared to enter the affray on my behalf and certainly wasn't offering any mantle of protection. There was no reassuring arm around my shoulder, he simply put his hands in his pockets walking on with careless disregard for my wellbeing.

Lucy calmly asks how I am feeling. I note eyes on the other side of the table disengage from their papers. If they were cats, I would also see their ears prick up. I feel unable to speak, there is a lump in my throat and I know if I say anything the words will be an embarrassment of incoherent sounds. I nod my head and she sympathetically does not pursue the subject but pushes a copy of the Daily Mail across to me.
Smiling she says. 'Ha, a little light reading!'

Alice Waite

The eyes on the opposite side of the table are disappointed I am not going to play to the gallery and brighten their commute. In no time at all we arrive and are navigating the stairs and coffee stands at the station. After my last experience at this court with only a broken-down drinks machine in the waiting area, I insist on buying a few bottles of water plus some magazines to keep Lucy happy, while I am in court.

Another taxi and with perfect timing we draw up in front of the now familiar grey concrete building situated on the ring road from hell. Lucy stepping out of the cab looks ahead to the entrance of the concrete monolith and says

'Puwahh…!'

As I turn from dealing with the taxi fare, I see a tall figure wearing a long black coat and Fedora, briefcases in either hand, striding up the steps to the swing doors.

'Wow! … Did you see *that*?' She enthuses.

'Looked pretty scary to me!' I respond.

'Come on girl, let's go, let's go…' She is striding ahead at a rate of knots. It's all about to happen. The lift and three agonising stops later, we arrive at the right floor. The Clerk is scanning his paperwork, to tick the box, confirming we have arrived.

'Oh yes. Mr Midgley and Mr Steele are here…. In the end room.'

I look towards the end of the waiting area… I call the bus station, where National Express declared *free refreshments this morning*. There are dead coffee cups, overflowing bins and Coke cans everywhere. It's 9am for heaven's sake. Perhaps there was a party last night?

I query 'The end room?'

There are three doors on the horizon, I do not want to open the wrong one, to come face to face with my husband. The Clerk is quite direct.

'Look through the porthole to the right, you can see Mr Steele's hat on the coat stand.'

Lucy's eyes lock with mine as we walk determinedly towards the icon the Fedora has now become. I would have knocked, but Lucy exudes such confidence, she walks straight in. Hugo Steele looks surprised, but then he sees me, and I introduce Lucy. We seat ourselves at the table next to Greg Midgley who as ever, has his head in his briefcase searching for something, a broken pencil to write with, no doubt?

Yet again he is wearing his court suit, crumpled, dark and shiny. Under his tie, the top button of his shirt is undone; he obviously thinks no one will

Only cry on Fridays

notice. His tie is in the worst possible taste. He is flustered and it's only 9.05. His hair is slightly wild, he can barely utter
'Hello.'
I know the look. I can see panic in his eyes. He is the antithesis to Hugo Steele, immaculate in his cutting edge, double breasted pin striped suit. Outside this court, Steele would look like Al Capone in charge of The Mob, but in this surreal legal world, it soon becomes clear, he commands huge respect. His bow tie is red, his shirt, fine red and white stripes. The tortoise shell specs add gravitas to his appearance and I am immensely grateful he is here, batting for me. Now tapping his fingers ever so gently on the laminate table, we are all sitting around, I sense the tension in the air. There are wodges of paperwork and numerous files all over the table. Steele now stands up, staring intently at Midgley.
Midgley, is still excavating another, larger briefcase, this one is on wheels. He is ill at ease; clearly there is urgency in his manic search. It seems best not to utter a word, there is something important unresolved, so I do not want to distract anyone. Suddenly Steele's voice cuts the silence.
'You have brought these files, haven't you Midgley?'
I realise Hugo Steele has reverted to his schooldays which clearly weren't at the local comprehensive. Greg is now only referred to as Midgley and Midgley is his fag.
'Yes, it's here somewhere.' Midgley bumbles
I can see beads of perspiration on his forehead. The very image of sophistication, he licks his fingers to control the recalcitrant paperwork.
Hugo Steele continues 'I told you yesterday, I wanted this faxed to me *before* 5pm.'
The silence, apart from the shuffling of paper work is leaden with retribution. Midgley, trying to recover the situation stammers
'Well… err… it didn't get to me until after four …'
Then he put in his nervous, most irritating postscript
'If you see what I mean.'
Hugo Steele clearly didn't. His voice is now raised.
'I needed the paperwork last night and I need it NOW!' he boomed.
Lucy and I felt like voyeurs in the headmaster's study. Midgley was in trouble, big time and was about to get a detention and probably a note to his mother. Hugo Steele fingered his Mont Blanc pen. Lucy caught my eye, I was feeling sick. The atmosphere suddenly lightened, as Midgley triumphantly pulled some sheets of paper from his case, now resembling a waste paper bin.

'Ah here we are.' He said, as if he had located a missing Tiddly wink.
'Date order?' Steele quizzed without a breath.
There was a pause that said it all but was too awful to contemplate.
Midgley muttered 'Err... yes.'
He would have been dead meat if he had said no. But tell one fib and if you have half a brain, you do not even consider the idea when your inquisitor is Hugo Steele QC. Quick as a flash Steele responded
'Current dates first?'
Midgley was unnerved
'Err, Um, not sure…err.'
Steele starts shuffling the pile.
'This isn't in bloody date order!' 'This is a mess; it's a fucking dog's breakfast!' He remonstrates.
I am surprised at the language and I think he sees me wince. Steele, quickly apologies. Bemused, I shrug my shoulders. At this point, I have no idea of the significance of this paperwork. I want to crawl into my handbag. I am cross with Greg but feel sorry for him at the same time. When embarrassed, cats groom themselves furiously, women, delve into their handbags and look for heaven knows what. I find some Polo mints in mine and breaking this calamitous silence muster,
'Polo mint anyone?'
Hugo looks over his glasses and there is a smile as he says,
'Thank you.'
I proffer the tube to Greg who looks like he wants to make a run for it. He has loosened his tie and his neck is bulging. He can barely muster
'No thanks.'
I am aware in the silence as we wait for the pile of papers to be put in date order, it would be preferable not to have embarked on crunching my Polo mint. Steele mutters under his breath,
'Waste of my fucking time… this is madness!'
Midgley squirms and tries to smile as if Steele is chastising someone else.

'Right!' Steele says, 'This is our position.' 'Firstly, we have Nat Selwyn standing by his affidavit saying you knew he was paying off your husband's debts… and technically they were your debts as well, as you were a Director of the company.' 'Selwyn says you knew he was being given one third of your French property in recompense.'
'Nonsense!' I respond. 'This is an arrangement between the two of them, to try to gain two thirds of the house.'

Steele continues 'Secondly, your husband maintains he is entitled to half your income as he was a partner in your business and as such deems you are responsible for half his tax.'

There is a deep intake of breath and Steele shakes his head in disbelief.

'Thirdly, the fraud issue.' 'Your husband clearly engineered a sub sale of your joint SIPP Property to the detriment of your pension fund.' 'He denies this and says the fact that the property sold again some twenty days later for an extra £110,000, is just down to marketing.'

'But look' I say, 'We have all this evidence stacked against him…The Ombudsman's Determination… how can he think he can get away with it?'

'Mrs Waite, I wouldn't believe your husband, if he told me Christmas day was the 25th of December!' 'I'm going next door to start negotiating.'

'Next door?' I query

The other side are in the adjoining room' he informs me as he bounces out of our room and without so much as a polite knock on their door, he enters the enemy camp. Greg, off the hook for a nanosecond, asks if we would like a coffee. At this point I could drink any brown liquid masquerading as coffee and in a flash, he is making his way to the vending machine.

'Well' says Lucy 'what was all that about?'

'I don't know' I say

'You are going to be OK' she reassures. 'You've got Steele…thank God you're not relying on Greg.'

She stands up to stretch her legs. Linking hands above her head, elbows either side she pulls hard. I think she is about to start her Pilates routine, as she twists from side to side. Moving over to the coat stand she pops the Fedora onto her head.

'Lucy!' I yell '*No!*'

She quickly hangs the hat back in position and as she does her hand touches the black coat on the hook beneath. She strokes it.

'Oh, just feel this ….my God, its sooo gorgeous!'

'Must be cashmere.' I muse

Lucy looks inside to find a label. 'Nothing so pedestrian darling.' 'It's Alpaca!'

'He'll be able to have one in every colour of the rainbow when he's finished my case.' I said.

Greg blunders in, slopping coffee from the styrene cups. It is warm, and I am grateful for anything as we wait for Hugo Steele to return.

The door opens abruptly, Steele breezes in. Like an emissary from the enemy camp he starts to appraise the negotiations so far. He is just in his stride when a face appears at the porthole of our door and the hand it belongs to tentatively knocks. Steele gets up, pops his head around the door and I hear him announce 'Five minutes.'

Sensitive to the strain on my face, he says, he is going to see the Judge. We are due in court any moment, but that seems of no concern. At this stage of the proceedings, my understanding of how final hearings work or might work, is equivalent to a five-year-old embarking on a PHD. I am totally at the mercy of those skilled (or not as the case may be) who are battling on my behalf.

Greg is writing notes furiously, about what, I have no conception, because no one has given him the time of day, never mind involved him in negotiations. His sole role seems to be Sherpa for our legal documents, which from time to time, he produces from his vast suitcase on wheels. The antithesis of urban chic, his yellowing grey locks are thinning and form an unflattering wave which is stuck to his perspiring forehead. His hands are slightly yellow stained, (surely not nicotine in this day and age?) hold a blue Bic biro with a chewed end. The atmosphere in this windowless room is close. I sense he would like to remove his jacket but remembering the last time, he did this, I am relieved the formality of the occasion, dictates it must stay stuck to his back. There can be no release for a cigarette break, hence, the perspiration.

Lucy picks up the styrene debris, announcing, as she swings out of the door, she is off to find the loos. Midgley continues to scribble away. He is probably writing to his mother. Hugo Steele returns with Lucy on his heels, my tension is palpable. Before he has chance to utter a word I blurt out, 'What about Court?' 'What is happening?'

Steele is calm and very much in control. I *love* this man.

'We may not be in court for some time…" It might be we can sort out some of the central issues beforehand.' 'It will save everyone time and money.'

Greg sits up straight, puts the letter to his mother back in his bag and pays attention. He is concentrating hard. I should hope so too, the hourly rate Garston and Welland charge for him.

Hugo Steele announces Nat Selwyn is interested in a deal. He has decided (more like, been advised) that, in non-legal parlance, he hasn't a hope in hell of proving he is one third owner of our French property. There is no paperwork, just his word, that a third of our joint property, was given to him in exchange for paying off my husband's debts. Thank heaven, he has

Only cry on Fridays

obviously given up on the idea of pulling my girls into court, to testify to the contrary. I concede the debts have been paid, but I point out that Nat's affidavit states, he paid these debts in cash, but then, he can't prove this, because he is unable to show where the money came from.

'Hasn't he dropped himself right in it?' I say. 'If the Revenue learn about his stash of cash…it will be the firing squad.'

'That's not one for this court.' Hugo Steele says 'Others will deal with that, but I do agree, he must be feeling nervous this cash issue has come to light, there could be consequences'… 'But then he didn't have to sign the affidavit.' He said and continued 'Something about cutting his nose off to spite the face comes to mind!'

It seems, Nat Selwyn will, apparently accept payment of his debt from my share of the equity of the French house. I must pay him 50% of the Company debt.

'But I didn't know about the Company debt.' I remonstrate.

Before I can utter another word, Steele firmly reminds me,

'You were joint Director of this Company and as such you had a duty to make yourself aware of the financial situation.' 'There is no escaping this.'

And I thought he was on my side. I want to cry.

Oh yes Mr Steele, in an ideal world, where people are honest, kind and civil to each other, of course I should have been able to have a say in these financial matters. But in my world, that was a fantasy,

Sisters, I know you are out there. You are paper Directors of a Company set up by your husband. You are a Director because you have been told, *this is tax efficient and the way these things are done. …. 'Don't worry darling I will handle all this ….'*

'It's just the best way, the accountant says to have you on board is a good thing….'

'Just leave it all to me.'

Does anyone have any comprehension of what the reality of *my* situation was like? I've mentioned it before and I still have nightmares, but you should know now, as here I am in this court, facing the consequences of my inability to say 'No' because I was paralysed by fear.

The manipulation routine…. That's the one where a knife is drawn from the knife block on the kitchen work top. It is menacingly fingered as *requests* are made for my signature… My husband's voice is calm, but his eyes are like ice and I know the score. Someone said *Eyes are the windows of the soul* and by God they are. One look from those cold, intimidating eyes would turn me into pulp, my mouth bone dry and the pit of my stomach churning. The anxiety levels this periodic procedure would instil in me meant that for fear of retribution, words would not leave my mouth, even if I tried. I suspect if I had, had my say, I wouldn't be in one piece now, to be hauled over the coals, for not acting as a responsible Company Director. And so, another document is signed, and the consequences are here to haunt me today.

Steele disappears next door again. Through our porthole I see the adjoining door open. I think I can smell sulphur. I ask Greg who is my husband's QC? He looks up from what now appears to be his shopping list.
'QC?' 'Oh, Peter Hutchinson is not a QC'. 'He is very much Mr Steele's junior.' 'Very up and coming you understand, but not in Mr Steele's league'.
My chest swells with pride. Now some things are making sense. There is deference, protocol and it is noticeable that *next door* never come into our camp. There have been tentative knocks on our door, but no one ever enters. On the other hand, Steele, without a bye or leave, barges into the next room with the confidence of a Boa Constrictor selecting his prey.

Lucy fishes out the bottles of water from her bag and puts them on the table. Greg is grateful. I need to find the loo and Lucy directs me. I stand up for the first time in two hours, wobbling on my heels. Squeezing around the table, brushing the heaven that is the Alpaca coat, I walk through the door with purposeful strides through the fluorescent lit waiting room. There are rows of turquoise bench seating and I see Nat Selwyn coming into view at the far end of the room. I suck my tummy in, tuck in my tail in, stretch my torso up, push my shoulders back, hold my head high and gloss my lips with saliva. Focusing above and beyond his baldness, I walk right past him, heels clacking, without so much as a wobble. Lucy has given me the security code to enter the loos. Security systems for the WCs? Perhaps someone might steal the soap? The lighting in here is worse than our so-called conference room and it kindly throws deep shadows and a jaundiced pallor onto my face. Fresh lipstick and some Touché Éclat on the shadows and I'm ready. Unexpectedly, there is a full-length mirror so then I check for VPL, mindful that Nat will follow my stride back to the sanctuary of our room.

Meanwhile Steele has been negotiating hard, he is back with more news.

The other side are making noises about offers to pay £ 20,000 towards my costs. He's kicked a wasp's nest! This is just the start. They are on the back foot. I am quietly feeling much more confident. Lucy on the other hand is exuberant waving her arms with a loud 'Whoop whoop!
Hugo Steele stifles a smile.

Chapter 32

Final Hearing 2

Steele doesn't do chit chat. He's onto the next stage which is my husband's claim for 50% of my business. I push a bottle of water across the table to him, apologising for not having any paper cups. He politely accepts the water and manages a most elegant swig from the bottle. Greg thumbs through his file looking for Harvey & Jenkins valuation. Hugo Steele has removed his copy from the relevant file and is walking out of the door before Greg has even located the right tab in his apology for a filing system. The valuation is good news and bad news. The good news is that the valuation, for court purposes is deemed to be excellent. On the other hand, the bad news is that the valuation, for my self esteem, is depressing. Harvey and Jenkins, have no compunction advising, that as a sole trader, my business is totally reliant on me.

Yes OK! This is not rocket science, why do we have to pay a specialist to state the flipping obvious? The business per se is worthless to any prospective buyer. OK! OK! Got it, message received and understood. I write the courses, deliver them, I do all the marketing, plan the advertising, answer the phone, lick the stamps, clean the loos, weed the drive. Delegation is something I must address, but delegation costs money, fluid funds and this depressing report of some twenty odd pages has just cost me over £500 + vat. So, delegation will have to wait, again. On the plus side, this disheartening report means my husband cannot make any claims against my business. So, forgive me if I over react…. But, Whoop whoop again!

Within minutes, Steele is back from the enemy camp.

'Right, that's blown that one out of the water' he says, 'now to the Pension Fraud.'

Steele advises, my husband is denying culpability despite the Ombudsman's Determination. This is the last hurdle, the inconvenient truth that is fraud. The collusion of two double dealing, conniving, treacherous crooks,

Only cry on Fridays

(yes, I know too many adjectives!) who have feigned innocence, until a mere woman, uncovered their corrupt, rotten scheme. While I have every confidence in Steele, my tummy is still churning, as we sit in this airless room, negotiating with the unseen camp next door.

Lucy chips in 'Alice must be compensated *more* than £20,000 for her costs ….'

'This divorce has been prolonged, and the costs have escalated because of the fraud… which surely now, is an open and shut case?'

Greg suddenly comes to life. 'Costs are a matter for the judge – if we go into court we might not get any costs … depends on the judge on the day'

'It's a risk you take.'

Lucy is aghast, 'You mean it depends what side of the bed he gets out of?'

'Pretty well.' Greg replies.

Steele, ignoring Greg the oracle, pulls out the Ombudsman's Determination from his briefcase and, as if wild dogs were at his heels, swings out of our room and is back with the other party next door. I wish I could hear what he said. They are trying to convince him black is white but clearly from his face when he returns he has said something that has put the fear of God into my husband.

'I've given them ten minutes' he said

'For what?' I ask

'Before I go to see the Judge and request the court hearing we are all here for.' He replies, 'If we go into court, the whole fraud issue is in the public domain.' 'I'm not sure they want to take that risk.'

Steele looks at his watch as he leaves the room. I see him stride in the direction of the loos. The ten minutes seem to take an hour. Lucy is working on The Times crossword.

'Five across' she says trying to give us all something else to think about

'Farm vehicle south of Washington?' 'Mmmm…'

Steele returns. He sits next to Midgley and sips some more water.

I ask, 'Are we going to be able to recover a serious amount of costs?' 'This case has gone on for nearly four years because of the fraud.' 'My costs are running at somewhere in the region of £60,000!' 'And that's not my fault… this divorce should have been over with, in six months.'

'I do appreciate that' he says checking his watch. Standing up, he buttons his double-breasted suit and strides purposely, out of the door. We sit, in silence, frozen to the spot.

Midgley, literally twiddles his thumbs. Lucy stares at her crossword. I can barely breathe; my neck is tense with anxiety. My fate is in Hugo Steele's hands. At some point today, I will know. It's the *not knowing* that is so ghastly.

When I discovered a breast lump, my GP arranged for me to attend a specialist Breast Clinic that was literally, a one stop shop. The appointment letter suggested taking someone along, presumably for moral support. All the Mammogram's were seen by the radiologists there and then and the results given on the day. No waiting weeks for a letter marked NHS to come through the post. Naturally worried, I told Steve the date of my appointment, so he could come with me. On the morning of the appointment, he was suddenly busy, with what I don't remember, but it was too late to enlist the support of anyone else, so off I went on my own. From discovering the lump, having waited a few days for my GP appointment, then a couple of weeks more for the Breast Clinic appointment, I had been in a state of *not knowing* for over three weeks. The nights and very early mornings during those weeks were so long. It's the not knowing. If you know, you can deal with it, make a plan. But when you don't know, the mind goes into overdrive.

After a nightmare parking ordeal (just what you want when dealing with a situation like this) I checked in with the receptionist. She asked if anyone was with me.

'No err…that didn't work out.' I said considering the waiting area, where there was not a single woman sitting on her own. I sat down feeling like *Norma no mates* as my girls would say. Burying my head in an ancient magazine, I wondered how many worried women had read these pages before me. It was early summer, I remember, as I stared at out of date features like *'New Year, New You'* and *'Eat yourself fit'* plus all the usual articles on *'Running a Business from your Kitchen Table'* and *'Great Family Suppers'*. It all seemed so irrelevant in my current location. Judging by this dog-eared copy, quite a few women had stared at these pages waiting for their name to be called. Apart from the women accompanied by their husbands, there were also women sitting side by side. It didn't take me long to work out which woman would be the one to have her name called out. One woman would be chattering away, trying to make conversation, pointing to magazine articles, while the companion at her side was lost in her own world. We were women of a certain age, young in the swinging sixties. Cleverly, the music playing in the background reflected our heyday. Perhaps someone had thought it would make us feel more comfortable, more relaxed. For me, the sixties were the zenith of carefree years. Leaving school, first job, art school and the freedom that comes when the only person you are responsible for, is your self.

One of the nurses came along with a form attached to a clip board.
'I will be back to collect it in a few minutes' she said.
Noticeably, the first question after the usual name, address, date of birth was Have you ever taken the Contraceptive Pill? If so, for how long? I was a young woman of the Swinging Sixties for goodness sake. Of course, I took the pill! The biggest sin at that time was to become a so called, Unmarried Mother. There was no blurring of the lines then, using the term, Single Parent. If you became pregnant (and of course one achieved this on ones own) that was it, your life was over. Many girls ended up in Homes for Unmarried Mothers, because the shame could not be borne by their parents. So, hey yes, I was on the pill. It was so new, there wasn't any research available about long term effects and quite frankly, if it kept us out of the Home for Unmarried Mothers, we didn't care. Next question: Have you ever taken HRT? If so, for how long? In no uncertain terms, here was the correlation. Oestrogen.
Women of a certain age have been popping pills containing Oestrogen; not only in their youth but at the other end of their reproductive life and now here we are, sitting in a waiting room, to find out what the long-term effects have been.
My form was duly collected, so I found another magazine to occupy myself with. The waiting room was slowly thinning out and at last my name was called. The nurse showed me to a cubicle asking me to remove my top and bra. Wearing a lovely hospital gown, I was shown into the room for a mammogram. They politely flattened my breasts this way and then that, between steel plates, saying,
'Now don't move.'
As if I could, then...
'Just one more.' And 'I think we'll just do that one again.'
What! Pleeese... I know you are only doing your job Mrs Radiologist and I'm grateful, thank you.

Now, in a different waiting room the Beatles are singing *Please Mr Postman*...Several of the faces from the reception waiting area are familiar. Presumably they have all had their Mammograms too? No one really engages in conversation, no one wants to make small talk. We all know why we are here. A Nurse appears at my side,

Alice Waite

'You can get some lunch now if you like; it will be some time before the Radiologists can look at your Mammogram.' 'The café is only just outside the unit, so we can come for you if needed.'
I thank her, pick up my bag and make my way towards the smell of school dinners. Walking along the hot plates displaying all manner of unhealthy food, I ask what the vegetarian option is. The lady in a blue catering hat offers something with leaden pastry and leeks, which I decline. I see she's disappointed but in all honesty my tummy doesn't really want anything, I am but passing time. Sitting with a mug of Earl Grey, I watch a world of ill people and their carers going about their business. Wheel chairs glide by, people on crutches hobble past. I muse why the Radiologist wanted extra shots. Had she seen something she needed a clearer picture of? Surely this is untoward? Time is hanging heavy now, I can't just sit here. Walking over to the shop to buy a newspaper, I see there is a section marked Gifts, so with nothing else to do I take a look. There are tins of talc, boxes of chocolates, some plastic photo frames and not much else. This selection makes a National Trust Gift shop look like the Harrods. Looking at my watch, I can see I have only managed to waste about three quarters of an hour but decide to make my way back to the second waiting room in the Breast Clinic.

Some of the faces I have previously been studying have gone, where, I do not know. There are new faces now, so I assume I have moved up the queue. Gerry and the Pacemakers are singing *Ferry across the Mersey*. After reading *The Times* from cover to cover, I start trawling the saddest pile of magazines I have seen in a long time. Resolving to buy the unit some magazines before I leave, I sit staring at the wall for another hour and a half. The Beatles are singing *'Please Mr Postman'* again. Time is dragging now. T*he not knowing* is getting to me. Eventually a nurse asks me to follow her to yet another waiting area, I must be getting near Gold Command surely? Some of the original familiar faces are here, looking like I feel, tired, concerned and rather grey. This time when a nurse directs a patient along a corridor, to an inner sanctum, both people are guided in. This must be it. Starring ahead into space, I wait. I notice those that have gone into Gold Command do not exit this way and for a reason. From where I am sitting I can see down the corridor, they have been directed along. A man and his wife leave one of the rooms, he has his arm around her, they are chatting away, and I can just tell she is OK. After ten minutes or so, another door opens and before I can see who is leaving, I can hear sobbing. Two women leave. I recognise the pretty blue cardigan from the first waiting room. Her companion has her arm firmly round her shoulders. It looks as if her legs are collapsing underneath her. I don't know this lady, but my heart goes out to her. I wonder if she is alive now. I continue to wait. I wait some more. It's the *not knowing*, again, the *not knowing*.

Suddenly, 'Mrs Waite, this way please.'
The nurse directs me to a windowless room and I take a seat. Dr Bailey introduces himself, he puts my Mammograms onto a back lit wall. I have no idea of what all the grey areas are but read from his demeanour it's OK. He tells me the lump I found is merely a cyst, so he will make arrangements for it to be removed. Seeing my face, he reassures me.
'This is easily done, by syringe.' he says, 'Your appointment will be through in a few weeks.'
We shake hands and I thank him profusely. Walking out past the café to the car park, my sense of relief is huge. Reaching the car, I realise I didn't buy the unit any magazines. Note to self, drop some in, next week. The car parking fee tells me I have been here for over six hours, but I don't care because the outcome is good. Driving home, I think about today. How vulnerable and alone I have felt waiting to hear if my lump is benign. How could someone be so heartless, so detached not to come with me, to give me support. What if the outcome had been different? When I pull into the drive, he appears promptly at the front door. There is guilt and regret all over his face, but I walk past him. I will not give this person the time of day.

Lucy tries another crossword clue, 'Fifteen down, Squirrel's nest?' 'I didn't know Squirrels built nests!' She said, 'I mean, are they made of twigs and moss like a bird's nest?' She queried
No one replied. The tension was palpable.
'I like to think of them living in a nice little tree house, like Squirrel Nutkin' she murmured to herself, knowing no one was listening. Poor Lucy, she was still trying to lighten the mood, but to no avail. Squirrel Nutkin couldn't have been further from my thoughts. Our door swung open. Cool as a cucumber, Hugo Steele walked in.
'They don't want to go into court' he said, 'they are offering a settlement of £40,000 towards your costs.'
'Not enough!' I heard myself say.
Hugo looked surprised.

'Look they don't want to go into court for two reasons.' 'One: It's a risk the Fraud issue will be referred to the CPS…. Am I right?'
'Correct.' Hugo confirmed
'And two: Nat Selwyn will have some explaining to do about all those cash payments.'
'Correct.' Reiterated Hugo
I took a deep breath'
So, we should call their bluff and ask for £50,000 towards costs… or we proceed to court without delay.'
I was ever the risk taker but could see Hugo was not exactly racing out of the room.
'Are you sure about this?' He said, 'I had to push for £40,000.'
Lucy chipped in
'Go for it Hugo, they will never go into court.' 'They are at a huge disadvantage.'
Lucy's gung ho irreverence made him smile.
'Certainly, I'm sure we can outmanoeuvre them' I said, 'They are running scared.'
Greg Midgley remained silent. He looked terrified by the brinkmanship he was witnessing. Hugo looked resolute as he took his new instructions from these two audacious women, to the enemy next door. Five minutes later he was back. Without showing any sign of emotion, he stood with his back against the door.
'Mrs Waite, in a *final* offer, your husband will pay £50,000 towards your costs.'

He wore the uniform
He looked the part
He delivered.

Chapter 34

With Wings

The last hurdle: I just wanted the Rectory sold, so that I might begin to pick up the pieces of my life, find a home I could call my own, close the front door and lick my wounds. It had been a tough four years chasing my freedom. Within weeks of the Final Hearing, a couple made an offer on The Rectory, well below the asking price. Occasionally, I would drive by and from the outside, at every turn, I could see how much my old home was deteriorating. Paint was peeling on the window frames. A gutter was overflowing, presumably blocked with leaves, resulting in water pouring down the stone work. There were weeds sprouting between the flags on the drive and I doubt the windows had been cleaned since I left. My old home looked sad and unloved. Strangely, there were no pangs of regret, no thoughts of buying him out, because the house was imbued with unpleasant scenes, ingrained in my memory, and deeply rooted in my spirit. Just when I thought they had faded, some little thing, some minor event, would trigger their renaissance. Like a deep shadow within the recesses of my brain, my thoughts were suddenly permeated with angst and consternation. There are still nightmares, even today.

Looking back, I was also cross with myself. How could I have let him get away with such destructive behaviour? Why did I allow him to police my life? The truth is no one wants to heed the warning bells. I can recall instances in our early married life, which should have given me a sense of misgiving, but no one wants to contemplate such negative thoughts, after all, he was probably just tired, not himself? We make excuses, when frankly there are none. Then life goes on with happy times, until the next time, the next episode, where we have not lived up to expectations, not given our all, so we try harder. The control is such a slow burn, so subtle. We know something isn't right but can't articulate it and then the problem goes away, until next time. The more demanding he became, the more I tried to fulfil his requirements, to give reassurance, I was there for him. But, enough was never enough; he always demanded more, until his controlling behaviour was not something that was happening occasionally, it was no longer a blurred memory, it had become my every day.

I wanted to accept the offer on the house but of course it was in his interests to refuse. Greg Midgley wrote a stiff letter (dictated by Hugo Steele) advising we would take the matter to court for resolution, if he didn't accept the one and only offer we had received in four years. Reluctantly he agreed to the sale and the ball started rolling with all the usual searches and questionnaires relating to the property. I had the luxury of being able to stay in my flat in St Phillips Square until I found somewhere to live. Where he would go? I had no idea, but it wasn't going to keep me awake at night that's for sure.

The next item on the agenda was to divide up our possessions. Long before I had taken that holiday in Sicily, remember that? It seems like a life time ago now. In my bones I knew our marriage was over and like a girl guide, I was prepared. With a new film in the camera (no digital cameras then) I had wandered around the house from room to room, taking photographs of every piece of furniture. every shelf, every painting, every lamp. I duly had the film processed. Yes, films were taken into places such as Boots to be processed and after a few days, we could collect a yellow Kodak folder, containing all our glossy photographs. I had two sets made and now in the privacy of my flat, I looked through the folder. There were antique tables, chests, mirrors, chairs and paintings, which were once the backdrop to my life. Every piece brought back memories. I could tell you where we had bought each and every item. Over the years we had managed to buy furniture as we could afford it, slowly relinquishing our Habitat pieces c1970 as we did so. I labelled every photograph with a number which corresponded with a list, Trish typed up for me. Greg Midgley had received a letter from Steve's solicitor with a list of items he wished to retain and of course, these were all the best pieces. When I cross referred with my detailed list I soon saw some pieces had just evaporated. He was still thinking I was a fool and I would just forget after four years, surely. On the phone, I could sense Midgley's impatience, dividing the contents of a divorcing couple's home. I think, he thought it beneath him to be dealing with this trivia, arguing over the contents was the last straw. I can only assume, the excellent outcome of my case, had given him a huge sense

Only cry on Fridays

of self importance. The truth couldn't be more different. Without Hugo Steele's input, I would be sunk. Midgley fulfilled a minor role, more like a clerk and was now, no doubt crowing around the office, about the success of *his* case. I had to explain we weren't dealing with a house full of MFI furniture, so I sent him the photographs with the list to forward. I asserted we should negotiate using the photographic inventory, so a date was set for me to go to, what was still my house.

Annie offered to accompany me. I hadn't been back inside The Rectory since the day I left and realised I was about to come face to face, with a very angry man. His case had been blown out of the water on every count. Not only was he caught with his fingers in the till, but had been left with a huge legal bill, pretty much of his own making. I knew he would be smarting. Now he had to deal with a photographic inventory, so he wouldn't be able to secrete anything away, as he had planned. He would be thinking *that damned efficient woman.*

Annie and I came in our own cars, so we met just up the road. We both looked super smart, we meant business. The front door was slightly ajar, so with a split second of deliberation, I decided to walk straight in, after all, it was still fifty percent my house. The air hung heavily with neglect. The smell of four years of fry ups with a back drop of cigars was ghastly. The hall carpet was filthy and if I wasn't another person now, I would have burst into tears.
We walked into the kitchen, my eyes skimming over spillages and crumbs on the work tops, inwardly I sighed. Our heels tapping on the floor, caused chairs in the adjacent dining room to suddenly move. Looking through the open door, I could see our neighbour Rachel was sitting with Steve at the dining table.
'Oh, it's *you.*' He said.
Unshaven, he was wearing an old sweatshirt I didn't recognise; it was grubby and fraying at the neck and cuffs.
'This is Annie' I said
'Hello Alice' said Rachel 'Annie, nice to meet you.'
From the girls, I had heard it was Rachel's mother who had been so attentive to this man, deserted by his wife. Rachel saw the confused look on my face as she sat down again.
'I'm going to help Steve go through this' she said
Irritated as I was, I could hardly complain, as I had Annie with me. On

Alice Waite

this fine sunny day, Rachel was clad in a mauve tee shirt vest, sans bra. You know, there is an age when a strappy number like this, barely covering pert young bosoms, looks charming. Then there is an age, Rachel's age, when a strappy number like this, barely covering a pair of slumped, languorous mammaries is *not* pretty. Rachel, did you even check yourself in a mirror before leaving the house?

I opened my file. I had two copies of the inventory just in case he had *lost* his. The accompanying list had three columns headed Alice, Steve and Auction. I also had packs of sticky dots and stars to attach to furniture, as we made decisions. I pushed the paperwork across the table along with the pack of blue stars. He gave me a withering look and said
'I don't need these we've got the lists my solicitor sent.'
'No matter.' I said going into efficient mode 'The typed copy, as you will see has three columns, so we can go through every piece systematically and decide who has what.' 'I will mark my pieces with the red dots and it's up to you if you want to use the blue stars for your pieces.' 'I suggest the items no one wants, can have the green dots and they can be picked up next week for auction.'
Now *he* was irritated. He hated to be organised. Rachel, leaned forward in earnest, the pendulous contents of her vest, reached the top of the table, before she did.
To her credit she said
'That's not a bad idea you know Steve.' 'It will make everything clear…. Won't it?'
He stared at the inventory, there were several pages organised room by room. I had left the furniture in the girl's rooms out of the equation, as I felt they should have these pieces. After all they were about to embark on life, post university and would have flats to furnish in the near future.
'OK' I said, 'Let's start shall we, there's a lot to get through.'
I looked longingly at their half Cafetiere, of now, cold coffee, but knew we weren't going to be offered so much as a drink of the green water, from the vase of dead flowers on the table. Slowly we haggled. I refreshed my memory, by going into the relevant room to look at the furniture in question. At every turn, I was followed either by Steve or Rachel. At one point, I was so irked by Rachel, walking two paces behind me, like a faithful dog, I said
'Rachel! Its fine." I really do not need you following me around *my own*

house...!' 'For Heaven's sake do you really think I'm going to secrete a painting inside my jacket?'
When we got to the sofas Steve piped up 'Hettie wants the Grey one.'
'Well, lets just divide the main list between us.' I said, 'Then we can make some decisions about our own things with the girls quite separately.'
'I'll go and talk to Hettie' Rachel said
'You mean she's here?' I queried
'Yes, she's in the coach house with Sam.' Steve said in a matter of fact way. He was putting the knife in; reminding me Hettie was living with *him*. *He* was the chosen one.
Standing up I said,
'I'll go over now and talk to her.'
Rachel stood up and, in a flash, was walking ahead of me towards the door.
'I'll ask her.' she said
This was a step too far.
'Rachel, I will talk to *my own daughter* and I don't want *you* to accompany me!'
My voice was raised. Rachel looked to Steve for back up, but he just shrugged his shoulders, as if to say, *see what I have had to deal with?* Yes Steve, a woman with a voice and an opinion, I am now, not too frightened to express. Annie's eyes darted from me to Steve to Rachel and back again. She sat at the table as a silent witness to this farce. I could hear Hettie's voice as I walked towards the coach house. I opened the door and called up the stairs,
'Hetts, I didn't know you were here!'
'Hey Mum!'
She was on the landing now and as I reached her we hugged.
'Thought it better I kept out of things... you know.' She said by way of explanation.
I asked about the Grey sofa and there wasn't any problem with it being on my list, for future discussion. She followed me down stairs, across the court yard and into the kitchen.
'Hetts, would you be a darling and get two glasses of water, please? "Oh, this is Annie by the way.'
They exchanged pleasantries as she brought the water to the table, then she said
'OK, must get back to Sam, we're planning an event, you know.' 'I'll tell you all about it later Mum....'
And with that she was gone.

Negotiations resumed. We had a pair of portraits of an 18th century lady and gentleman, of unknown provenance. We were both very fond of them but could not agree who would be allocated the lady or the gentleman. The lady had a rather stern demeanour but the gentleman, in his velvet jacket had a much kinder face. On the toss of a coin, I walked away with the gentleman. Frankly I wouldn't have minded either way, but as the years go by and he still hangs on my wall, I have become, more and more fond of him.

Next on the list were the contents of our bedroom. Standing in the doorway, I could see the bed was badly made. It looked lumpy, as if someone was still in it and there was linen spilling out from underneath the bedcover. I didn't dwell on it because my eyes were drawn to a gap under the window, where there had been a mahogany chest. Of course, he was hot on my tail, so I asked where it had gone.
'Ah, it had to be repaired and err…. treated… wood worm you know'
I didn't believe him for a minute. Clearly this was a piece he wanted, and it had been moved to ensure he retained it. I know he thought the chest was circa Queen Anne, but anyone researching historic styles, would be able to see that with bun feet it was Victorian. This gave me a strong negotiating hand for a Georgian side table and an early demi-lune table, in lieu of the chest. *Result!* Rachel called up the stairs
'Steve you're wanted on the office phone.'
With that he left me in my former bedroom to wander into the dressing room and bathroom without my shadow. Half thinking, I might have left some clothes in the wardrobes on opening the doors, I was confronted with lots of clothes, but they weren't mine. Here were rails of multi coloured clothes I simply did not recognise. It took a moment for the penny to drop. Of course, Rachel's Mother… she must have moved in. Clearly today she was keeping a low profile… probably at Rachel's house which was only opposite after all. More than likely, she had seen Annie and I arrive. The mahogany chest was almost certainly at her side, I was intrigued. In the bathroom were lots of products on the marble top. They were all decent brands, Lancome, Clarins, Estee Lauder. It was a slightly surreal experience. Another woman in what *was,* my domain. I wonder how she felt sitting in *my* bath and sleeping in *my* bed to boot? I just hoped she hadn't been sucked in by this poor boy in need of so much tlc.

Standing in the bathroom for some time, I stared at the little cupboard underneath the hand basin. This had been my safe. This cupboard was where I kept Tampax and pant liners and so on, so it was no-go territory for Steve. Saving cash had become an art form for me. From the days when money was handed out in more or less the amount I would require, I knew I had to find a way to have some funds of my own. Maybe it was a sixth sense, an intuition that first made me embark on this money saving venture? But no, the reality was, that being dependent on his moods, as to whether I would be given the autonomy, *his* money might allow, was so demeaning, I had to put something in place.

So firstly, there was the family allowance. Steve didn't seem to notice this and as it was always paid in cash at the Post Office, it meant I could save it for things like birthday presents. Then, when supermarkets started giving cash back, I could put extra onto the grocery run, to add more to my safe. In my head, I was saving for a birthday party for him, His fiftieth was the next significant number, so ever wanting to please, I did throw a party. After the party, realising with funds diminished, I didn't like the lack of security I was feeling, I started seriously building up my reserve. With every new bout of destructive behaviour, my resolve to save cash became stronger. I thought of it, maybe for a night in an hotel, if I had to get out, or to fill the tank with petrol… I don't know, but that nest egg, call it what you will, gave me the peace of mind that I might have choices. Without money, girls your life is at the behest of those that hold the purse strings. You are at their bidding. They can dictate and demand. *You* have *no choices*.

When we came back from a trip overseas or just a holiday, where he, as ever, had been in control of all our foreign currency, he would just throw the money into a drawer or empty it into an envelope and well… who knows where it went? I knew. After a few weeks, I would pop to American Express to change it into sterling. This furtive behaviour, didn't make me feel like a very nice person. To be honest, I felt double dealing and underhand, I didn't like the person his behaviour had forced me to become. This was my failsafe, a game plan for survival, some day…. in the distant future. Regardless of the guilt I felt surrounding my deceit; I knew it was significantly better to experience this, than the vulnerability I had known without money. Every fifty pounds would be changed at the bank for a fifty-pound note (less bulky to store) every £500 would be stored as follows.

Girls, remember those sanitary towels… with wings? OK, well they all came individually wrapped, in a sachet… so discreet for the handbag, I know. Opening the sachet, by pulling the top edges apart, *very carefully*, so there was no damage to the packaging, I then removed the towel. Laying it flat, unfolding the wings from the sides, I placed my £500 on the pad, then, bringing the wings around to secure everything in place, the towel was folded back exactly as before. It would still slide back into its sachet, the open edges secured together, invisibly, with double sided sellotape. My freedom indeed, came with wings.

After we had worked through every page of the inventory, I took my packet of sticky dots, with the list to assign myself the right pieces of furniture. Annie ticked our inventory and held the tape measure as I measured each piece, because everything would be going into store. When I was in a position to look for my own house, I wanted to be able to plan where everything would go. I also labelled the pieces for auction and then advised Steve my furniture would be collected the following Wednesday.
'I don't know if that will be convenient' he said, controlling to the last.
'Well it will have to be' I said because Dave Davies is booked.' 'I can organise the collection of the auction pieces too.'
'I will deal *that'* he said 'I need to check the best auction houses, first.
I should have been more insistent about getting this organised, but my tummy was rumbling, and I had, had enough. It was mid afternoon by the time we were finished and with only a glass of water since breakfast, we were both starving. I called to Hettie to say goodbye, but she had left, for where I don't know. I wished she had just popped in to say, *bye Mum*. I felt rather sad about this, but pulled myself together and taking Annie by the arm said,
'Come on Annie, my treat. I think afternoon tea is called for, don't you?'
We stopped off at a nearby hotel, ordering rounds of cream cheese and cucumber sandwiches, a pot of tea, with scones to follow.
'Annie, I am so grateful for your support today.' I said tucking in.
'What a fiasco' she said, 'I mean… that Rachel woman…what was she thinking… spilling out of that little strappy top?' 'And… she was like a guard dog following you around!' … 'Didn't you find it painful going back after all this time?'
'No not really.' I said, 'It didn't feel like my old home any more …it was so shabby and dilapidated……..and Rachel's mother must have moved in, because all her clothes were in the wardrobes.'
'You're kidding!' Annie said pouring more tea.
'It was really strange, seeing that, with all her lotions and potions were

where mine had been.' 'Well she's welcome to his underpants, that's what I say!'
Annie spluttered her tea 'What are you talking about?'
'I won't go into it here!' I said, 'It will spoil our tea!'

Chapter 35

The Move

Dave Davies, a tall, gangly man, who I swear cut his own hair, had been introduced to me by a friend of a friend. Since the very first removal, he had been my go to man for collecting and moving props, *nothing* was too much trouble. Always client presentable in a clean sweat shirt and chinos, as long as the kettle was constantly on the boil for tea, he worked like a Trojan.

Dave was booked for the following Wednesday. Looking through my list of furniture he decided his Luton van would be the most suitable, mainly because of the huge mirror and the kitchen dresser on my list. He told me the move to the storage unit would take two men, as he couldn't manage some of the furniture on his own. So, all good! Arranging to meet at 8.00am at The Rectory, I warned Dave to bring along a thermos as we wouldn't be offered so much as a used tea bag. Concerned I had stretched the kindness and goodwill of my girlfriends to breaking point, I didn't like to ask the usual suspects, but I badly wanted some support for the moving day. Barbara had telephoned out of the blue, so I just blurted out,

'I don't suppose you would be free next Wednesday… would you?' 'I would really appreciate an ally on the day of the move…. you know, to get all my furniture from the house… it's not going to be pleasant.'

'Err… well I need to look in my diary' she said…. 'It's in the car.' 'Can I get back to you?'

Barbara's diary was *always* in the car. I ask you, what's the point of keeping a diary in the car? The times, in the past, Barbara was going to get back to me about a theatre visit or seeing a film…. And do you know what? By the time the diary had been unearthed from the car, the film had gone to DVD and the super star cast of the theatrical production, were in a home for thespians, by the sea. I therefore didn't hold out much hope, anything would be different. Of course, the diary was always to hand if Barbara required my assistance, to talk to the architect about one of her interior

projects. But that's the luck of the draw with friendships, isn't it? Some friends would walk over broken glass to help, others like Barbara, fall into, what I would call the flaky category, they are the fair-weather friends. *Alice, stop bitching about Barbara and get on....*
Well no surprises then. There were several days of silence from Barbara, as she excavated her diary from the car. I decided not to phone her, I didn't want the humiliation of being turned down, because of a must have pedicure. By Tuesday evening, I hadn't heard a word, so resigned myself that I would have to deal with this one on my own. I started wishing I had asked Annie or Lucy or Dee or anybody but Barbara. Even though everything had been agreed and documented, it should all be just plain sailing, but what I dreaded most of all, was one of *his* intimidating looks. One of these looks could blacken a sunlit day, crush myself esteem in seconds and turn my legs to jelly. One of those looks, was a mental bludgeon, giving rise to haunting anxiety. There was no logic to my fear. I had become stronger; I had stood up to this man, left a thirty-year marriage at the age of fifty-three and uncovered his fraudulent, double dealing scheme. Nevertheless, for all my coherent reasoning, the night before this finale, I was sick with apprehension.

It was gone ten pm, so I ran a deep bath and sinking beneath the rose scented bubbles, tried to calm myself, as I had done on so many occasions, before having to see him at court. Inhaling the delicious scent, I closed my eyes visualising the imaginary suit of armour, I would wear tomorrow, when the landline suddenly burst into action with its annoying trill ring tone. I knew from past experience, I could not get from the bath, to the sitting room telephone, in the time it takes for the answering machine to kick in. I heard Barbara's voice.
'Sorry to be late getting back to you' she said
'Well it's only a week Barbara, no worries' I muttered from the depths of the soap suds.
'I can't be with you tomorrow...'
She gave no reason. 'But hope it all goes well...'
'Yes, the sun will shine... I'll have a really fab day Barbara!' 'It will be a breeze' 'Looking forward to it actually.'
Her voice continued. 'So, let's catch up soon?'
'What when you've found your bloody diary?' I yelled
The answering machine purred to a halt.
Now I really need to polish my armour for the morning. I tried to run

more hot water into the bath, but the venerable immersion heater hadn't had enough time to work its magic, so I called it a day.

I slept remarkably well, but woke with that churning in the pit of the stomach feeling, as the reality of D Day kicked in. With a flask of coffee, bottles of water, a packed lunch and a supply of Dave's favourite biscuits, all in a carrier bag, I made my way out of the building. I have neglected to say, my outfit……..casual but smart, and make up were all impeccably in place. Can't, no *won't* let the side down. I wonder if Rachel's mother will be ensconced in Rachel's house, keeping an eye on things from behind the curtains. Although I was bang on time, Dave was already outside The Rectory. I looked at the grubby windows of my old home with a Sold subject to Contract sign on the end of the driveway. When Dave saw me pull up, he jumped out of the Luton. His co-worker Big John came over. Big John was both big in girth and height. Standing next to tall lanky Dave they were a sight to behold.

'How you doing?' He said in his Bristolian best.

'Well, I'll be glad when today's over and everything is safely in store.' I murmured 'Come on, let's make a start.' I said, leading the way towards the front door.

Dave and Big John followed behind like Lions about to stalk their prey. As ever, the front door was slightly ajar, so I pushed it fully open and calling 'Hello' walked into the hall.

The usual nauseating smell greeted my nostrils. No one appeared to be about, so handing Dave the list and photographic inventory; I walked them from room to room on the ground floor, pointing out the furniture still embellished with red sticky dots and at the same time, checking everything against the list, just in case any little dots had been removed. I called up the stairs

'Hello, anyone in'?

There was no response. Still calling out, we ventured up the stairs and into the main bedroom, as the door was wide open. Dave, I could see was making a mental packing note of every item and the order he would pack things into the van. Trailing back down stairs he said

'Right… we'll get the steps John and the tool kit, to get this mirror off the wall first.'

'OK 'John said bustling out of the sitting room into the hall.

'Who are you?' Bellowed a voice, I knew only too well.

Only cry on Fridays

'I'm with Dave Davies removals.' A slightly unnerved sounding John responded.
I moved quickly into the hall, to see Mr Angry blocking John's passage.
'I didn't know you were here…' He boomed.
'Well it's now twenty past eight.' I said looking at my watch. 'And we said eight am… so, as you weren't here, we are just carrying on with what we have to do.'
He gave me a withering look, but I kept strong, pulling down the visor on my armour. Turning to Dave to avoid any further difficulties, I saw Big John was back with the tool kit and ladders. Work commenced. The mirror was huge and incredibly heavy. Steve came back as they were slowly unscrewing the coach bolts from the substantial metal brackets. Leaning against the door frame, coffee in hand he advised,
'It took four men to carry that mirror when it came in here.' 'I mean …. it's *so* heavy when those coach bolts are out of the wall… nightmare that one!'
Dave and Big John remained resolutely silent, concentrating on the task in hand. Both were perched on steps either side of the mirror, their screw drivers slowly releasing the bolts. Somehow, determined not to show a grimace of strain, they lowered the mirror behind the steps to floor level. Clearly, irritated, Steve walked away. Within seconds, I could smell cigar smoke wafting from wherever he had gone to lick his wounds.

At 11am Dave signalled it was time for a break. They had worked tirelessly moving some of the allocated pieces to the drive ready for packing into the van. As we sat on the tail gates of the Luton, grateful for our thermos flasks of coffee, I passed the favourite biscuits over.
'Well look at that!'
Dave beamed as he dunked his chocolate Hobnob into his mug. Big John, followed suite. Carefully wrapping the packet of biscuits and putting them in his lunch box he said,
'He's a nasty piece of work, isn't he?'
'Tell me about it!' I nodded
He shook his head
'Now you just keep with us Alice love… don't stay in the house alone with him.'
'OK' I said, reassured someone was looking out for me.
'Back to work!' he gestured to Big John.
As he looked at the load amassing on the drive Dave was scratching his

head, but not saying anything. There was still a fair amount to come, plus a huge stone, garden urn.

Next on the list was a fruitwood wardrobe. A heavy piece, but moved with professional aplomb from the bedroom, they struggled with it on the first flight of stairs, because they couldn't manoeuvre it around the return, as the newel post was in the way. Steve took up position at the bottom of the stairs, smouldering cigar in hand. As they tried in vain for nearly half an hour, to lift the wardrobe up and manoeuvre it over the newel post, it became clear there was insufficient space on the landing to turn the bulky carcass. Big John looked like he might have a heart attack. Dave would have killed for a cup of tea. He instructed,
'Let's get this lying on its side.'
They carefully slid the wardrobe down the stairs, propping it against the landing wall. With tape measure in hand, Dave started measuring the landing window. The window was a half level sash, only a few feet off the ground.
'The best way forward' he said to Big John, 'is to take this window out.'
'We can easily slide the wardrobe through the window then, onto a trolley.'
Steve ran up the stairs like a rat up a drain pipe.
'*No, no*, you are not touching *that* window!' He remonstrated loudly.
'Well I think…that's the way it came in, in the first place?' Dave said, 'I mean, did it?'
'Yep, I think so.' Steve said in an idle tone.
'Well why didn't you tell us?' Dave said in exasperation.
Shrugging his shoulders and blowing cigar smoke, Steve said
'*You're* the removal people.' 'AND DON'T TAKE THAT WINDOW OUT!' He shouted as he wandered off to a ringing phone.
Dave wasn't having any of it. He proceeded to take down the Roman blind in preparation. In an expert jiffy, the blind was removed, carefully folded, then placed on the landing table. Dave proceeded to remove the window. Steve reappeared and was visibly shaken, at the sight of the window, now leaning against the landing wall.
He yelled 'What the f**** do you think you are doing?' 'I told you DO NOT TAKE THE WINDOW OUT!'
Instructions I think they could probably hear on Mars. Dave turned to Steve but didn't say a word. He just calmly went about his business.
'Look here!' I said 'This wardrobe came in *this way, now* you, kindly tell

us…. So, it will have to go out the same way.' 'This house is still half mine; the decision isn't just yours to make.'

Steve's face was thunder. He sucked on his cigar with anxiety. His authority on the matter had been eclipsed. The fruitwood wardrobe sailed out of the window to Big John, poised with his trolley waiting on the other side. It was duly wrapped in one of Dave's immaculate blankets, then secured to the interior of the van. Big John and Dave carefully re fixed the window and then re-hung the Roman blind, while Steve watched intently, anger etched all over his face.

Chapter 36

The Move 2

We broke for lunch. Thank heavens it was a dry day. Sitting on the tailgate again with our lunch boxes Dave said,
'I think some of this will have to be left for tomorrow… we haven't started on the attics yet and…'
Big John butted in 'You can't do this tomorrow Dave… we're in Cheltenham….'
Dave saw my face turn to panic.
'I can't leave some of it Dave…. I'll never see it again.' 'You can see what I am up against.'
Dave sucked through his teeth
'We may be OK with the bulky stuff, it's just all the lamps and books and …. pictures and other things...' He said.
Looking into the distant space across the road to Rachel's house, I wondered if Rachel's mother was being given a blow by blow account.
'Look Dave, I'm sure with careful packing of the smaller stuff in my car we can manage this… can't we?'
He didn't reply but feeling stressed at the thought of having to leave things behind, then negotiate another day to collect them, I went back to my car to fold the seats down flat. The look on his face didn't make me feel one hundred percent confident, but he just continued methodically, to load the Luton with the larger pieces of furniture. They were watched by Steve like a hawk, hovering over his prey. Nothing went into the van without him checking it against his list. He even opened cupboard doors and drawers to be sure we weren't secreting unauthorised goods inside. Dave thought we might be able to pack paintings, books and smaller items into the cupboards once they were secured to the sides of the van.
I just concentrated on packing books into boxes. I had to stop myself dipping into lovely Art books and well, thumbed biographies. There were guide books to pretty much every European city. Each one had a memory

attached, as I always wrote the date along with my notes inside the cover. Some were purchased over thirty years ago. Flicking through Fodor's Italy, through a splotch of olive oil radiating into the text, I could just make out, Venice 1973. I was twenty-four years old and had been Mrs Alice Waite for three years. Then at the back of the shelves were my ancient GCE text books. I thought of my hopes for the future at the tender age of sixteen. Steve and I met when I was eighteen. In awe of his self confidence; he seemed to have an answer for everything. After all, he had been to Art College in London, he had *A Plan*… he was going to succeed, whereas I was still struggling to get the education I craved.

Looking at my watch it was just before three' o clock, our Thermoses were empty. We all badly needed a cup of tea. Gathering up the flasks, I rinsed them out under the outside tap and walked up to the Lamb and Lion at the end of the village. They were on the point of closing but agreed to fill the flasks with tea. You would have thought I was proffering Champagne, the way Dave and Big John fell upon the nectar. Ten minutes sit down with mugs of tea lifted our spirits like nothing on earth.

'Now!' Dave muttered from the depths of his mug, 'we must get started again… mustn't slack… so much to do.'

Big John started to laugh, and a wry smile flickered across Dave's face. We were up against it. Time was ticking on and energy levels failing. I relentlessly started on an ancient grey filing cabinet containing all the girl's old school reports. I couldn't bear the thought they might just end up in a skip. There were Brownie badges, still waiting to be sewn onto Brownie outfits, (bad mother!) Then I came across swimming diplomas and handwriting certificates. A whole raft of their childhood housed in this utilitarian metal box. I placed all of it in a dutifully labelled cardboard box of its own. Steve was hanging around, surveying the boxes.

'No room in the van then?' He smirked.

'No problem!' I responded in a haughty voice

I was dammed if I was going to admit we might have a problem. As far as I was concerned, I didn't care if I had to hire roof rack and trailer, all my goods and chattels were leaving this house tonight!

Let me take a minute to describe the location of my old home in the village itself. The Rectory was sited on the corner of Mead lane, a narrow lane, fronting a much wider, Norton Street, which was the main village street. Mead lane was the route of the local bus, still a double-decker, despite being half empty most of the time. When the bus arrived at the end of the lane, that is, at the junction with Norton Street, it had to turn on a sixpence to make its way along the street and through the village. Passengers on the upper deck always had plenty of time during the manoeuvre, to look intently into the upper windows of The Rectory. The timetable of the buses coming into and out of the village was arranged so the buses would not meet at this pinch point. (Oh really)?

This normally quiet village had been alerted to the goings on outside The Rectory. Not only were curtains twitching, but the bolder residents were out of their front doors pottering in their front gardens, trying to look purposeful. More dog walkers cruised past than I have ever seen in the village before. I noted the same dogs walk past, time and time again, eyes diverted to the melee of boxes near the pavement.

We soon had a system. I packed into boxes, Dave Davies and Big John manhandled the boxes onto the drive where some were decanted into cupboards already in the van. Dave wheeled a filing cabinet to the edge of the pavement, followed by a wing chair, a footstool and a marble topped table. How those residents gawped. This was better than any view from the top of the bus. Here it was piece by piece, right in front of them, for close inspection. I carried out a tall lamp and wedged it between the back and front seats, of my car, most of it protruding out of the sunroof. Thank God it was a dry day. By now we were running out of Dave's immaculate packing blankets but still had bubble wrap and corrugated card board to pack around things. I checked through the inventory we had about a quarter of the list still to remove and pack. On it went….

We were just manoeuvring a pair of Box Trees in terracotta pots to the edge of the pavement when the 116X bus appeared at the end of Mead lane, hoping, as is its usual practice, to turn on a sixpence, onto the main road. However, the 116X a few minutes behind its schedule, taking its passengers in the opposite direction, was poised on the so-called sixpence. Both buses honked their horns, hoping the other would reverse. There were about twenty or so passengers on each bus, who as one, focused through the inhospitable condensation on the windows, to watch my married life of thirty years on the drive, spilling onto the pavement. I smiled an embarrassed smile at the drivers, who didn't smile back.

The passenger's watched intently, more interested in the goings on outside The Rectory, than the stand-off between the two buses. There was more honking of horns, then, both drivers dismounted. High Noon style they began to slowly walk towards each other. I thought pistols were about to be drawn.

Only cry on Fridays

A balding man bursting out of his Direct Route uniform called out 'Brian'… 'Brian, you're ten minutes late!' 'I've got to get this bus moving….' 'Now look ere' mustered Brian 'Traffics terrible on the bye pass, there's road works an all…be reasonable Kev… it's not my fault!'
Brian was a slim build, probably in his fifties, with more hair than Kev, wearing a navy Direct Route pullover with a tie parting company from a crumpled end of the day collar he said, 'It's not my fault either…!'
'Too bad… just reverse out of the way' remonstrated Kev, whose paunch was a taut button hole away from a heart attack, waiting to happen. Brian's arms were folded across his slim frame in defiance. Their eyes were steely, their faces hard, no one was going to back down. I continued piling I don't know what, into boxes, when out of the corner of my eye, I saw Dave Davies calmly walk past me. He could have been wearing his U.N. Peace Corp blue helmet, because on his arrival, an aura of calm surrounded the High Noon stand off. His back towards me, I could see Brian and Kev's faces clearly. Not able to hear what was being said, I noticed they had stopped shouting at each other. Then, Brian unfolded his arms and I saw a flicker of a smile appear across his face. Dave stepped back and fishing in the pocket of his chinos, pulled out a coin. I heard Kev shout
'Heads!'
The coin was tossed into the air and allowed to fall onto the pavement. Both stepped towards the coin bending over to examine it.
Jubilant, Kev called out
'Heads it is!'
With a huge smirk across his face, he made his way back to the bus, to a faint cheer from his passengers inside, all anxious to get home after a day at work. Brian tried not to look disappointed and giving the thumbs up sign to Dave Davies standing on the pavement, dutifully reversed his 116X out of the way, allowing Kev's bus to squeeze around the tight bend. After a playful honk of horns, the two buses continued their journeys in opposite directions. Meanwhile Dave Davies sauntered back to the van to continue organising his load. Looking up as he walked past me, I congratulated him on his mediation skills. It felt like half the village had now turned onto the street to watch Kev's, Gary Cooper moment. This madness would be the talk of The Lamb and Lion for weeks to come, never mind the Post Office and village shop, which incidentally (for those of you that haven't got a life) was run by the equivalent of Susan Carter.

Within the hour the last boxes were loaded into the van and my car. The inventory list was double checked, then I took a final walk through the house. Mercifully I was on my own, Steve had lost interest and disappeared, I presumed to Rachel's house. It was eerily quiet, my foot steps echoing on the wooden floors. I wondered in the two hundred years since the house had been standing, what other scenes of such heartache, its walls had witnessed.

The remnants of my home now looked so dejected. There were marks on the walls where pictures had once hung. Fluff on the floor where sofas had been moved and general detritus on every surface. An air of despondency and neglect filled every room. I was confused by the mixed emotions running through my entire body. Was I experiencing loss, or freedom? But I knew my heart had long gone from this house, it was no longer a home. The positive memories associated with it, had faded along with the childhood of my girls. All I could see now were reminders of the happy confident woman who once lived here, who was reduced to believing all the pain she was in, was her own fault. I could still hear Steve's voice in my head, criticising, battering my self esteem, ensuring I felt worthless. Only since I left, did I realise how utterly exhausting my life had been, living on the edge, walking on egg shells. Learning how to anticipate his moods was a necessary survival tactic. The scars are brutal, there are so many internal wounds yet to heal; erasing these memories will take some time. Brushing aside a tear, I had to swallow hard to keep my emotions in check. Standing in the kitchen amidst the muddle of unwashed breakfast things, I could see through your chaos, to all the family meals I had cooked there. Looking out onto the garden, it seemed only five minutes ago, that the paddling pool was full; tents were pitched, with the rabbit and guinea pig, Flopsy and Squeak, freely running around the garden, to your squeals of delight, my darlings.

Upstairs now, standing at the open door to our bedroom, another woman's dressing gown lies across our bed. I don't know you, or hold any grudge against you, who ever you are, but I fear for your soul. It will start slowly, you won't really notice. You will blame *yourself* when he's not happy. He will trivialise the things you love, the people who care for you. Then you will get caught in a trap of catering to his every need, to keep *him* happy. *Your* needs will be extinguished in preference to his. He will play on your sympathy. If you try hard enough, you may just win his approval. But you will have to keep trying harder, because the goal posts will move. His personality will have a public face and a private one. His mood changes will be particularly perplexing. He will twist your words around to make you feel stupid. You won't be able to do anything right and somehow you let him get comfortable disrespecting you. At other times, he will be emotionally needy, deflated and even tender, so you will be supportive of this man, who you think you know. But with no notice, he will return to the angry, controlling person, you don't know. You will be confused, incapable of understanding what has caused this, and start to blame yourself. Dear Lady, I wish you well, because Leopards don't change their spots

The girl's rooms were untidy but intact, waiting for them to decide what to keep, what to put in store and what to lose. I remembered Betty's kittens being born under Cesca's bed in the middle of the night. In all of this, I have forgotten to mention that dear Betty, the family cat I had to leave behind, had died the year before. As I wandered from room to room, I fancied I caught sight of her a couple of times.

Chapter 37

Is anything familiar?

So, all my furniture was safely loaded into the storage unit and the sale of The Rectory went through, leaving me with a deposit for the cottage I eventually bought. Yes, dear reader, it's even got Roses around the door. Every time I arrive home, my heart lifts. Every time, I open my front door, I bless the day I plucked up the courage to leave my marriage of thirty years. This was the bravest thing I have ever done in my whole life.
The second bravest thing I have done, is to write my experience down. Everything you have read here is true. Locations and the names of the guilty have been changed, to protect the innocent, whose names have also been changed. Of course, I have had to approximate speech, but the gist of the speech is, as I remember it. Everything else has been written from my diaries and notes made at the time.

Standing on the edge of the cliff, thinking about jumping into the abyss was terrifying and I am not exaggerating. Where would I go? How would I survive? Would I become a bag lady? Magically, arms came out to catch me. We all have that negative doubting voice in our head, but it must be quelled. Sometimes it takes a reasoned voice, from a trusted friend, to tell you what you already know, but can't bring yourself to admit.
Someone said to me 'Life isn't a rehearsal Alice, *this is it.*' This phrase went around and around in my head, as I tried to find reasons not to acknowledge what was going on. Surely things will get better? We are going through a difficult patch. He's tired/ worried, it *must* be me... *I've done something to upset him...?*
Really? Blaming yourself is part of the game, but let's see this, for what it is. Abuse. So please do not fall into the trap of defending the indefensible, because the alternative for you, is too frightening to contemplate. This behaviour has serious effects on every aspect of our lives, mental and physical, as well our social interaction with the outside world. The degrees

of control seem trivial at first and to make life more confusing, they are often disguised as loving behaviour.

Isolation:
'Don't go out (with your friends) in the evening, *I worry about you driving back at night on your own.*'
'Don't invite... (other people) around, *I want you all to myself!*'
These sound like the comments of someone who cares for us. They are not. Gradually our social circle diminishes and therefore we have less people to confide in. Do you avoid having family and friends around because his behaviour has been difficult and embarrassing? We close doors to those who might support us and the self confidence that comes when social exchange is eroded. Our partner has us exactly where he wants us and thus, he is ever more powerful in our lives.

Criticism:
Sometimes he will insult you, put you down, both privately and in front of others.
'Alice has always struggled with that hair of hers, haven't you darling!'
He will insist you are just being too sensitive... so whatever hurt *he* has caused is *your* fault.
'I wouldn't let Alice drive your new car... know what I mean!'
Then, when you are upset, he asks, if you can't take a joke?
With a daily barrage of negativity, our opinions are dismissed with derisory comments or our suggestions are called *crazy ideas* and it is therefore easier not to proffer an opinion at all. We slowly shut down, we disappear. In silence there can be no rejection, so we retreat into solitude, it's a coping mechanism and a safer place. Belittling comments, undermining us are the bruises no one can see. This is really a subtle form of brainwashing, infiltrating our personality like a mantra. We hear the negative messages over and over. We find ourselves repeating versions of his words to others.
'Silly me!'
'Don't listen to me...!'
'What do I know?'
Self-confidence crumbles, because we lose the ability to connect verbally.
'Who would want to hear what I think?'
'They will probably think this is a silly idea.'
Even when he's not around, his messages are in our head, developing insecurities and impacting on our self-esteem. Socially and at our

workplace, confidence is diminished. The way we approach a situation, gradually changes from an assured woman, to someone we do not recognise. We might tentatively start a sentence with
'Well I'm not sure what you think about this…' rather than,
'I've had this great idea…'
It takes time to regain control of the demons lodged deeply in our psyche. Even now, I castigate myself when I have done something silly, like forgotten to switch the kettle on, I hear myself say…. *You stupid woman!* *His* mantras must be replaced. Choose your own, choose words that mean something to you. As soon as a negative, demeaning thought enters you head, replace it with your own positive mantra.
I am a strong woman, I will not be compliant any longer.
I deserve to be treated with respect.
I won't be a victim.
I don't give you permission to treat me like this
I will take back control of my life.

There is no truth in the adage
'Sticks and stones will break my bones, but words will never hurt me.'
Those words go around and around in our head until we believe them.

Financial control:
Is it the case, that he keeps control of the family finances, so that you are left with no autonomy, no choices? Do you have to ask for money for the smallest things? Is every financial transaction trawled through?
'Why did you get cash back at the Supermarket?'
'What's this on your credit card?'
Are there occasions when you have had, no say, regarding financial decisions you will be jointly responsible for? Do you hide purchases, because he will be *so* angry you have spent money on yourself? However, does he find the money to buy things he wants, leaving you inexplicably short of money for household expenses? Do you find yourself secreting money away, for whatever reason? Does he prefer you to be financially dependent on him? Of course, if you are financially dependent, you are unable to leave, you are reliant on him for your survival.

Guilt:
Does he make poor decisions and then deflects the blame onto you? Are you made to feel guilty when you spend time away from him? Do you

Only cry on Fridays

return, to find him morose and angry, you have been out without him, with the house in a mess, waiting for you to clear it up? Does he suggest you do not love him, because you have left him on his own? Are you apparently responsible for his depression because you haven't supported him, cherished him, given him *more* time? Would he have got that promotion, if he could stay at work late without you nagging him? Does he sulk, if you do not comply with his wishes? Are you given the silent treatment as punishment? Making *you* feel guilty, for all the problems in *his* life, is the trap. You will try harder, put your own needs to one side, *to be there, for this man.* You mistakenly think, if you get it right, he will love you... more? But he won't, you will *never* be able to do enough.

Lack of Emotional support:
When there have been difficult times in your life and you have wanted some emotional support, is he there for you? If he doesn't want to acknowledge your pain and therefore you must deal with it on your own, he's telling you, it's *your* problem. You must have brought this on yourself. Does he give you the minimum time to discuss what's on your mind and then shrug you away, as if your problems aren't as important as his? When you try to discuss how he's hurt you, does he shut down? This is a pattern, because it keeps you running after him, needing him. He feels important, but you are subjugated, craving his attention.

Self- Doubt: (Gas lighting)
Have you made arrangements that have been categorically denied? This makes you start to feel confused and worry you have memory problems. Have you put something in a safe place, to find it has disappeared? Then heard,
'Mm!' 'You do keep doing this don't you...?' 'That's worrying.'
Has your recollection of an event been questioned to the extent you feel uncomfortable? Then he says, in a concerned voice,
'Your memory isn't what it used to be, you know.'
Before long you start to question your own instincts, memory and sanity. This puts him in control, as you no longer trust yourself; you have become totally reliant on him. Manipulating situations, so that we think we are going crazy, are the tools of an abuser, subtlety eroding our sense of self-worth and sanity. Does he switch from Mr Nice Guy to Mr Nasty, when the front door has closed? Then, when you are at your wits end with verbal abuse, does he change again, becoming the charming tender man, you fell

in love with? A bunch of flowers might appear, or a cup of tea by the bed. Then you doubt yourself again, you start thinking you have over reacted.... maybe even imagined it.

Sexual Abuse:
Does he make lewd comments about you in front of friends? Has he insisted on sexual practices you find abhorrent? Have you had sex, when you didn't feel like it? Were you verbally coerced?
'Prove you love me then…'
You're my wife.' 'I provide for you, isn't that enough, aren't you grateful then?'
'Well show me.'
'A man's got needs' 'The trouble is you're just frigid …!'
Or, if you have refused, did he have sex with you anyway? This is called rape, there is no other word for it. It is a criminal offence. Does he need you to tell him how great his performance has been and how much you enjoyed it? Have you been woken from your sleep in the night with his demands? Is he libidinous at inappropriate times, such as when the children are around? Reclaiming your body will be part of the recovery process.

Strategic Kindness:
Can you think of acts of kindness, you have welcomed at the time, but have left you unable to perform some basic tasks? Maybe, he always sorts out I.T. problems, so you don't try to deal with them yourself, you just ask him, because it's easier. Often these are tasks we don't like or have no interest in, so we go into Damsel mode, because someone else will deal with the issue. So, have you signed a document, he has explained, without reading and understanding it yourself? Does he take care of the central heating timer or always insists on driving when you go out together? Does he decide what type of mortgage you have, what ISA's to buy? These apparent acts of kindness, in reality, erode our skills. We are less self- reliant. We are reliant on another person who, by *our authorisation*, has been given control.

Depression:
Loss of confidence and self- esteem can mean we feel so hopeless in our situation. Everything is too much effort and we are filled with despair. Is it any wonder, when we are constantly trying to second guess his mood, to keep the peace, ensure he is not upset in any way? Meanwhile, daily we are demoralised and damaged by senseless harassment and criticism, which compounds the misery. Someone else is holding the reigns of every aspect

of our lives, we have no autonomy. This leaves us feeling inadequate and a shadow of the person we used to be. Sadness permeates every fibre of our body. We feel guilty our partner finds us so pathetic and we are fearful for the future. *How has it come to this?*

Do you recognize any of this?

Sisters, if you feel the slightest discomfort reading this, or indeed any of the above is familiar, it is *time to take action*. Believe me, *I do know* it is not as easy as those few words imply. *I do know*. Unfortunately, some of us choose to ignore the truth. I know this too, because I did for many years. I am incredulous how long it took me, a reasonably intelligent woman to understand what was happening. You might even recognise some of these scenarios in a friend's relationship, but whatever your good intentions, don't wade in, pointing these things out, because if she is not ready to acknowledge her predicament, you will no longer be her trusted friend. Just be there for her to confide in when she is ready.

The abuse is a slow burn, it's sketchy but confusingly layered with loving gestures. The control is vague to start with, but over time gathers pace. When we love someone, it is difficult to believe they are acting in a way to hurt us, especially when there are loving, tender times. But understand this; emotional abuse is a cycle of extreme psychological behaviour. He will swing between playing mind games, throwing belittling comments, maybe you will receive the silent treatment, then inexplicably, be showered with praise, flattery, and caring loving behaviour. Then, without warning, he will revert to the climate of fear, he can so easily generate. This is highly manipulative behaviour and it is the pattern you need to recognise. You must break the pattern of control. Don't give anyone permission to treat you this way. You might get good at hiding the pain, but it shows in your eyes.

We insulate ourselves with optimism and we do so at our peril. Bear in mind, there will always be a reason, why *now* is not the right time to leave. Maybe there will be a holiday, a birthday, or a child's exam on the horizon. You must choose the right time, but **do not let it drift**. Do not keep finding reasons for staying. If you have children, what kind of role model are you? Do they see a shadow of the mother they once knew? Are your daughters being subliminally taught that this is how partnerships work, with their mother under their father's control? If you have sons, will they think it acceptable, to treat their future partners, the way their father treats you? On a plane, the safety instructions tell you to put on your own oxygen mask first. Then you can help others. Think on that. Remember that person who was carefree and happy? She is still there, buried in a litany of abuse, and you must reclaim her from the shadows.

Make a plan, my thoughts below will help crystallise your thinking. Write it all down… you will know where to hide it, safe from prying eyes.

So, where do you want to be in five years' time?
In the same place, suffering as you are now?
Or with a new life for yourself and family? Maybe a job you've always dreamed of, with your own money to plan as you please. Above all, happy with your new life!

Where do you want to be in three years' time?
In the same place, suffering as you are now?
Or free to do things you love. Go for a swim, meet friends for a coffee, enjoy the company of your family, enrol on evening classes…? And have happiness in your new life!

So where do you want to be in one years' time?
In the same place, suffering as you are now?
Or maybe divorced or separated…? You will still be in recovery, but with a front door of your own, you will be in a safe place and day by day, you will begin to reclaim your sense of self. If this is the plan, start saving money now. No matter how, you must secrete it away…find a way. No matter how little you can save, it will all help in the end. Open your own on-line account but delete every trace. Or a local building society account, but remember, every so often they will send statements, so find out when they are due and watch the post. Save from the family allowance/ cash back at the supermarket/ selling things on eBay… be creative, because this maybe the key to your new front door.

So where do you want to be in in six months' time?
In the same place, suffering as you are now?
Or with a real plan in place? You will have started to save money, maybe researched a change of schools, if you are moving out of area. Are you

planning a divorce? Citizens' Advice will be able to guide you to a solicitor, who specialises in cases like yours. Maybe you have talked to a solicitor to find out what your rights are? Most solicitors will offer the first half an hour free of charge, so having confirmed this, make sure you go armed with a bullet pointed list, and with all the relevant information to hand. If you engage a solicitor, make sure they understand the difficulties you will face if post comes to the house. Enlist the help of a trusted friend, where your mail can be sent. Get a copy of your credit file from Experian or Equifax, the major credit agencies, to check if there are any issues. If you are planning to rent accommodation you need to know you have a good credit rating. If there are problems because of his credit record, ask your solicitor or Citizen's Advice about a notice of disassociation. (Or Google, template letters of disassociation.) Will you have researched rental properties? What prices, in what areas and what deposits are required. If he trawls through the phone bills, buy a pay as you go phone, switch it off when you have used it and make sure you hide it somewhere he never would look. (Maybe buried in a box of Tampax!) Be hypervigilant with every step.

So where do you want to be in three months' time?
In the same place, suffering as you are now?
Or with that plan to leave, taking shape? No one can do this for you. It is a ladder *you* must climb, to be free again. Make sure your behaviour doesn't change, be compliant as ever. He cannot suspect your bid for freedom. But inside, although you will be terrified, and I do know this, there *will be* hope. Visualise your five- year plan.
Walking through your own front door, knowing you have choices, is beyond priceless. Painting the walls in your new accommodation, cooking the food you like, playing your favourite music, having friends and family around for meals, is a joy.

Plan ahead
Keep a diary. Note down all the hurtful things he does, on a day to day basis, no matter how trivial. Then, to show the pattern of abuse, note the kind, normal things he does, when he's pushed you to the edge. Photograph any injuries, no matter how minor, such as bruises on wrists, missing clumps of hair. If he sends abusive texts and emails keep records. You may have to forward them to another phone (maybe a trusted friend's.) Smart phones can record well, from inside a pocket, but take extreme care

that the recording is not discovered. (again, this can be forwarded, all the information is on Google.) Practice switching to record mode, so that in an abusive flare up, you could take yourself off to the loo to switch to record promptly, but please be very careful. This, plus any other digital evidence, such as phone records and from social media platforms, will be useful for your solicitor to use in court. From May 2018 new guidelines come into force, making it clear that domestic abuse is no longer confined to human contact. For the first time there is reference to abuse perpetrated through email, text, social networking sites or tracking devices. Further information can be obtained from www.cps.gov.uk Coercive Control became part of The Serious Crime Act in 2015.

Other useful reading www.theconversation.com

Whenever you plan to leave, look at all the practical things:
Passwords:
Change all your online passwords.
Finance:
Take details of the mortgage, or tenancy agreements, any savings accounts in joint names. Or, if he has an account solely in his name, see if you can turn up a statement to copy, or a way to take screen shot if you can possibly access the account on line. Bank accounts/ credit cards, check whose names they are in, and copy statements.
Documents:
You will need passports, marriage certificate and birth certificates.
Utilities:
Check if utilities are in joint names, because when you leave, you will need to extricate yourself from these bills. On leaving, take a photograph of the meter reading, advise the supplier you are leaving the address, to ensure you are no longer responsible for future bills. Or pay the account if it is in your name. Do not give your new address, give the address of a trusted friend. Your solicitor or Citizen's advice will advise further.
Cars:
Whose name are the cars or car in? If you have your own vehicle, changing the owner's address will be no problem with the DVLA. Make sure you take both sets of car keys though. However, if you share a car, get appropriate advice, because the value will be considered, as a joint asset when everything is divided up.
Mobile Phone:
Arrange for a new phone contract, with a new number, or use your pay as

you go, giving the phone number only to trusted friends. If the contract for your existing phone is not in your name, take a note of all your contacts, then delete everything, leaving it behind, otherwise, you could be traced by the *Find my Phone* App.

Computer/iPad:

If you use a shared computer, delete all search history, then delete the Trash/ Recycle bin.

Social Media:

At least two weeks before you leave, delete your Facebook Account (this can be reactivated for up to two weeks by anyone with the password.) In time, open a new account, but be careful with access from joint friends. Google up-to-date information on covering your tracks re Instagram/ Facebook etc as this information can easily change.

Redirect your post:

A month before, organise redirection of post. Bear in mind, this will be confirmed by letter, to your existing address, so watch the mail like a hawk.

Aftermath

You will know, he will react badly. The person he blames for everything, will not be around to reproach. He will think, you can't do this, and after your moment of madness, you will come back to him. He may turn on the charm, telling you he can't live without you… Mr Nice Guy will be there in full force, but read through your diaries, remember the pattern, don't be lured back. *He will not change.* He may even threaten to commit suicide, he may even try, but his life is not your responsibility. You will have taken one huge, brave step, and no matter how hard it seems, do not look back, you are on your way to reclaiming who you are and retrieving the good things in life. Look at your five- year plan, visualise your new life, repeat your mantras, to help you stay on track.

If you are older, don't be afraid of being on your own. You *can* do it. Ask yourself what is the alternative? Do you want to spend the next twenty years living like this? You will find yourself again, there is so much support out there. You *can* do it. The day you walk away, is the first day of the rest of your life. Your life, your future.

Eventually, when there is so much insidious pain and the luxury of hope has gone, we know we must act. This is the tipping point. Talk to a friend. Make that plan, whatever it takes, because if my experience is anything to go by, I can tell you now, that if I had stayed, I wouldn't be here today, to write this. Some of the demons are still with me. Yes, there are moments when time stands still, and he can get into my head, whispering negative, belittling things, but I also know now, how to banish them.

This has not been an easy write, but today, I am a stronger woman than I have *ever* been in the past. I am my own woman, I make my own decisions. I am a self- reliant and resilient woman. I close my front door at night, knowing I have the luxury of peace in my own home. Believe me this is magic. I have come through the most difficult years, not only in my marriage, but also for four demanding years afterwards, trying to extricate myself from it. The latter experience has empowered me, more than I can say. I am not afraid to make waves if something is wrong. I will not be spoken to as if I am a fool. I will not be interrupted when making a point. I am happy in my own skin.

Finally, I love this song… the chorus, I used to sing in my head to keep going.

Don't tell me what to do,
And don't tell me what to say,
Please, when I go out with you,
Don't put me on display.

You don't own me,
Don't try to change me in any way,
You don't own me,
Don't tie me down cause, I'd never stay.

To any of you about to make the leap, good luck, I will be thinking of you.

Sincerely

Alice Waite

Chapter 38

Sources of Help

DOMESTIC ABUSE

Women's Aid & Refuge

www.nationaldomesticviolencehelpline.org.uk
24- hour National Domestic Violence Freephone Helpline
0800 2000 247
helpline@womensaid.org.uk

Women's Aid defines domestic abuse as an incident or pattern of incidents of controlling, coercive, threatening, degrading and violent behaviour, including sexual violence, as in the majority of cases by a partner or ex-partner, but also by a family member or carer.

Domestic abuse can include, but is not limited to, the following:
- Coercive control (a pattern of intimidation, degradation, isolation and control with the use or threat of physical or sexual violence)
- Psychological and or emotional abuse
- Physical or sexual abuse
- Financial abuse
- Harassment and stalking
- Online or digital abuse

STALKING

The National Stalking Helpline is run by the Suzy Lamplugh Trust

Alice Waite

www.stalkinghelpline.org

Freephone **0808 802 0300**
The helpline is open 09.30 to 16.00 weekdays, except Wednesday, when it is open 13.00 to 16.00

Calls are free from all landlines and also from mobiles using the O2, Orange, T Mobile,
Three (3), Virgin and Vodafone networks. Calls will not be shown on BT landline bills. If you are using another telephone provider, please enquire with them about whether 080880 numbers will appear on your phone bill.

Printed in Great Britain
by Amazon